Beyond Criminal Justice:

An Anthology of Abolitionist Papers presented to conferences of the European Group for the Study of Deviance and Social Control

Edited by:
J.M. Moore, Bill Rolston, David Scott
and Mike Tomlinson

The European Group for the Study of Deviance and Social Control

Published by the European Group for the Study of Deviance and Social Control, Weston-Super-Mare, England

www.europeangroup.org/

ISBN 978-0-9511708-4-7

All authors' royalties are being donated by the editors to the European Group for the Study of Deviance and Social Control

The European Group for the Study of Deviance and Social Control held its first conference in Italy in 1973. Since then, annual conferences have been held at different venues throughout Europe with academics, researchers, activists and practitioners in criminology and related fields participating. While initially class and certain political hierarchies were the focus, the European Group gradually sought to address other national, linguistic, class, ethnic, sexual, and gender barriers in an effort to develop a critical, emancipatory, and innovative criminology. This was to be done through the topics of members' research and in the conduct of conferences, with the ultimate aim being to provide a forum for, and recognition of, emancipatory science and emancipatory politics as legitimate areas of study and activism. One goal of the group has been to highlight social problems in the field of deviance and social control which are under-exposed by criminologists in many other contexts; thus to create a forum not commonly provided at other conferences and international networks for academics, practitioners, and activists working towards the promotion of social justice, human rights and democratic accountability.

Cover Photo: Kjersti Varang

Dedication

This book is dedicated to the memory of Louk Hulsman (1923-2009)

A leading member of the *European Group for the Study of Deviance and Social Control*, Louk was an active and influential critic of penal policy. He was renowned not only for his gentleness and kindness as a human being but also for possessing a remarkable intellect and intensity of political commitment. Louk is perhaps remembered most as an educator. He could captivate and inspire an audience through the spoken word like few others. He participated at a number of European Group conferences, his last being at  Utrecht in 2007, and his humanistic values and principles not only echo those of the European Group, but indeed helped to shape them. His teachings have played an important part in the development of abolitionist arguments all around the world. Indeed, his influence on penal abolitionism is reflected in a number of chapters in this volume. Louk lived his beliefs and politics and encouraged others to do so. Louk asked people to re-think human problems and troubles and constantly problematised the application of the penal law. The best way to honour his legacy is to continue to advocate abolitionist values, principles and visions today within the European Group and beyond. This is the intention of this book.

Acknowledgements

This project would not have been possible without the efforts of all those who took part in the conferences at which the papers in this collection were first presented. In particular we are indebted to the authors and those who contributed to the production of the ten volumes of Working Papers in European Criminology; in particular Bill Rolston and Mike Tomlinson who edited the volumes from which most of this anthology are drawn from.

In addition we would like to thank Corina Rogerson who transcribed the majority of these papers, Mills Owens for proof reading and transcribing and Thomas Blok who reviewed (and corrected) the transcribed Dutch references.

Throughout this project we have benefited from the support of Emma Bell and Monish Bhatia, the co-ordinator and secretary of the European Group for the Study of Deviance and Social Control. We have also received personal and intellectual support from members of the group and through our continuing participation in the European Group. Thank you friends and comrades.

Any errors however are entirely our own.

J.M. Moore & David Scott
April 2014

Contents

Introduction

Section A:
Theoretical contributions

Section B:
Exposing and resisting criminal justice's harms

Introduction

1.

Beyond Criminal Justice

J.M. Moore and David Scott

The *European Group for the Study of Deviance and Social Control* has, since its first conference in 1973, provided a space for critical academics, students and activists to explore issues related to, among others, harm, power, social control and regulation. These examinations have been from a range of critical perspectives and the group has been characterised by its lack of a uniform dogma and openness to new and emerging ideas. For many of us who have been involved in its conferences it has offered the opportunity to meet in a supportive environment, largely devoid of hierarchies, to explore our ideas and to develop new ones. The group remains vibrant and relevant to contemporary debates as it approaches its 42nd conference in Liverpool in September 2014.[1]

In 2013 (with Joanna Gilmore) we edited *Critique & Dissent,* an anthology of papers presented at the first 40 conferences of *the European Group for the Study of Deviancy and Social Control* (European Group). As we read through the available papers we were struck by the rich vein of abolitionist papers delivered to conferences. In particular the ten editions of European Working Papers,[2] published between 1980 and 1990, included a number of important abolitionist papers which we, as more recent participants of the European Group's conferences, had not previously know existed. Although we were unable to include most of them in *Critique & Dissent* we resolved to compile them into a further collection. *Beyond Criminal Justice* is that book.

A question of values

The *European Group for the Study of Deviance and Social Control* has for over 40 years provided opportunities for scholars, activists and students to critically engage with issues connected to state punishment, 'crime' and 'deviant' behaviour.[3] Its 41 conferences have seen well in excess of a

---

[1] For more information about the group and its history see its website www.europeangroup,org/
[2] The full contents of the ten published *Working Papers in European Criminology* are listed in Appendix B of this edition.
[3] Gilmore, J., Moore. J. & Scott, D. (eds) (2013) *Critique and Dissent* Quebec: Red Quill

thousand papers delivered which have reflected the wide range of philosophical and political viewpoints the European Group has always been open to. Many of these have focused on state punishment which has consistently been exposed as an instrument of dominance. From the first conference the influence of penal abolition on the group has been both clear and welcome.[4] This influence has been both intellectual – how we see and understand the state's penal apparatus – and in defining the values of the European Group. These core values can be summarised as:

- *promoting craftsmanship, intellectual autonomy and integrity;*
- *fostering mutual support, cooperation and sisterly and brotherly warmth;*
- *nurturing comradeship, collegiality and solidarity with sufferers and the oppressed;*
- *emphasising political commitments, direct engagement in struggle and compassion for fellow human beings in need;*
- *And, facilitating emancipatory knowledge that can be used to challenge existing power relations.[5]*

These 'European group values' – promoting mutuality, solidarity and political commitments with the oppressed and holding the explicit aim of utilizing scholarship as a means of facilitating emancipatory change – when focused upon issues of 'crime' and punishment, dovetail perfectly with the principles and theoretical priorities of penal abolitionism. One of the aims of this book therefore is to emphasise these interconnections and indicate how the European Group and penal abolitionism have historically had a symbiotic relationship.

Abolitionism

Abolitionism historically has had many forms; the most significant being the eighteenth and nineteenth century movements for the abolition of slavery and the continuing campaigns for the abolition of the death penalty. What characterises all abolitionist movements is a rejection of the possibility of reforming their target institutions. Neither slavery nor the death penalty needed reform. They required abolition. For penal abolitionists the same

---

[4] For a discussion of the early relationship between abolitionism and the European group see Bianchi, H, Simondi, M. and Taylor, I. (eds.) (1975) *Deviance and Control In Europe,* London: John Wiley & Son
[5] For further details see Scott, D. (2012) *Opening address of 40th Annual Conference [available online at http://youtu.be/YOBsQjQ5xus]* and Gilmore et al (2013:21)

principal applies to state punishment in general and prisons in particular. In this collection Marijke Meima describes abolitionism as:

> The movement – grass-roots as well as academic – that tries to reach the diminishing and finally the abolition of the criminal law system, its rational as well as its institutions.[6]

Whilst reformers seek to find ways of making penal sanctions more effective abolitionists represent a much more fundamental challenge; for us the penal system is not malfunctioning but fundamentally flawed, it needs abolition. Included within the broader abolitionist movement are more specific abolitionist campaigns including those arguing for an abolition of the imprisonment of women,[7] people with mental health problems[8] and children.[9]

Penal abolitionism has a long history. For example William Godwin's *Enquiry into Political Justice* 'precluded all ideas of punishment or retribution'[10] whilst Edouard Desprez published his groundbreaking text *De L'Abolition de l'emprisonnement* in 1868.[11] Abolitionists recognise the reality that harmful acts, inter-personal conflicts, violence, problematic behaviours and a multitude of other troubles exist. What is distinctive about their thinking (and action) is the ways they chose to interpret and respond to such phenomena. By recognising that the way acts can be interpreted is socially constructed – for example by being classified as 'crimes' – abolitionist's offer the opportunity of seeing these acts in a variety of different ways. This in turn leads to the opening up of the possibility of a wide range of solutions.[12] Whereas the paradigm of 'criminal justice' funnels a wide variety of acts into the category of 'crime' – and thereby resolvable only through firstly the identification of someone to blame and secondly through the deliberate infliction of pain – what we popularly refer to as *punishment* – abolitionism seeks to understand each act in its own situational context and thereby offers the possibility of a multitude of possible resolutions. For abolitionists the sanctions of the criminal justice system in general and prisons in particular neither addresses the underlying issues nor provides any restoration to victims. Instead these 'solutions' are counter-productive, generate additional

---

[6] This volume p. 195

[7] Carlen, P. (1990) *Alternatives to Women's Imprisonment* Milton Keynes: Open University Press

[8] Hudson, B.A. (1993) *Penal Policy and Social Justice* London: Macmillan

[9] Goldson, B. (2005) 'Child imprisonment: a case for abolition' in *Youth Justice* Volume 5, No 2. pp. 77-90

[10] Godwin, W. (1793) *Enquiry into Political Justice* London: G.G.J. and J Robinson p. 237

[11] Desprez, E. (1868) *De L'Abolition de l'emprisonnement* Paris: Librairie De E Dentu

[12] Hulsman, L. (1986) 'Critical criminology and the concept of crime' in *Contemporary Crises*, Vol. 10, No. 1, pp.63-80

pain, produce social divisions and create further problematic behaviours.[13] By returning conflicts to the parties involved, by addressing them in their context and seeking to allow the participants to invent their own solutions, abolitionists offer a creative alternative to the crude infliction of blame and pain.

What's wrong with criminal justice?

In chapter twelve of this book Jolandeuit Beijerse and Renée Kool refer to the 'traitorous temptation' of criminal justice. This is both an incisive and appropriate description. Criminal justice language and thought has become embedded in our 'common sense' understanding of our world; it has, in a Gramscian sense, established its hegemony. But like much common sense we only need to scratch the surface, to see that its reality is far less impressive than its ideology.

Criminal justice's *claims* are impressive. It, in the name of the people, ensures fairness and 'justice'. It protects all equally and is enforced on all in society in a uniform manner. It protects society by controlling people who are dangerous, responding appropriately and proportionately to harmful and damaging acts. Through both its very existence and through its operation it prevents future problematic behaviour. Its operation benefits 'victims', who are portrayed as being at its core and against 'offenders'. These two groups, who are at the centre of its focus, are portrayed as belonging in separate and distinct categories.

Central to abolitionist thought is a deconstruction of these claims based on an empirical observation of the *reality* of criminal justice practice. In its day to day operation criminal justice reinforces the structural inequalities that characterise our socially unjust and unequal societies.[14] Its energies are focused predominately on controlling marginalised and powerless people whose 'crimes' are relatively harmless whilst failing to exercise control over powerful actors who are responsible for many of the most harmful behaviours.[15] With its focus on the infliction of pain as its ultimate outcome it is concerned with creating more not less harm.[16] Despite its philosophical claim in practice it fails to provide either security or protection for society.[17]

---

[13] Christie, N. (1993) *Crime Control as Industry* London: Routledge
[14] Scraton, P. (2007) *Power, Conflict and Criminalisation,* London: Routledge
[15] Hillyard, P. & Tombs, S. (2004) 'Beyond Criminology' in Hillyard. P, Pantazis, C., Tombs, S. and Gordon, D. (eds.) *Beyond Criminology: taking harm seriously* London: Pluto
[16] Christie, N.(1981) *The Limits of Pain* Oxford: Martin Robertson
[17] Mathiesen, T. (1990) *Prisons on Trial* London: Sage

Whereas victims are a relatively recent discovery for criminal justice, abolitionist critique has always taken victims seriously. A major part of the abolitionist project has been to return the conflict to the victim; to actually place them at the very centre of the conflict resolution process.[18] However in so doing it rejects the false dichotomy between the victim and the 'offender' instead recognising that often they have great similarities.   Crucially they share a common interest in successfully resolving their conflict. Abolitionist critiques have also highlighted the differential treatment victims' experience - based around their class, 'race', gender, sexuality and age – at the hands of criminal justices agencies. They have also challenged claims that reforms have sought to address the needs of victims. These reforms have often focused on reducing the rights of the accused and increasing the severity of pain inflicted on the convicted; changes which do nothing to address the marginalisation of victims and their needs. In their implementation such reforms purely exploit victims to justify enhancing the repressive capabilities of the state which continues to be deployed to consolidate and extend unequal power relations.

At the heart of abolitionist critique is a questioning of whether justice can ultimately be delivered through the criminal process. Abolitionists have argued that rather than contributing to the creation of a just society criminal justice undermines it. In unequal societies criminal justice reinforces social inequalities and focuses on inflicting pain on the least powerful.[19] Instead, they argue, to create a more just society and to meet the needs of both the 'victim' and the 'perpetrator' we need to develop alternative non-repressive conceptions of justice that can meet the needs of human beings.[20] In other words we must think **beyond** 'criminal justice'.

Book Overview

All the papers included in this anthology have been previously published in editions of the *Working Papers in European Criminology* published between 1980 and 1990. This series, long out of print, represents a rich source of critical and emancipatory scholarship. It was also a major logistical triumph of publishing. The papers were delivered at a European Group annual conference, by scholars and activists whose first language was often not English, written up, revised, edited and printed in time for distribution by the following year's conference. In the era before word processors, e-mail and publishing software this required immense effort and dedication. We therefore wish to thank Manfred Brusten and Paul Ponsaers, (the editors of

---

[18] Christie, N. (1977) "Conflict as property" *British Journal of Criminology,* Vol 17, No. 1, pp. 1-15
[19] Mathiesen, T. (1990) *Prisons on Trial* London: Sage
[20] Hudson, B.A. (2003a) *Justice in the Risk Society,* London: Sage

volume 2); Paddy Hillyard (who jointly edited volumes 3, 4 and 5); Peter Squires, (the joint editor of volumes 3 and 4) Mike Tomlinson (the joint editor of volumes 5, 7, 8, 9 and 10) and Bill Rolston (who edited volume 6 and was the joint editor of volumes 5, 7, 8, 9 and 10) as well as the anonymous editors of volume one. Without their commitment to the European Group and their scholarship this anthology would not have been possible.[21] It is planned that the full series of *Working Papers in European Criminology* will be electronically republished by the European Group in the near future allowing the full collection to become widely available.

This collection has been organised into three sections. The first of these focuses on the theoretical contribution of European Penal abolitionism, whilst the second contains essays that expose and resist the harms generated by criminal justice. The final section highlights abolitionists' capacity to look beyond criminal justice and advocate alternative responses to conflicts, harms and disputes. In the next chapter, in a paper originally published in 1989, Jacqueline Bernat de Celis provides reflections on a how we can foster greater cohesion of the abolitionist movement as a whole. Locating her discussion in an international context rather than just a European one, her central premise is that for penal abolitionists the prison is 'unacceptable' and must be rejected as a legitimate response to human conflict. This is because of three fundamental reasons, which should be reiterated today with equal vigour – first, the prison is counter-intuitive to normal human values, ethical codes and commitments to human rights and well being; second, the prison reflects an abstraction of humanity and its continued existence can lead only to further reification and alienation; and third, the prison has a clear political function in maintaining social inequalities.

The prison cannot be humanised and therefore a further central unifying theme of penal abolitionists is the demand for radical alternatives to prisons and other forms of penalisation. This requires radical transformation of the social system which perpetuates penal incarceration alongside pragmatic interventions for handling human conflict and problematic conduct that respect human diversity. To be an abolitionist means bearing witness to the violence of incarceration and being prepared 'to stand up against it'.[22] Jacqueline Bernat de Celis points the way forward by considering strategies that could be adopted by penal abolitionists to challenge the power to punish on both an individual and collective level.

In chapter three Heinz Steinert explores the relationship between Marxism and abolitionism. He recognises a natural sympathy between these two

---

[21] Such is the contribution of Bill Rolston and Mike Tomlinson to the papers selected in this volume that we felt it appropriate to acknowledge this by including them as co-editors.
[22] Bernat de Celis, this volume p.22

radical and emancipatory traditions – both abolitionism and Marxism have similar value bases and to differing extents draw upon the assumptions of a libertarian socialism that pre-dates the emergence of both perspectives. Writing in the 1980s, however, his initial focus is to critically review a then recent perspective that appeared to have its roots in Marxism but was often considered as hostile to abolitionism – 'left realism', and especially the issues and debates rehearsed in Roger Matthews and Jock Young's 1986 reader *Confronting Crime*.[23] Identifying the limitations and contradictions within the (then fashionable) left realist perspective, Steinert systematically outlines the close relationship between Marxian analysis and penal abolitionism. In so doing he draws attention to their shared philosophical underpinnings in libertarian socialism and the ideas of socialist diversity, ironically fundamental to the Marxist abolitionism found in the 'new criminology' proposed by the later 'left realists' Ian Taylor and Jock Young.[24]

Pat Carlen has observed that whilst the history of penology has been characterised by 'the failure of punishment in general, and imprisonment in particular … (p)hilosophies of punishment, by contrast, have enjoyed a continuing success.'[25] Most abolitionist critique focuses on this failure of punishment in practice but in chapter four Willem de Haan develops a powerful abolitionist response to the justifications of punishment articulated through moral and political philosophy. His essay sets out a rational challenge to the assumptions underpinning the incorporation of punishment as a social institution into philosopher's theories of justice and their attempts to reconcile punishment with a just social order.

Of fundamental importance in de Haan's critique is a rejection of the direct association of the concept of punishment with justice. How can one person's rights be restored by inflicting pain on another person? Surely, he argues, compensation or restitution are more effective expressions of justice than punishment. By separating out the concept of sanctions from that of punishment de Haan provides for the possibility of just responses which are not based on the pain-infliction. His 'plunge into moral and political philosophy' provides abolitionism with a much firmer theoretical grounding and shows how a just social order is not only possible without punishment but requires its rejection.[26]

---

[23] Matthews, R. and Young, J. (eds) (1986) *Confronting Crime* London: Sage

[24] Taylor, I., Walton, P. & Young, J. (1973) *The New Criminology* London: RKP

[25] Carlen, P. (1983) "On Rights and Powers: Some Notes on Penal Politics" pp 203-216 in David Garland and Peter Young (Eds.) *The Power to Punish: Contemporary Penality and Social Analysis*. London: Heinemann Educational Books p. 203

[26] de Haan, this volume p.72

Sebastian Scheerer in chapter five considers why the abolition of the prison failed to materialise as predicted by influential social commentators in the 1970s. Indeed, rather than seeing its end we have, instead, witnessed the expansion of the prison at a frightening pace in many countries, with Scheerer focusing on the case study of the Federal Republic of Germany in the mid 1980s. Drawing upon the insights of key thinkers such as Max Weber, Scheerer explores the interrelationships between what he refers to as 'autopotetic subsystems'.[27] In this chapter his primary focus is on the relationship between the 'relatively autonomous fields' of prisons and the criminal law. Scheerer starts by considering right and left wing arguments about the 'death of law' as a coherent and rational set of principles guiding human conduct and the implications of this dissolution for the meaning and practical application of the 'rule of law'. Throughout Scheerer presents an analytical framework that incisively and insightfully explains why the criminal law must be located within a wider administrative 'system' that has created not the 'death of criminal law' and penalisation but rather their enormous expansion. He concludes with a consideration of exit strategies and alternatives to current forms of 'over-criminalisation'.

The next section opens with Ida Koch's critical evaluation of the use of isolation in the detention of suspects before trials in Denmark. In 1985 when this paper was written Denmark had the highest per capita prison population in Western Europe and routinely solitarily detained those remanded in custody. Many of these prisoners were held in these conditions for months and sometimes years and Koch explores the harms caused by this isolation. Through a combination of interviews with prisoners, second-hand accounts of prison staff and documentary evidence Koch details the impact of isolation. The harms suffered by the prisoners are extensive and include: nightmares, anxiety, suicide attempts (sometimes successfully), self harm, difficulties concentrating, a loss of memory, fatigue, rage, declining physical health, hallucinations, and paranoia. The impact of isolation continues beyond release, with great difficulties being experienced in engaging in social interaction and with some reporting themselves 'no longer (able to) cope with physical and emotional intimacy and contact ... They feel severely handicapped.'[28] Koch's conclusion is that detention in isolation is both unnecessary and 'inhuman and cruel treatment'; a violation of the detainees human right.

---

[27] Scheerer, this volume p. 78
[28] Koch, this volume p.104

The next two chapters explore the political context in which prisons operate in Italy and in England and Wales. Raffaele Calderone and Piere Valeriani in chapter seven explore developments in the operations of Italian prisons in the 1970s and the relationships between prisoners' struggles and the wider left wing movements. In their review they identify, from the 1960s, an attempt to develop significant progressive reforms in penal policy. These included a greater focus on rehabilitation and maintaining prisoners' contacts with their families and communities. However despite this they highlight how these reforms have been systematically clawed back with the core functions of order and security reasserting their dominance of penal practice. In a Marxist analysis Calderone and Valeriani see the conflicts taking place within prisons as reflections of 'the political and social conflicts taking place in the world outside (and) as a theatre of class conflict.'[29] Their account emphasises the various attempts made by the prisoners' movement to link their campaigns with those of workers and others outside the prison.

Calderone and Valeriani were writing at a time when the constitutional parties of the left, the Socialists and the Communists, held considerable political power, particularly within local government. It was also the time when an extra-parliamentary left was emerging. They suggest the failure of the political parties to utilise the (limited) power they had to realise progressive change in prison conditions had resulted in the prisoners' movements becoming dominated by what they describe as 'counter-power organisations'.[30]

The political situation Joe Sim describes in mid-1980s England in chapter eight is very different. The Thatcher government had recently defeated the miners' strike and was implementing economic policies which represented major defeats for working people. Prison populations had grown significantly amid an increasing strengthening and militarisation of policing. The government's rhetoric focused on their alleged concerns about serious crime whilst their actions displayed an increasing capacity to maintain 'public order' and ruthlessly respond to dissent and political resistance.

The increasing resort to the use of imprisonment is seen by Sim as a direct result of this political situation. However, it placed considerable strain on the penal estate's capacity and contributed to a deepening of the crisis within the prison. This crisis he explores in detail, highlighting that it extends beyond the impact of overcrowding and includes conflict between prison staff and management; conflict between prisoners and staff; increased resistance by prisoners (including peaceful direct action and legal challenges); and ultimately leads to the questioning of the legitimacy of the prison. In response

---

[29] Calderone and Valeriani, this volume p. 116
[30] Ibid, p.121

the state has sought to increase capacity and to introduce a range of control techniques intended to isolate and neutralise the most 'difficult' prisoners. Re-reading Sim's article nearly 30 years after it was written is sobering. The English and Welsh prison system's expansion has accelerated and resistance within prison has, at least to date, largely been successfully managed. In a time of austerity for the majority of the population Sim's reference to 'an increasingly fragile social order beset by economic decline, industrial stagnation and political conflict' remains highly relevant.[31] In such a context the abolitionist's challenge to the very legitimacy of the prison and penal system is particularly important.

The consequences of the reality of imprisonment are explored in the next chapter by Phil Scraton and Kathryn Chadwick. They focus on the Glenochil Complex in Scotland, which when this paper was delivered incorporated both a detention centre and a young offenders institution, and critically evaluate an official inquiry into it following the death of seven young teenage prisoners in the early 1980s.[32] Such deaths threaten the legitimacy of penal institutions and Scraton and Chadwick highlight how in seeking to defuse this challenge the inquiry team led by Derek Chiswick sought to focus on the individuals who had died at their own hands rather than the institution in which their deaths had occurred. The inquiry report by-passed the 'broader structural and political contexts' and instead sought to establish a category of particularly vulnerable prisoner at risk of attempting to take their own lives.[33] Although Glenochil utilised a medical model to identify vulnerability Scraton and Chadwick highlight how in its practical management of those defined as vulnerable it adopted an entirely punitive approach. Rejecting the report's naïve belief that the institutions exist for the care and treatment of the young people confined within them, Scraton and Chadwick firmly locate the cause of the deaths in the violence and pain inherent in penal institutions. Those who have killed themselves they argue should not been seen as deficient, instead we should consider them as 'responding *rationally* to inhuman policies and practices which are inherent in harsh regimes'.[34]

In the first chapter of the third section of this anthology Rene van Swaaningen argues for following Michel Foucault's advice and avoiding the mistake of 'thinking we can present another – better – "law and order" so as to create a more righteous society.'[35] In examining the relationship between criminology and abolitionism he highlights a major difference – abolitionism

---

[31] Sim, this volume p. 148
[32] Glenochil currently (in 2014) operates as an adult male prison.
[33] Scraton and Chadwick, this volume p. 155
[34] Scraton and Chadwick, this volume, p. 168. Emphasis in original
[35] Swaaningen, this volume pp. 173-4

extends beyond criminology and its focus on 'crime' and punishment. Abolitionist alternatives don't only seek to redirect the responses to conflicts and harmful acts away from the criminal justice system but also to critique the authoritarian nature of those alternatives. For real change 'punitive and repressive attitude(s)' need challenging as well as specific institutions. Central to this is the rejection of the 'authoritarian idolatry' that comes from abdicating responsibility to the 'professionals in charge' and state agencies. Ultimately, abolitionists are arguing for us all to reclaim our collective responsibility, or as Swaaningen argues:

> If we want to put a stop to an undesirable situation, and we want our personal views and wishes to play a role in the settlement of the conflict, we should not just rely on some kind of authority to do it for us. We should take up our personal responsibility as well; before, during and after a criminalisable conflict.[36]

Swaaningen's analysis touches on the way the women's movements campaigns against sexual violence have been 'defined in' by the criminal justice system. This theme is central to the next three chapters which all provide abolitionist insights into gendered violence and possible responses. Common to all three is an acknowledgement, from a feminist perspective, of the seriousness of sexual and other gendered violence. In the first of these papers Marijke Meima sets out to critique both existing criminal justice responses to sexual violence and potential abolitionist alternatives. For Meima the criminal process has a number of fatal flaws. The most serious being the number of possibilities of escape — in the police investigation, in the decision to prosecute and in the trial — offered; the ineffectiveness of the sanctions available in the event of a conviction and the way criminal justice formalises and removes the conflict from the parties. Echoing critique from earlier chapters, 'neither the 'culprit' nor the 'victim',' Meima argues, 'will recognise himself or herself in the legal version of what has actually happened.'[37]

The absence of a single authoritative abolitionist approach is highlighted by Meima. Instead abolitionists argue for enabling people to find ways of resolving their own conflicts. This raises the obvious problem of the co-operation of the alleged perpetrator. However by moving away from criminal justice's focus on blame and penal sanctions (and the associated legal protection of a defendant) an abolitionist approach promotes this co-

---

[36] Swaaningen, this volume p. 184
[37] Meima, this volume p.200

operation. Meima draws on the conferencing approach of restorative justice allowing for the parties to reach a resolution without the need for judicial intervention (although some form of civil judicial intervention may be necessary where agreement has not been reached).[38] But does this mean effectively the 'rapist' will get away with their sexual violence? For Meima this is not the central question, instead she prioritises the objective of stopping sexual violence. She argues that under an abolitionist approach not only is the necessary message about the unacceptability of sexual violence communicated, but also that:

> The chance that a rapist will learn from this procedure, being confronted with all the suffering and problems he has caused, is much bigger than the chance that he will learn from the distant, authoritarian and uniform procedure we know now.[39]

In chapter twelve Jolandeuit Beijerse and Rene Kool explore the relationship between the Dutch Women's Movement and the Criminal Justice System in respect of responding to violence against women. Their starting point is the encounter between women as victims and the criminal justice system. They conclude, like most research, that criminal justice largely fails to hold perpetrators to account and where it does it can only offer women 'that the violator will be punished.'[40] This failure has led to a number of responses from the women's movements. Initially their focus was firstly on a political understanding of sexual violence which located it within the context of power relations and secondly on the provision of direct services to women victimised by this violence. This political understanding has led inevitably to a critique of criminal justice and its potential role in responding to sexual violence. For significant sections of the women's movement this has led to calls for reform of criminal justice to make it more effective through for example revised legal definitions of offences and the training of police and prosecutors. The authors highlight how such moves have largely failed and will prove 'a dead-end street'.[41] Such a failure is, they argue, inevitable when women rely on an institution whose primary function is the maintenance of social order. The women's movement they conclude must avoid 'the traitorous temptation of criminal justice'.[42]

---

[38] For a critical discussion of some of these points see Hudson, B.A. (2003a) *Justice in the Risk Society* London: Sage and Hudson, B.A. (2003b) *Understanding Justice,* London: Sage.
[39] Meima this volume p. 203
[40] Beijerse and Kool, this volume p.211
[41] Ibid, p. 219
[42] Ibid, p. 207

In chapter thirteen Willemien de Jongste seeks to explore the understandings of power that underpin feminist theory and the abolitionism of Louk Hulsman. Like the previous paper de Jongste's analysis is based on the experience of law reform and the women's movement in the Netherlands. She identifies a conflict between the movement's theoretical understanding of both sexual violence and the operation of criminal justice as strategies of patriarchal power and its increasing advocation of criminal law as the appropriate paradigm within which to respond to sexual violence. By deploying Hulsman's apple model of criminal justice this essay identifies how the attempts to reform criminal law inevitably lead to the reinforcing of existing power relations. Whatever success is achieved in changing the wording of the penal code with respect to sexual violence the reliance on criminal justice leads to 'an implementation of a dominant view of rape rather than a means of fighting against it.'[43]

The section concludes with Marti Gronfors's account of a mediation scheme introduced in 1984 to the city of Vantaa in Finland. The paper provides an account of the scheme's first two years of operation before drawing some important conclusions. The project had been set up on good abolitionist principles – for example recognition that conflicts are normal, best resolved quickly and between the people directly involved – although it operated alongside criminal justice interventions. This meant that some cases were both resolved in the mediation scheme and processed through the courts. Gronfors's evaluation reaches some important conclusions. Firstly mediation operates at its best when deployed to resolve a conflict between the parties. Where someone has a more general problem expert advice is required rather than the communicative skills offered by mediators. Secondly whilst the scheme was initially characterised by mediation resulting in creative solutions it rapidly lost this aspect and by the end of the two years was exclusively trying to resolve disputes by financial compensation, often at levels far higher than would have been awarded by courts. Thirdly participants reported high levels of satisfaction with a significant proportion feeling they were getting 'justice'. His final point is to raise the danger that such schemes, particularly when funded by the state, will be co-opted. There was already evidence of this happening in Vantaa.

The books comes to a close with a chapter by David Scott and J.M. Moore which locates the key themes and issues raised in the previous thirteen substantive chapters within our contemporary social and political contexts. Scott and Moore point to a number of lessons that can be drawn from these European Group Working Papers which abolitionists can adopt today in 2014.

---

[43] de Jongste, this volume p. 236

Bibliography

Bianchi, H, Simondi, M. and Taylor, I. (eds.) (1975) *Deviance and Control In Europe,* London: John Wiley & Son

Carlen, P. (1983) "On Rights and Powers: Some Notes on Penal Politics" pp 203-216 in David Garland and Peter Young (Eds.) *The Power to Punish: Contemporary Penality and Social Analysis.* London: Heinemann Educational Books

Carlen, P. (1990) *Alternatives to Women's Imprisonment* Milton Keynes: Open University Press

Christie, N. (1977) "Conflict as property" *British Journal of Criminology,* Vol. 17, No. 1, pp. 1-15

Christie, N. (1981) *The Limits of Pain* Oxford: Martin Robertson

Christie, N. (1993) *Crime Control as Industry* London: Routledge

Desprez, E. (1868) *De L'Abolition de l'emprisonnement* Paris: Librairie De E Dentu

Gilmore, J., Moore. J. & Scott, D. (eds) (2013) *Critique and Dissent* Quebec: Red Quill

Godwin, W. (1793) *Enquiry into Political Justice* London: G.G.J. and J Robinson

Goldson, B. (2005) 'Child imprisonment: a case for abolition' in *Youth Justice* Volume 5, No 2. pp. 77-90

Hillyard, P & Tombs, S. (2004) 'Beyond Criminology' in Hillyard. P, Pantazis, C., Tombs, S. and Gordon, D. (eds) *Beyond Criminology: taking harm seriously* London: Pluto

Hudson, B.A. (1993) *Penal Policy and Social Justice* London: Macmillan

Hudson, B.A. (2003a) *Justice in the Risk Society,* London: Sage

Hudson, B.A. (2003b) *Understanding Justice,* London: Sage

Hulsman, L. (1986) 'Critical criminology and the concept of crime' in *Contemporary Crises,* Vol. 10, No. 1, pp.63-80

Matthews, R. and Young, J. (eds) (1986) *Confronting Crime* London: Sage

Mathiesen, T. (1990) *Prisons on Trial* London: Sage

Scott, D. (2012) *Opening address of 40th Annual Conference [available online at http://youtu.be/YOBsQjQ5xus]*

Scraton, P. (2007) *Power, Conflict and Criminalisation,* London: Routledge

Taylor, I., Walton, P. & Young, J. (1973) *The New Criminology* London: RKP

Section A:

Theoretical Contributions

·2.

Whither Abolitionism?

Jacqueline Bernat de Celis

This paper was delivered at the European Group's 15th annual conference in Vienna and first published in Working Papers in European Criminology, Volume 9 'Justice & Ideology: Strategies for the 1990s' in 1989.

Introduction

The third international meeting in Montreal on the Abolition of the Penal System should, I believe, prompt every 'abolitionist' to take stock of the present state of the movement not, as I see it to note the possible progress of abolitionist ideas in the various circles where they are proposed or attempted—an attempt which would be premature—but to explore the internal cohesion of the movement and each one's place in it. Can one clearly define what the different practitioners who spoke in Montreal are demanding? Do all abolitionists have the same objective? Is there a minimum of agreement among them that could lead to the elaboration of a basic abolitionist proposal? I personally feel the need for such a consummation. In proposing my ideas, I would also like to evoke others, which would finally enable the abolitionists to gain credibility and the possibility of action.

A Conviction Shared, but without Definite Objectives

The participants in the Montreal conference expressed, at least implicitly, a profound common conviction: prison and punitive imprisonment, such as conceived and applied in the penal system of the western world, is *unacceptable*. A consensus of this kind can be hailed as an event, and from two points of view—first as a development of the movement itself. The meetings at Toronto and Amsterdam, which preceded that at Montreal, still fell back sometimes on the idea that the prison can be *transformed*. In Montreal it was a question of *abolishing* the prison. Second, to consider the prison impossible to reform is a radical position compared with other types of conferences where the problems of criminal justice are dealt with in the traditional way. Although in these meetings too—and for a long time—the negative aspects of incarceration have always been denounced, since there are no alternatives it is generally agreed that imprisonment is a necessary evil that our society cannot do without.

In Montreal there was a definite and unanimous rejection of prison. Whatever the origin of the participants (nationality, ethnic origin, professional activity, social status and so on) and whatever their particular approach to the problems at hand, all confirmed in one way or other the need to eradicate the existing state-controlled punitive model in western type democracies. But it must be said that in spite of the unanimous nature of this desire no precise common objective, immediate, long-term or middle-term, emerged from this conference, and I would like to find out why. An analysis perhaps may discover one or several lines of action with which everyone thinking about abolitionism may be able to go along.

Many Points of View

The participants in the Montreal conference were involved in the abolitionist movement in many different ways, which was natural, considering their great diversity. Among them were university professors; criminologists; researchers in sociology and psychology; representatives of various Christian churches; members of native Canadian groups; a prosecutor from the Republic of the former Belgian Congo; lawyers; social workers; educators working in the prison milieu; members of associations for the rehabilitation of ex-prisoners; feminists; former prisoners; students; and so on.

The enormous number of approaches and points of view was striking. In workshops an attempt was made to analyse the forces of alienation at work in the prison world; the over-representation in the prison population of the most disadvantaged elements of society; the ineffectiveness of so-called 'alternative punishments' on the the ever-increasing number of prisoners, and so on. Other workshops discussed the methods used by native peoples to settle disputes before colonisation or by the people of the Bible, as well as the efforts made here and there to revive or adapt these same methods of appeasement in the villages and cities of post-industrial countries. In another group where questions were raised concerning the opportunity to decriminalise certain causes of litigious matters the irrationality of the penal system was pointed out, its legitimacy questioned. Elsewhere the participants looked into the concepts and mentalities of those who created the present punitive model in the western countries and the structures and values on which the societies of advanced capitalism are based. A well-represented group in several workshops expressed the desire, in the name of a born-again Christian ideal to bring about a 'justice of reconciliation' to replace the present 'vindictive justice', or to revive 'places of refuge' where the perpetrators of violent 'crimes could stay during the period of negotiation or mediation'.

Prison, the Focal Point of every Discussion

When going from one workshop to another it was obvious that the participants were not dealing with the same problems, nor did the content of the discussions concern equivalent issues with some drawing up reports others expressing desiderata while others were proposing ways of making changes with some strategies should the occasion arise. It was difficult to see what common ground there could be for the various demands.

The common denominator, of course, was the prison with many expressing the regretful premonition that it would still be with us for a long time to come. For some, to abolish the prison was the ultimate goal for others, however, this was not the point of arrival, but the point of departure or if you will, a step that would lead to others—merely one phase of a complex process to be considered in its entirety. To simplify matters it might be said that the discussion in Montreal revolved around three main issues:

1. the prison seen as a place for the implementation of an *unacceptable desire to punish*, going counter to both the values upheld in native societies and the principles proclaimed in the charters of human rights;
2. the prison seen as the product of a system, itself unacceptable because very far removed from reality and revealing a dim and *pessimistic view of humanity* and human relationships;
3. the prison considered the *symptom of an unequal, marginalizing society*, founded on a domination/submission relationship that the penal system supports and maintains.

A Gradual Awareness

These three areas of discussion, using different theoretical approaches— the prison world, the penal system, and the ethical and institutional bases of society— could be regarded as levels of awareness that everyone is called upon to acquire. Faced with the inanity of the efforts made to try to open up, humanise and empty the prison, the realisation comes that it is not really the *transformation* of the prisons that must be programmed, but their *elimination.* To accomplish this, we must see the penal system in perspective, as it is conceived, legitimised and implemented; it can only cause useless suffering. To eliminate prisons, however, we must first remove the system that produces them. But we have to look even further; the penal system is merely part of the economic, political, ideological structure on which society is founded. Thus abolishing the penal system must necessarily be part of a more global movement to change the entire order.

To be aware of the implications involved in any action regarding the prison is to understand the strength and tenacity of the resistance against abolitionist thinking at every level, this obtains not only among the backers of the penal system, but in university, political and journalistic circles, where discourse naturally falls within the framework of traditional political philosophy. If the abolitionist point of view did not profoundly question, at least implicitly, the forces that maintain the dominant groups in power and the simplistic Manicheism that affects all social groups it would be more easily accepted. The fear of chaos it engenders when proposed (within the framework of intellectual thought) shows that in essence it is an element of ideological opposition to a certain form of state.

What is to be Done?

A presentiment about the final stakes concerning the movement invites a certain modesty in the formulation of our project and a great deal of care in the elaboration of strategies for the transition from theory to practice. An analysis of the penal system is far from finished. Its connections with the economic, political and ideological structures of the surrounding society are still little known. Decision-making mechanisms, the very essence of power are the subject of much controversy today. Under these conditions, how can we suggest actions that would not immediately be crushed or reprocessed by the reigning conservatism? To concentrate on our incapacity to foresee how our alternative proposals will be utilised gives one a feeling of helplessness, and the participants in the Montreal conference who had made a point of this tended to adopt a wait-and-see policy. As long as we lack additional information on all the issues that are still not clear, as long as we have not proceeded with all the demystification necessary, and as long as we have not reversed the order of values on which our advanced capitalist societies are based, it would serve little purpose—or could even be counter-productive— to speak of abolishing the prison or the penal system.

This attitude can easily lead to an impasse of pessimism and immobility, but this did not happen in Montreal. There is another form of attack, which does not attempt to reverse the existing order all at once. On the contrary without minimizing the complexity or power of that order every blow it receives, undermining it bit by bit contributes to its destruction. It seemed to me that most of the participants shared this point of view.

Abolish What?

Not everyone spoke of abolishing the same thing, of course and some would have preferred that under no circumstances should such a radical term as 'abolish' be used considering it uselessly provocative, since the final object of the 'movement' is impossible to define just now. The term, however, is historically recognized. Today we are demanding the abolition of the prison or the penal system just as we have demanded in turn—and finally largely obtained—the abolition of slavery, of the death penalty and of corporal punishment. The abolitionist movement is not trying to specifically do away with this or that. It is critical awareness embodied in the reality of the moment and which never ceases to be on the alert in the face of mechanisms for the submission of humankind or specific groups of people. The 'abolitionists' of today, at whatever level their demands, are obviously part of this dynamic. Of different conceptual views or varied experiences they set in motion a multiform process of questioning the administration of justice that not one of them can claim to really control, that necessarily remains open, 'unachieved' and whose value in the possible results obtained—ever to be surpassed—will be less than in the ferment of liberation they introduced in a domain where the relationship of forces is expressed with a particularly intense and significant violence. To be an abolitionist today is to be a witness to this violence whether discovered in theoretical thought or in one or other aspect of the penal process and to want to stand up against it. If we accept this criterion, all the participants of the *International Conference on Penal Abolition* (ICOPA) were certainly 'abolitionists'.

The Creative Spirit of Abolitionism

The paradox of the abolitionist position is its creative aspect. The abolitionist would rather create than abolish. S/he sees what would make society more just and what stops it from being so, what exists already that is hopeful and what must be fought so that favourable alternative elements can develop. To consider people equal because they are different and not because they are identical; to recognize the diversity in groups rather than a false homogeneity; to see in the 'social contract' an assumption of the domination of a majority over minorities; to seek to engender a society no longer based on *consensus* but on *assensus*; to believe that truth is not one but many things, that truth is neither behind us nor already moulded for the future, but must be created each moment; to consider the values of solidarity and tolerance as priorities, today stifled by contrary values—these are some of the basic ideas taken up in Montreal. They give a creative aspect to 'abolitionism', a term whose very meaning makes it prejudged as a pure and simple desire for destruction.

The penal system must disappear, according to abolitionist theory, because it is based on principles of death and humiliation of the weak; on a simplistic and simplifying view of humanity and human relationships; because it gives priority to the 'system' over the 'real world'; and finally, because it legitimises the prison, which is a product of an authoritarian and violent intervention of the state in people's lives. In order to destroy the mechanisms of alienation, more destructive in the penal system than anywhere else, the abolitionists mean to introduce in society as a whole a respect for differences and the emancipation of the individual.

Dispute over Corrections

Abolishing the penal system is not regarded as *an end in itself* by all theoretical abolitionists.   Everyone at the Montreal conference, in fact, seemed to agree that it was a *means* to an end. While considering it necessary to analyse the interface between the organisation of justice and the other existing socio-political organisations, we can agree to consider corrections *ad intra* as well, and to convince ourselves that actions that tend to make this system less active—indispensable, incidentally if we are to start resolving the problem of prison—could at the same time help in precipitating the socio-political change desired. Those who have chosen to carry on a direct fight against the penal system find support in the recent contributions of penal sociology. The latter has already shown:

1. the non-specific nature of the situations dealt with in the correctional field;
2. the absence of natural characters among the persons selected for this field;
3. the historically recent origin and the marginal character of corrections as a system for the settling of interpersonal conflicts.

These essential findings should make it possible to eliminate the discriminatory concept of crime and thus the penal system itself, in favour of a model for resolving conflicts based on negotiation and mediation and universally attached to the civil domain. The penal system, however, is not a simple techno-legal organisation. At the same time that penal sociology is discovering, statistically and normatively that it is a particular field that has no rational reason for its existence, it gradually reveals its socio-political aspect, showing the link between forms of correction and forms of the state. Consequently, it may be imagined that the adversaries of the project aimed at its elimination will multiply their forces in order to prevent its realisation.

The abolitionists now know better than they did in the past that they must not hope for the political authorities to topple the penal system, as it would be easy to do in theory—gradually and quietly. Whereas the over-population of prisons worries almost all governments, why, for example, is there no decision to turn some correctional disputes over to civil jurisdiction, to stop public action when a victim withdraws his/her complaint, reduce the delays of prescription, offer interested parties the possibility of conciliation outside the penal process? Instead of trying to suppress penal production, however, governments prefer to plan, at great expense, the construction of new prisons. Under the present circumstances, with the return in full force of repressive ideologies and the hardening of official crime policies (plus ignoring the teachings of science), those who would abolish the penal system know that their proposals to weaken the system 'from the top' must be kept in reserve for a more opportune moment.

The Prison in the Forefront

Thus it was perceived at Montreal that in the end prisons themselves would have to be largely counted on to bring about the expected awareness. Experience has shown that it is practically impossible to rouse crowds against the 'penal system', the significance of whose machinery is hard to understand without using difficult concepts that have no emotional impact. On the other hand, we know there is considerable public awareness of all that concerns the prison world.

As a result of the endless discrimination suffered by the helpless, prison at a given moment, could become intolerable to many and start a movement toward important changes. This was clearly expressed at Montreal, where the fight for prisoners' rights was regarded as a strategy to be developed. If all the rights recognized outside the walls were respected inside the walls the prison would explode of itself. Demanding rights for prisoners—such as the right to medical care citizenship self-education a trade, to meet with family members, to receive a normal salary—were all seen as one way of attacking the socio-political foundations of the system.

An Active but Cautious Approach

Prevented from developing openly by all the forces it opposes, the abolitionist movement has been forced to think of indirect or underground strategies and to find allies among groups that have already undertaken acts of emancipation on their own behalf. Feminists, homosexuals, ecologists, the non-violent, Christians engaged in 'liberation movements' and ethnic minorities organised for the defence of their rights in a society in which they are browbeaten have something in common with the abolitionists, and the latter must explain their cause more clearly. These groups should know that the abolitionists were on the march toward a utopia that closely concerns them. The abolitionists in turn can learn from these groups the alternative non-authoritarian political forms they are trying to proclaim. Besides the urgent need to promote active dialogue with these natural allies, it was declared imperative at Montreal for every abolitionist to work relentlessly on him/herself. How? By being attentive to the discoveries of the social sciences and learning to draw useful data from them, as well as freeing oneself from the hidden grip of the penal system on the life and being of people in the West.

Are those who call themselves abolitionists sure they have completely banished the guilt/punishment perspective of the penal system from their minds? Do they speak a language that no longer borrows from the ideas that found, implement and legitimise this system? To free oneself from penal ideology is a long-term undertaking, for it surreptitiously colours all spheres of thought. For example, we hear philosophers of law speak of the penal system as if it were the *entire* law or the *original form* of the law, thus we still find in the writings of informed sociologists the words 'crime', 'criminal', 'victim', *etc.* used as provided by the criminal law, the very system they are trying to demystify. Moreover, we have seen at Montreal one of the pioneers of *decriminalisation* suddenly distrust a step that, based on the definitions of the system, he wondered might possibly reinforce it in a way. To track down and denounce the unsuspected totalitarianism of the penal system, to be absolutely sure of taking a new departure, the last recommendation heard at Montreal, the message that the abolitionists repeated one to the other was *let us decolonise ourselves.*

3.

Marxian Theory and Abolitionism: Introduction to a Discussion

Heinz Steinert

This paper was delivered at the European Group's 15th annual conference in Vienna and first published in Working Papers in European Criminology, Volume 9 'Justice & Ideology: Strategies for the 1990s' in 1989.

Under ordinary circumstances I would have thought that there is a strong and natural affinity between Marxian theory in criminology and abolitionism. Where else do we have a formula like the 'withering away of the state' (and where should such a 'withering away' start if not with prisons)? We could, of course, see anarchism as a strong rival. But then, I must confess, I have always, in spite of everything that went on between Bakunin, Catalonia, the anti-authoritarian movement of the 1960s and their respective 'Marxist' counterparts, seen anarchism as very closely related to Marxian thinking, the main difference being an empirical question: do we still have to bet on even further development of the forces of production as a pre-condition for a thorough 'revolutionizing' of the social formation, or are we already far beyond that point, especially in the concomitant development of the means of destruction and of domination. If the latter should be the case, the anarchist type of analysis of the historical situation and the strategic options it offers would be the more appropriate one. And I cannot see that anybody in the 'first world' could assume that what we need is still further 'progress' of the kind that brought us all the wars of this century[1], Auschwitz, the atomic bomb, widespread starvation in regions of the world and the impending breakdown of the ecological system which can mean the end of the habitable world. I cannot believe that anybody in his/her right mind could opt for 'more of the same' as a solution to present problems and a hope of emancipation and liberation.

---

[1] Editors' note: 20th Century.

But circumstances are not as 'ordinary' as some hope and others fear. In criminology we see very little Marxian analysis anyway and still less in which the question of liberation is the focus—and some of it is explicitly anti-abolitionist, some simply ignores it, but does not share its assumptions. On the other hand, there seems to be a direct line from labelling theory to abolitionism, but this approach has not been carried on towards a grounding in a wider framework of social theory, *i.e.* in some variant of Marxian analysis (unless we want to convert to systems theory, the only serious competitor, and give up the idea of liberation). Is the idea that in criminology Marxian analysis and abolitionism should go together simply wrong, or is it just historical contingency that empirically they mostly do not.

My impression that Marxian analysis and abolitionism should go together is probably first derived from 'liberation' - what can a liberating development in respect to police, criminal law and prison mean, if not that these institutions should lose their power and if possible disappear? And since Marxian theory is oriented towards liberation, it should analyse the conditions and possibilities of such disappearance. But surprisingly, some explicitly Marxist analyses come to a conclusion that is exactly opposite to the results of this simple syllogism. Criminal law is itself seen as an instrument of 'liberation', which should therefore be strengthened and not abolished at all for it provides liberation from oppression by criminals and the fear of them. The pre-supposition of such an idea, of course, is the judgement that criminal law *can* do such things—deter crimes and make us feel secure—and can do them better than other organisational measures. A further pre-supposition is that it is crime that we are most victimized by (and not for example house ownership and speculation which are perfectly legal and even protected by law and can still make a neighbourhood deteriorate). Such assumptions can only be the result of a pretty deficient analysis of the functions and workings of criminal law, in the background of which we can easily see a state-centred idea of social development that does not (in spite of the 'dictatorship of the proletariat') necessarily derive from the theory.

Before presenting what I think touches the crucial elements of a Marxian analysis of 'crime' and criminal law that deserves the name, and relating it to abolitionism, it seems necessary to lake a good look at what presents itself as 'Marxist' these days[2] and at the pre-conceptions implied by such theorizing.

---

[2] Editors' note: In the 1980s

When Marxists are 'Confronting Crime'

We have learned from Lea and Young's *What is to be Done about Law and Order?* that British criminology has been hard hit by the rise of racist crimes[3] on the one hand, and by the imputation of 'racism' to leftist writers who stated that blacks are more criminal than Asians and whites by other leftist writers on the other. Since, then, those first-mentioned leftist criminologists (Lea, Young and company) are determined to 'take crime seriously', rebuke and deride 'left idealism' and develop a 'left realist' policy against crime which is to counter the breakdown of community and political marginalisation of the coloured immigrants as well as the destitute whites who populate those disintegrating areas of Brixton, Walthamstow and Toxteth and innumerable other places. The only problem we had when reading that book was why all this should be treated as a problem of 'crime' and not as one of racism, the breakdown of community and the general brutality of conduct under deteriorating conditions of living as was shown in the book itself. And this, as we know, is not just a matter of words but one of programmes of action. If the problem is one of 'crime', then the course of action is to get hold of the individual perpetrators and punish them, and the relevant institutions are the police, the judge and the prison. If the problem is one of 'breakdown of community', then the police will not be the first institution that comes to mind when thinking about how to restore social relations.

This theoretical weakness of the book with the practical consequence of concentrating heavily on the police in its polity sections was a slight irritation only. I at least deeply sympathize with a policy orientation towards impossible programmes on a local and very concrete level instead of the impossible abstract ones (like 'heightened class consciousness' or 'mass resistance' or even 'revolution')—like finding ways of *managing* conflicts instead of hoping for a society in which there will be no conflicts at all—like thinking about ways to alleviate the financial consequences and to creatively use the situation of unemployment (which is Utopian enough in that it means a re-balancing of the respective values of wage labour versus unpaid/household/reproduction work, *i.e.* of 'masculinity' and 'femininity') instead of hoping for a reconstruction of full employment at 40 (or even 15) working hours a week in the future— like trying to reform the police (and the dichotomy of 'community' versus 'military' policing is quite useful here) so that it may become adapted to the needs of the people instead of seeing them as 'the enemy' only, a pure agent of repression of the masses in the service of

---

[3] Lea, J. and Young, J. (1984) *What is to be Done about Law and Order?* London: Pluto. See in particular their lively depiction, p. 55

capital, and so on. I do appreciate pragmatism.

But with Matthews and Young's reader *Confronting Crime* this mere irritation with a theoretical weakness ends.[4] In this book the consequences of the theoretical weakness are spelled out unmistakeably: the means to be used are punishment and threat of punishment. So from an 'innocent' theoretical sloppiness we have actually gone on to a position of advocating punishment with all its implications as to freedom and domination. We have—from a left realist position—fallen back on 'who rules' instead of 'how do we get nearer to a society without rulers?' Interestingly, this is especially obvious in the feminist articles, and this strand of 'left realism' has been strengthened since 1984. Two related quotations from Jock Young can illustrate this shift. In *What is to be Done about Law and Order?* we read:

> There was a schizophrenia about crime on the left where crimes against women and immigrant groups were quite rightly an object of concern but other types of crime were regarded as being of little interest or somehow excusable. Part of this mistake stems, as we have noted, from the belief that property offences are directly solely against the bourgeoisie and that violence against the person is carried out by amateur Robin Hoods in the course of their righteous attempt to redistribute wealth. All of this is, alas untrue. Indeed, the irony is that precisely the same kids who break into the next door neighbour's flat sit around the estates wearing British Movement badges and harassing Asians.[5]

The stress here is on the racist nature of crimes, or rather of the juveniles. In 1986 domestic violence is in the foreground.

> Crime is not an activity of latter day Robin Hoods—the vast majority of working class crime is directed within the working class. It is intra-class *not* inter-class in its nature. Similarly, despite the mass media predilection for focusing on inter-racial crime it is overwhelmingly intra-racial. Crimes of violence, for example are by and large one poor person hitting another poor person—and in almost half of these instances it is a man hitting his wife or lover.[6]

---

[4] Matthews, R. and Young, J. (eds.) (1986) *Confronting Crime* London: Sage

[5] Lea, J. and Young, J. (1984) *What is to be Done about Law and Order?* London: Pluto. p.262

[6] Young, J. (1986) "The failure of criminology: the need for radical realism" in Matthews, R. and Young, J. (eds.) *Confronting Crime* London: Sage p. 21

The punitive consequence is spelled out most outspokenly in the three (of nine) chapters pertaining to traditional feminist themes. Jill Box-Grainger, who takes great pains to tell unidentified co-feminists in a soft and unobtrusive way that their hopes for what the criminal law can do against rape are unfounded, still ends in her own recommendations for rape sentencing with the programmatic confession that she 'can see no reason why tempered punishment should not quite openly form part of a feminist rape sentencing policy'.[7] And even she, a member of Radical Alternatives to Prison and co-editor of their journal *The Abolitionist*, recommends that 'short but mandatory custodial sentences should be imposed upon first-time rapists', whereas for multiple or aggravated rape and for recidivists, 'there should be a restricted availability of *long mandatory*, fixed-term prison sentences where the length of sentence would be a protective measure as well as a punishment'. I cannot see how this differs from what is current male chauvinist judicial practice anyway—except that it is perhaps a bit harsher on the first-time offender if he is young.

Jeanne Gregory, in a programmatic article on 'Sex, class and crime', criticises 'radical feminists' who lean heavily towards the introduction of more 'punitive measures', but quotes without comment that they want to 'protect women from the *more extreme* manifestations of male power, particularly domestic violence, rape and pornography'.[8] And even though she speaks for campaigns against the imprisonment of women which might later be generalised to men, she also says towards the end of her article.

> When we see how crime impacts on women, whether as prisoners or the wives of prisoners, as mothers blamed for juvenile delinquency or as the victims of rape, it becomes increasingly difficult to regard crime as a politically motivated response or to cast it in a romantic light. The freedom of one person too often involves the oppression of another. An essential component of an alternative penal policy would be to devise human forms of treatment and containment for those instances where neither decriminalisation nor decarceration is appropriate.[9]

At last we can say openly that Marxists also like to see a criminal *punished*

---

[7] Box-Grainger, J. (1986) 'Sentencing rapists' in Matthews, R. and Young, J. (eds.) *Confronting Crime* London: Sage p.50

[8] Gregory, J. (1986) "Sex, class and crime: towards a non-sexist criminology" in Matthews, R. and Young, J. (eds.) *Confronting Crime* London: Sage p.66. Emphasis added.

[9] Ibid p. 69

and put into prison (as a protective measure, the well-known difficulties of a diagnosis *of dangerousness* notwithstanding), at least if he is a rapist and then even an intra- class, intra-race one. I will not comment on the bit about pornography as one of the more extreme manifestations of male power.

We get one more illustration of the punitiveness of 'left realism' in the paper on prostitution by Roger Matthews. Here it is found that making it illegal has not put an end to prostitution. Therefore, we need a new 'socialist or radical regulationism' that uses 'selective illegality'. There are:

> four general legislative strands through which the general aims of a radical regulationism could be formulated. These involve a) a clear commitment to general deterrence b) the reduction of annoyance harassment and disturbance, c) protection from coercion and exploitation, and d) the reduction of the commercialization of prostitution.[10]

The following section on 'general deterrence' states the moral aim very openly; women *and* clients should be kept from turning to prostitution by threatening them with punishment. This includes 'broadening the base of illegality to include the punishment of clients', but also keeps prostitutes firmly inside this threat, which, of course, is to be used judiciously.

> Of course, not all forms of solicitation can be effectively or reasonably policed, and intervention should be limited to those forms of soliciting or importuning which involve annoyance, harassment or public disturbance.[11]

It is worth considering in some detail the reasons given for the punishment of clients.

> Punishing the client would be an obvious strategy to pursue if the aim was to reduce prostitution, not only because clients are numerically greater than prostitutes, or because their sexuality and emotion are cramped and distorted by existing social conditions but because clients would almost certainly be more systematically deterred by the kind of sanctions currently directed towards female prostitutes.[12]

---

[10] Matthews, R. (1986) 'Beyond Wolfenden: Prostitution, politics and the law' in Matthews, R. and Young, J. (eds.) (1986) *Confronting Crime* London: Sage. p.204
[11] Ibid, p.205
[12] Ibid, p.203

Let me repeat this, punishing clients is advisable because:

- they are numerous;
- their sexuality is distorted;
- they *can* be deterred (implying that prostitutes cannot).

I can only understand the third reason given, I must confess, whereas the first reason would in my judgement be a reason *against* because a great number makes control more difficult. It only makes some pretention of sense here if it is to mean that the greater the number of those involved in this kind of despicable transaction, the more urgent the need to start reducing it. This again only can be partially understood if the aim really is a moralistic one, namely, to get people to give up the kind of sexuality implied by prostitution as a physical event that can be brought about by a service person, with few emotions and certainly no long-term obligations attached, comparable to buying a good dinner (with the cook personally attending at the table). To pay for sex, I suppose, means to buy a service *and* to buy off the obligations otherwise going with it. It is conceivable that such free encounters happen on a basis of mutuality and without payments involved, as they sometimes, in very rare instances, do, and we could be of the opinion that they should happen more often, but certainly this is nothing the state should be concerned with and punishments of whatever and whomever surely are the last thing that could further such freedom. We could also be of the opinion that sex without obligations should not be possible—but I would be most surprised to hear somebody say this is a leftist position ('realist' or otherwise). The second reason given above ties in with this – clients should be punished because their sexuality is distorted—implying that this shall and can be put right by punishment. I cannot believe this.

There is no mistake here, because it is said explicitly socialist regulationism:

> would not necessarily be preoccupied with the public and visible aspects of female prostitution, nor with the elevation of *expediency over justice,* nor with denying that the mobilization of legal sanctions is based on *moral concerns.*[13]

The criminal law is seen here as an instrument in the struggle for changed relations between the sexes. The contents of these 'moral concerns' are also clear for:

---

[13] Ibid, p.204. Emphasis added

the critical role of legislation of this type is to question and potentially undermine the widely-held male expectation that women and/or young men ought to be purchasable to service their sexual desires and fantasies.[14]

There should be no commodity relations between the sexes. There may be other instances in which people are reduced to commodities (we have heard of occasions when labour power is bought)—perhaps we should tackle those with the criminal law too. (In fact, the Austrian Criminal Code speaks of 'exploitation'—*Ausbeutung*—in the context of pimping and does criminalise it). Or perhaps there is something very special in the sex relation that makes it imperative and possible to simply forbid and threaten to punish any commodity relation that should crop up here, whereas in other areas, like production, it can be tolerated at least for the moment (if only the price is good). In that case, we cannot stop with prostitution, but have to go on to pornography, to striptease and related exhibitions. I am not certain that ballet dancing can be saved from the prohibition—and what about the exploitation of other sex-related work, like nursing? I will stop here, because I am not all that interested in prostitution and what to do about it (there are other problems higher on the agenda). What I consider striking, though, is the unabashed moralism transported back into a criminal law that is at the same time 'sharpened' to a new punitiveness by left realism. If nothing else, are you sure moralism and punitiveness will not get the wrong people in the end? Are you that sure of *your own* respectability? And of that of the proletariat? And if so, doesn't that frighten you?

But then the approaches used or recommended in different chapters of the book are not really consistent. There is the paper on 'black juvenile crime' by John Pitts which quite 'conventionally' concentrates on 'coloured offenders' and how they are discriminated against in the justice system, starting with the police. There is just one mention of their 'victims'. 'Furthermore, evidence suggests that black citizens are very likely to be the victims of crime perpetrated by black offenders'.[15] It sits at the end of a section more or less as an afterthought which is not followed up any further. Policy consideration accordingly follows the lines of giving these young people a chance in life:

---

[14] Ibid, p.205.
[15] Pitts, J. (1986) 'Black young people and juvenile crime: some unanswered questions' in Matthews, R. and Young, J. (eds.) (1986) *Confronting Crime* London: Sage. p. 124

we must move from a bland critique of welfare as a manifestation of creeping state control to a critical discussion about the ways in which public resources might be more effectively employed to create opportunity and the means whereby a dispossessed generation of young black people might be offered some resources with which to construct a life which is not just concerned with bare survival.[16]

Not much difference here from the old liberal programme of 'helping instead of punishment'—which isn't a bad programme at all, only neither original nor radical (nor very 'realist', it must be feared after all those years with much better than the present conditions in which this kind of programme could have but has not been realised). Similarly, in their discussion of heroin use Auld, Dorn and South[17] come to the conclusion that legalisation *alone* would only result in more use and therefore more harm (they do not say to whom) and demand programmes (educational ones are those they mention) aimed not at use-minimalisation but harm-minimalisation—which always has been the philosophy behind demands for legalisation for substitution programmes: take the illegality away and (thereby) create circumstances under which the drug use can become less dangerous and more 'cultivated'. This again is simple and straightforward liberalism.

'Left realism' has at last and uniquely discovered what criminology so far— traditional as well as critical—has missed: it hurts to be beaten up; it degrades to be raped; it costs money to replace a stolen object. We have learned these exciting new insights not only from feminists but also from the fascinating new science of 'victimology'. The chapter on criminal victimization by Alan Phipps therefore has a central role (although it only comes as number five).[18] It is a historical survey of the development of this speciality, which makes it obvious enough that at its origin there was (and to a large extent still is) the wish to find 'more crime'. Victimization surveys were and are one way to get at the 'hidden figure of crime'—with the implication that there are lots of more sinister things going on outside that circle of bright light in which the police work, which something could be done about if only they were known to the authorities. What is ignored (also by Phipps, sad to say) is the simple fact that 'the authorities' are not able and/or willing to do anything even about the greater part of sinister goings on that *are* brought to their

---

[16] Ibid, p. 144

[17] Auld, J., Dorn, N. and South, N. (1986) "Irregular work, irregular pleasure: heroin in the 1980s' in Matthews, R. and Young, J. (1986) (eds.) *Confronting Crime* London: Sage

[18] Phipps, A. (1986) "Radical criminology and criminal victimisation: proposals for the development of theory and intervention" in Matthews, R. and Young, J. (eds.) (1986) *Confronting Crime* London: Sage

attention, and that there usually are excellent reasons why people do *not* call the police, one of them being that there is a lot of danger in the 'attention of the authorities'.

Phipps does mention that 'radical criminology has largely failed to generate its own concepts. By choosing as the object of its studies "crime", it has allowed its subject matter to be determined by mainstream criminology and the state',[19] but he does not analyse the reification in the *pair* 'criminal/victim'. The instrument provided by criminal law is the image of an 'innocent' victim 'harmed' by a 'guilty' criminal. If people want to 'use' this instrument, they have to cast themselves into this 'innocent' role and the other into the 'guilty' one. If they do not succeed in doing this, they cannot have whatever services they may hope for from the law. But there are costs in doing this. As 'innocent victim' you have to be weak and helpless, you have to trustfully hand over your problems to the state agency defined as relevant, you have to gratefully accept whatever they do for you. As 'innocent victim' you have to give up activity and social competence. In other words, you bow to domination in an extreme way in order to give an occasion for a demonstration of the same domination over the 'guilty criminal'. To identify with the 'victim' role is to declare yourself powerless and ask for the protection of 'good government'. This may be an acceptable emergency action if the 'protection' is effective and the powerless is not taken advantage of. Obviously, with criminal law both conditions are not given. Accepting the victim role means legitimating the *form* of rule there is and the powers that be.

What Phipps asks for in the end is, of course further research, victim support schemes (he does mention that these already exist on a large scale, but does not mention that they do so on a legal and state-organised basis in several countries—like Austria—where the experience is that, since they exclude restitution of material damage, they are not used very much, because with this provision they are simply redundant in a moderately functioning welfare and health care system) and—somewhat unconnected and in a last sentence—'the development of alternative concepts and frameworks for justice.'[20] So, the outlook is abolitionist.

It seems that 'left realism' is a somewhat incoherent, but amazingly moralistic position, based on a short-sighted analysis of 'crime' that does not see the ideological function of the whole vocabulary of crime, law, victim, criminal, guilt, justice, *etc*. It rather falls back onto a 'naturalistic' conception of 'crime'— which we could have been beyond with interactionism and

---

[19] Ibid, p. 112.
[20] Ibid, p. 119.

should be even more with a Marxian analysis. This is what can be learned from this example: there is a type of Marxist analysis of 'crime' which seems to take this 'naturalistic' approach as an expression of materialism. Obviously we have to do better. It is exactly this crude materialism that depends on and allows for the moralism that we had to note. We need a more coherent Marxian analysis, not a theory but a *critique* of 'crime'.

The Criminal Outline of a Critique of Criminology

The distinguishing characteristic of Marxian analyses is that they start out from a *critique* of current wisdom, the latter understood as necessarily false consciousness, *i.e.* ideology. So, an analysis of 'crime' is first and foremost a critique of criminology.

A radical critique of criminology has to start with the very existence of this specialised field of study. History clearly shows it to be knowledge for the inquisitor, the policeman, the state attorney, the prison administrator, the legislator who wants to comply with the professional needs of these diverse state functionaries. History shows that criminology is the 'scientific' side of policing and punishment: It is police—and prison—science. As such, it takes for granted what is really the question whether (or for whom) it is prudent that a class of events is abstracted as 'crime', which means that a specific individual is blamed and punished for its occurrence. For the person victimized, this is in contrast to events conceptualized as 'due to higher forces' (in which case nothing can be done, although a prayer will do no harm), as due to 'accident' or 'negligence' (in which case compensation can be demanded) or as due to 'legal power', as when by a system of taxation and subvention of certain investments you lose the chance to earn a living and your part of the town is left to deterioration, or when some planning authority confronts you with an airport or an autobahn next to where you live, or when the police break down your door in their search for drugs or political subversion (in all of which cases again very little can be done and prayers are definitely useless). Certainly, in terms of victimisation the first case—'crime'—is far less frequent and consequential than the other three, especially the third case—'domination' by legal means.

History shows that the category of 'crime' as demanding punishment substituted earlier ones which demanded compensation; that its introduction meant that a new instrument of domination by a centralised power was established and instruments of social self-regulation and autonomous conflict management were taken away. Historically *and* in actual practice, then, to define and denounce an event as 'crime' is just one possible reaction to being victimised and it is just one means of domination by a centralised power (and certainly not the most important one). The public concentration on this relatively small class of damaging events is the main ideological effect of the concept of 'crime' and it is certainly underscored by the existence of a scientific discipline of its own. (There is no systematic investigation into the diverse kinds of damage that people suffer, but lately the new discipline of 'victimology' has been pushed by various academic and not so academic interests, which is only interested in the victims of 'crime', thus being a direct ideological corollary of criminology).

Lately, that is since the introduction of the idea of 'resocialisation', the concept of 'crime' can be anchored in welfare policy as well. Welfare policy is one part of politics pertaining to the reproduction of labour (other parts being population policy and labour market policy), the measures of which, as far as the state is concerned, can be ordered according to the directness of their impact on the reproduction of labour, which must always be understood as the reproduction of *wage* labour, of course, in a capitalist formation. The highest ranking measures (from the point of interest of labour) would be those which prevent damage to labour like the shorter working day, prevention of unhealthy working conditions, moderate speed of work, no piece work, *etc.* Next in order are measures which support reproduction on a day-to-day basis, like a good transport system, sufficient supply of good housing, not least the level of income which in this system is the precondition for being able to use all these services. A third level comprises all measures of qualification and re-qualification of labour, including medical services aimed at bringing the person back into the labour market. On a fourth level we find measures designed to support people who will not go back into the labour market, but whose treatment may have a feedback on the motivation of those who are in it or are to be drawn into it—like old-age pensions or support after an accident. It is possible to distinguish a fifth level, which is the negative side of level four measures used to demonstrate where it leads to not to be disciplined and willing to work—into prison or some other kind of institutional programme.

In this context, then, 'crime' and punishment is one measure (and not a very central but a 'last resort' one) among the many used to secure a labour force that is willing and otherwise qualified for the tasks of wage labour – one that is disciplined and has the proper work ethic. Again, considering the whole array of instruments that bring about discipline the criminal law, the police and the prison are pretty unimportant. (There have been historical changes in the importance of these apparatuses). Much more important are the immediate demands of the arrangement of production (not least the machines used); the promises of success, of the good life; the arrangement of the family in which every member looks after the discipline of every other;

the high demands upon people in all spheres of life which make it necessary to be very circumspect and calculating (in some spheres—like road traffic—in order to simply survive) *etc.* Criminal law comes in very late here and is not immediately instrumental. It has more of a symbolic or ideological value. Punishment is a *demonstration of domination* and as such does not necessarily bring about specific actions or abstentions. But it dramatizes what actions and what persons are on the wrong side of domination. It also dramatizes less what is to be found in specific paragraphs (because we do not need a criminal law to know that we should not steal and rape and murder) but what can be generalized from this and from the factual working of the law there is in all sections pertaining to private property a symbolization of the wage-consumption nexus. There is in the sections concerning violence a re-affirmation of the state's monopoly of force. There is in the statutes concerning sexual behaviour an affirmation of the monogamous heterosexual family (and not of sexual self-determination, as feminists want it to become).

Next to the ideological implications of the very existence of a differentiated field of 'criminology' stands the fact that these studies have in their classical form been concerned with constituting a separate class of *people*—'criminals' as a species set apart from the rest of mankind—or, to be more exact, set apart from mankind be they born criminals, degenerates, psychopaths or traumatised by a broken home. And this approach was by no means 'traditional' or self-evident, but had to fight its way to hegemony against the more sociological studies that went under the name of 'moral statistics', in which 'deviance' was taken as a statistical indicator of the moral status of the community, dependent on for example the price of grain or on 'anomie'. This concentration of criminology on 'the criminal', on the classification of people with the aim of identifying the good prospects and the hopeless cases, both with very practical consequences, is a good illustration of the more general process of 'reification', at the basis of which lies the treatment and categorization of people in terms primarily of their labour power.

We have an interesting problem here, in that the category of 'criminal' is certainly older than capitalism. But it seems that a lot of things later included in 'crime' triggered proceedings designed and suited to find out whether the perpetrator 'belonged' or not. If s/he was found to do so, the process could be steered into the more or less civil questions of compensation and restitution. If found not to 'belong', s/he was expelled, either by robbing him/her of honour (pillory, bodily punishment, often with the consequence of lasting bodily stigmata), by banishment or by (more or less cruel) killing in extreme cases. There is certainly 'reification' in this, but less in terms of 'usefulness' as in terms of 'belonging' or being 'alien'. In a warrior society the important thing was to find out whether somebody was a *bona fide* member of the community or an 'enemy' on whom the rules governing social behaviour did not apply. In a capitalist social formation this categorization of people according to 'inclusion/exclusion' is gradually changed into one of 'usefulness', which allows much finer grading and thus 'discipline'. The difference is that the capitalist formation is not built on such exclusive categorising of people, but on the presumption of equality. Therefore, 'reification'—now in terms of economic usefulness—can become a scandal in the first place.

In a feudal society it is obvious and self-evident that people are *not* treated as (equal) human beings but as exemplars of a certain caste, as nobles or peasants, clergy or artisan, merchant or serf. Individualisation, as far as it exists at all, can only mean to be a more or less exemplary embodiment of such a category. 'Reification', if being stuck in a caste category can be subsumed under that same concept, was so all-pervasive that the idea of a human being with nothing but 'human' qualities and a dignity and political rights deriving from exactly this abstract quality could not be understood, at least not in a way that had social and political consequences.

In contrast, in a capitalist society the abstract principles of market and commodity produce an abstract 'equality' that breaks up those earlier categories. It is in contrast to this abstract humanity that the factual 'reification' of men and women according to their usefulness makes itself felt. A social arrangement, in which men and women have exchange value in the first place, makes them 'free' on the one hand, reified into commodities on the other — *and* constitutes this as a contradiction. With capitalism, reification changes its character and its contents *and* becomes contradictory, so that a social dynamic and a struggle can crystallize around it.

The designation of some people as 'criminals', then, is just one instance of a mechanism of domination by grading and sorting out people instead of changing the task (so that it would be adapted to what people can do and want to do). Production is designed according to expediency, high output and technical possibilities — and, if in consequence jobs are dangerous or repetitive or exhausting or dirty or whatever, it is necessary to find or educate or bribe people who are or will be able and willing to do those jobs. This grading and sorting is mainly done according to criteria of 'ability'; but there is also a second sorting along criteria of 'morality' or 'respectability', of being disciplined in one's whole conduct of life. On the whole, the two dimensions seem to be linked, with the better jobs demanding perhaps not more ability but at least more formal education (and the self-assuredness going with it) *and* more discipline, but there are dissociations too. The rare talents of the artist compensate his/her bohemian lack of respectability. Similarly success (or even mere wealth) can make such extravagancies of conduct permissible without moral degradation, and at the other end there are low jobs in which—beyond a minimum directly related to doing the job at all—the question of respectability does not arise. This can work the other way round, since there are people who are 'beyond respectability', certain jobs can remain unchanged and be offered to these people. But on the whole moral degradation—which goes with punishment but has other instruments, purely verbal or symbolic ones, too—is not a means of immediate economic domination, but one delegated to the state and instrumental for its task of regulating the labour market as well as external relations. Moral degradation can be used to 'externalise' a part of the labour force be they immigrant workers foreigners in the first place or internal groups that are to be set apart and ghettoized if necessary, and it can be used to define an external enemy, as shown in war propaganda, and, of course, against internal enemies as well. In such a 'moral division of labour' economic institutions tend to neutralize this 'moral' sorting to a degree by referring to a moral 'ability' alone. Thus the big corporations in South Africa tend to be liberal and anti-apartheid, blacks can be good workers, so why discriminate against them? On the other hand, a lot of work does depend on 'moral' qualities of the workers, their trustworthiness, their endurance, their general 'willingness'—which always means a willingness to do more than one can be forced to do under a work contract, to function adequately also in situations that cannot be fully controlled. So this 'moral' sorting certainly is not just a historical remnant and far from easily dispensable.

The elegance of moral degradation as a technique of domination lies in the fact that usually this domination can be delegated to the population itself. All groups 'above' the one that is degraded are allowed to spit on the degraded ones, to use them as props for self-esteem—and especially groups only slightly above are most motivated to do so. Moral degradation of one group allows others to take part in domination for once, with the small but nonetheless real gains this includes. For the population moral discrimination is always useful in a competition, and very much so where the demands on ability are low or hard to operationalize. (In the latter case, ideas of a conspiracy seem to be convincing, like homosexuals or Jews keeping a whole branch of business or culture to themselves, letting nobody in who does not belong).

That it is *people* who are given a morally degraded status (and not types of acting that are criticized or situations that are seen as having to be avoided) and the easy combination with economic or other 'usefulness' at the lower end of the spectrum make for a quite dangerous position for those who are a 'failure' on both counts. The Nazis have demonstrated what a reifying, instrumental rationality has in store for 'life unworthy to live'. The link is punishment, the use of people for a demonstration of power and domination, and in the modern version by making them work and forcing them to be very disciplined. Within instrumental rationality there is an easy transition from punishment to extermination, especially if the old category of 'enemy' or 'alien' is added. Reacting with moral degradation against allegedly threatening persons still leads to social exclusion, which can take on more or less 'thorough' and brutal forms.

That certain events are singled out as 'crime' with the consequence of 'punishment' of a person, then, can be translated into functional terms as follows. The designation of certain events as 'crimes' is an instrument of social exclusion that is at the same time used to demonstrate power and domination and the 'work ethic' that is in force at the time (or is to be enforced). It is an ideological state apparatus that uses human victims for its demonstrations. The elegance of it is that this instrument is further offered as a resource of protection and conflict management to the population and that it is to the greater part set in motion on demand from the population only as soon as they notify the police. This also makes it useful as an instrument with which competition can be cut back a little, especially (but not exclusively) at the lower end of the labour market. The sorting of people as to ability is complemented by a sorting out as regards morality/respectability.

We must be very clear that this designation as 'crime' and the 'punishment' connected to it *does not* in fact 'protect' people. Criminal law and police are a resource in a very limited way only and under the condition of other resources (like an insurance or a routinized access to the police) being available. It is a central part of the ideology of criminal law that it can protect us and prevent us being victimized. Apart from these inabilities it is not even very useful in helping us come to grips with the situation after the damage has been done (as the civil law sometimes is). Instrumentally the criminal law is just a disappointment — and most people know this and do not try to use it. But it is dependent on the input from the population and therefore the false promise of instrumentality has to be kept up. In fact, the criminal law and the institutions connected to it (from police to punishment) are an *ideological* apparatus — with effects of its own kind, but not instrumental ones. The belief that we are 'protected' by the state is not the least of these effects. And — to repeat it once more — we should not overestimate the importance of this apparatus. Society is not kept going by laws and punishments, or norms and sanctions, as sociology only slightly more abstractly assumes, but rather by immediate economic and social forces. Criminal law is just one — rather helpless — last resort and an ideological apparatus in the first place.

On the contrary, a lot of what is puzzling about the function of criminal law falls into place when we – generalizing what Foucault has shown for the prison — assume that it is part of its function *not* to function.[21] This alone makes symbolic politics possible — a show of energetic state action that does not do any harm to important social interests while at the same time eliminating single persons who have no social backing. For a state suspended between functions for capital that have to be fulfilled and the need for mass loyalty such a flexible instrument is useful enough. This way you can at a time when mass incomes are cut back and at the same time welfare expenditures are reduced make a big show of going against 'economic crime', especially 'subvention fraud', which gives everybody a good feeling of not being the only one who has to make sacrifices. (It is a bit unfortunate if at the same time massive illegal financing of parties by firms and corporations and some cases of outright corruption become known, as has happened in the Federal Republic of Germany, on a smaller level in Austria, and, I am sure, in other countries as well). You can also, when under pressure for security or purity regulations make stiff impositions and be generous with the apparatus of implementation (or use them to give big firms an advantage in competition, because the smaller ones are unable to comply). Or you can, when a reform movement has to be stopped, go against 'terrorists' and confirmed 'enemies of the state' who have grown out of that movement and thus make the message clear without having to actually fight the movement itself (I refer here, of course, to the German Social Democrats and how they went about cutting back what had begun as the student movement, the groundswell to which they partly owed their coming to power, but which at the same time they had to 'tame'). Legislature can thus make concessions to popular demands without actually having to effectively disturb things as they stand — except on an ideological level, of course, which is not totally without effects. But very often the situation is as described for prohibition in the United States – I do not care whether they break the law as long as they know *whose* law they break.

This leads to an interpretation of 'crime' as acts of domination on which the state wants to keep its monopoly, *i.e.* acts of 'private domination' that are only to be tolerated if licensed by the state, and given that they also *have* to be accepted, resistance would be illegal and very easily labelled a crime itself. Such 'private domination' may be at odds with monopolized central state domination or it may be an outcome of it — and quite often it has aspects of both. The German bandits of the 18th and 19th centuries were the product of the process of disowning and displacing peasants, and especially the poor, by

---

[21] Foucault, M. (1977) *Discipline and Punish: The Birth of the Prison*, Penguin, London

a new concept and practice of 'property' which excluded traditional rights of use (like hunting or, later, collecting wood) and thus the beginning of the 'capitalization' of farming and food production. When people went on hunting and gathering wood and thus exerting their traditional rights, these attempts at 'private domination' certainly acted against central power. When they took to robbing merchants and preferably Jews (as some famous bandits, among them 'Schinderhannes' did), they simply imitated acts of domination as exercised by the old knightly gentry (in their decline) and by military troops of the day, in addition making use of widespread popular resentment against Jews as 'early capitalists' — resentments that were certainly shared by at least part of the political and administrative class. And aspects of the organization of banditry (like their international network and the internal mode of operation) were definitely capitalist and socially *avant garde.* So we get the whole range of contradictions here this kind of crime was in a way anti-capitalist, but it was so in an opportunistic way, choosing the most vulnerable victims. It thus reacted against the emerging form of domination *and* imitated elements of both the earlier and new forms of domination. It would later be romanticized by the literary bourgeoisie (as in Schiller's play or Vulpius' successful novel *Rinaldo Rinaldini)* because the old form of domination could in relation be interpreted as 'honourable' and as 'freedom'. And the moral panic over banditry (on which there is a lot of documentation) was staged in attempts to modernize the police, to turn it from a purely local to a regional force, and it certainly had the function of dramatically displaying for everyone to see and honour the dominant rule, including its emergent 'modern' elements.

What the criminal law pretends to offer is help in cases of 'private domination' in exchange for an opportunity to demonstrate the state's monopoly of domination. But any *real* help for the person who has been scandalized by being illegally dominated and has mobilized state intervention is accidental, the primary aim of the state powers mobilized is the show of legal domination. Therefore, there is very little effort (if any) on the part of the police to regain property that has been taken away illegally (except as evidence about the crime and its perpetrator), but all efforts (if any) are directed at getting hold of the 'criminal' in order to punish — which does not help the person victimized very much. The help that can be got is the product of the competent instrumentalization of elements of the state's show of legal domination. But, more often than not, there will be no help to be obtained from the police and the criminal law — and most people know that and act accordingly.

Abolitionism: Towards 'Socialist Diversity'

Historically, abolitionism has been a strange sort of liberating movement; in all instances the drive was to liberate a group that those who were the exponents of the movement did not belong too – *i.e.* slaves, prostitutes and convicts. In this respect, there is an analogy with 'moral entrepreneur movements' – they want to suppress certain elements of the lifestyle of groups the moral entrepreneur does not belong to s/he wants others to live as s/he lives. Liberating or going for more repression — both kinds of movements are concerned with *other* people's lives. In this sense, abolitionism is a 'disinterested' movement. Or is it?

Movements of convicts and ex-convicts very rarely demand the abolition of prisons. Usually their concern is for better conditions and more rights *in* prison. The institution itself is attacked for the usual and popular reasons; it is inhumane, ineffective and counterproductive. But we rarely hear from there that prison should be totally abolished and not replaced by something else either. So, how do people get that kind of idea? It seems that to a great extent abolitionism is in fact motivated by considerations of inhumanity and ineffectiveness again, only with a historical perspective added. Reform of the prison becomes very unconvincing when there is some knowledge of the history of prison reforms which — as Foucault showed — are part of the prison as institution and not unsuccessful attempts to really change it. To become an abolitionist, the idea of prison reform must have been abandoned.

But I think it goes further. Abolitionism becomes more than a do-gooder movement in that it radically turns to the question of punishment. Is it conceivable that somebody can legitimately be *punished* by somebody else; *i.e.* used as an opportunity for a show of domination? And then even by the state? It is the same question that was put by anti-slavery abolitionists: is it conceivable that human beings can legitimately be kept as serfs? That they can legitimately be used as instruments and treated as things? The same question was put by the Austrian professor of criminal law, Julius Vargha, in his book of 1896 *Die Abschaffung der Strafknechtschaft* (The Abolition of the Serfdom of Punishment), in which he speaks of the 'torture' or even the 'butchery' of punishment on the one hand, the 'serfdom' it puts people into on the other, and demands 'punishment without revenge'.[22] He does so in the name of 'human dignity' and 'unconditional respect for man', from which he derives the duty 'never to hurt anybody intentionally except in a case of just

---

[22] Vargha, J. (1896) *Die Abschaffung der Strafknechtschaft* (The Abolition of the Serfdom of Punishment) *Volume 1: Studien zur Strafrechtsreform.* Berlin: Ulan Press

self-defence'.[23] I will not follow his thought any further here, because in the end he turns out the 'solution' of 'rational punishment' and speaks of 'rendering criminals harmless' ('unschadlich machen') — and I certainly do not intend to share this consequence of instrumental rationality. But this 'solution' only follows because of the 'instrumental optimism' that Vargha had. There is no reason to share that. But it makes us aware of one more condition of a radical abolitionist position – not to believe in an instrumental effectiveness of punishment and criminal law and the possibility to 'order social life' with this kind of instrument.

Abolitionism, then, is a moral position oriented at the bourgeois idea of freedom, based on some factual propositions prison cannot be reformed to harmlessness, social life cannot effectively be regulated by criminal law, and there are alternative autonomous, social ways of managing problems and conflicts that should rather be developed. There is no legitimation for punishment.

Abolitionism has also given up the traditional idea of justice in its classical variants, the idea of 'just deserts', as well as that of 'compensatory treatment'. Instead, there is an orientation towards the avoidance of harm and pain as the basic minimum (and that includes a rejection of the absurd idea that one pain can be compensated by another, state-inflicted one), towards something like 'equity', which means a moderate version of 'from each according to his/her abilities, to each according to his/her needs', and towards 'practicability', a principle of least necessary effort and commotion. Abolitionism does not assume that problems should be dealt with under conditions of mutuality and solidarity, *i.e.* of powerlessness — conditions which have to be created by social and political action, but certainly not in the Hobbesian way of giving all power to a sovereign who thus will put things into 'order'. There is also a tendency not to believe in 'solutions', still less in permanent ones. There will not be a perfect society, so there will always be troubles and conflicts. There will always be change and development, so there will always be troubles and conflicts. There will always (hopefully) be diversity and incongruent, even opposing, interests, so there will always be troubles and conflicts. The number of such troubles and conflicts can be reduced (mostly by quite banal means), but not to zero. On the contrary, troubles and conflicts are what life consists of and they therefore have to be managed, but certainly not eliminated or delegated to specialized agents. There is also a strong disinclination towards 'experts' in abolitionism and a lot of trust in the autonomous abilities of people to manage their lives — if power (including experts) will not intervene and conditions of solidarity are

---

[23] Ibid, p.19

created, and even under conditions of competition, reification and domination, a lot of cooperation, solidarity and equitable pragmatism can be found exactly in the 'underlife' of informal relations that springs up under oppression. (This 'informal' life may include some oppressive features, but usually they are at least not as systematic as institutionalized ones. And private oppression very often imitates and is legitimised by official forms of domination).

I would add that, at least in my brand of abolitionism, 'prevention' does play quite some role. A lot of troubles can be 'abolished' technically instead of having to be treated morally. Instead of having rules of politeness, morality and law not to intrude upon our neighbours by noise we make at night, we should rather have better noise insulation in our flats and houses. Instead of having a law that penalizes fare evasion on public transport, we should rather have conductors who can do all kinds of useful things on the tram besides collecting the fare — if it is not wiser to take no fare at all, or only a symbolic one. Instead of penalties for speeding, we should have under-motorized cars ('under-motorized' by today's standards, of course) and technical, built-in speed reduction that can be regulated from outside (which can be no problem in this age of electronics)—if it is not wiser to have a system of taxis instead of private cars substituting for what public transport cannot do. And so on wherever possible, we should put technical 'solutions' to more moral problems.

'Justice' means general principles or rules that can be appealed to in single instances. Abolitionism puts a strong stress on the singularity of events and of people and their constellations. This, of course, is a general principle, but one to end all generality beyond that. Besides, what are the conditions under which such appeals are made? Very often 'justice' is invoked when we are hindered in doing something that others can do. We are given a traffic ticket for speeding and point to the others speeding by while we bargain with the police, asking and why don't you fine these? This looks as if 'justice' meant that all be punished equally. But in fact the question goes against exemplary and arbitrary punishment and can be translated as since you cannot fine all perpetrators, not even all you find out, you might as well let me off too! The appeal is possible here because state action is to make no difference between people nowadays. It would be absurd addressed to a private person in his/her dealings with members of the family versus other persons. We would be most surprised *not* to find him/her prejudiced *e.g.* towards his/her children. Social (in contrast to political) relations are mostly particularistic. Questions of 'justice' do not apply.

'Justice' is an ideal that only makes sense under conditions of domination, and even then it does not make much sense. Rather than fight for 'justice' in domination, we could put the same effort into fighting for *less* domination. 'Justice' is not more than the elimination of arbitrariness—and so far it has not succeeded anywhere even in this limited aim. All formal systems of justice have a class bias, work unequally in different local and regional contexts, and very rarely (and then coincidentally) bring about 'good' or even 'wise' decisions. Their biases are usually to the disadvantage of exactly those people who suffer under the domination anyway, which means that they do not compensate private oppression, but systematize the bias of the given kind of domination and perfect the latter's grip. The best that can usually be said about them is that they do not inflict *much* harm.

It is especially this dim view of what 'justice' is good for in social life that is well suited to link abolitionism and Marxian analysis. Contrary to what many people seem to think, socialism is *not* the quest for more justice in society but for more freedom. Exploitation cannot be overcome by higher wages but only the the abolition of wage labour. Liberation is not achieved with equal and 'just' domination, but with collective self-determination and the reduction of domination. The problem is not 'better' laws in the first place, but the possibility to work on troubles and conflicts without being fenced in by domination and its prefabricated 'solutions' that have to be accepted. The problem is how to make *diversity* possible.

Abolitionism may be idealist in that it simply posits this possibility without stating the contradictions that energise a development in that direction. But this can easily be supplied: it is the contradiction of 'discipline' that was developed to make freedom (in the sense of mastery over nature) possible and which at the same time makes social freedom impossible, which constitutes an intimate and refined form of domination. But 'discipline' can be understood as not only a form of domination but also as part of the forces of production, a quality of labour power that is developed for the needs of capitalist production and in constant adaptation to them ('work ethic') it is also a competence. Being disciplined as they are, people are competent to manage conflicts and troubles without the dubious help from external 'sovereigns'. By discipline the possibilities of self-determination have been so far developed that external domination becomes an obstacle to possible further developments. It is mainly this contemporary state of the contradiction that has, I think, led to a widespread and popular (theoretical and practical) critique of criminal law: that it is useless and unnecessary, given autonomous competences, and it is in fact only used in a minimal fraction of the cases in which it could be used. This need not necessarily hold true for everybody. There are disadvantaged positions in which autonomous competences are also lacking and therefore we get — in a helpless and short-circuited way — the demand for law and order. And there are advantaged positions in which it is convenient to use the criminal as well as the civil law and from where we therefore also get the call for law and order. In neither case is there a need or even a justification for the theoretician to literally take over this demand.

Abolitionism ties in with a Marxian analysis if we assume that it is not the main historical task today to further develop the forces of production (plus destruction and domination) but to adjust the relations of production to what has long been achieved and has therefore long been *possible*. Today we have an excess of what Marcuse called 'additional repression' and the destruction of nature by the very kind of mastery over nature that has been developed. The problem today is not under-developed forces of production but over-developed forces of destruction and domination. Obviously this speaks rather against progress, at least of the kind we have had.

Secondly, abolitionism ties in with a Marxian analysis that realistically reduces the historical role of the proletariat as it has turned out historically. Today, at least in Europe, the politically dominant parts of the proletariat have been manoeuvred into a firm coalition with capital in a 'productive bloc' that also dominates the state in what has been called neo-corporatism (The English experience of the Thatcher regime can perhaps be interpreted as the labour organizations being beaten into readiness for this coalition).[24] Together they go for development of the world market, *i.e.* an international division of labour suitable for 'high tech' production and are willing to have others pay the price of this 'high risk' project – risks of a destruction of environmental conditions, of a splitting of society and of a deterioration of democracy as a consequence of 'security measures' of a technical and political kind that become 'necessary'. It seems that we cannot expect too much liberation from a labour movement that is in such a situation. On the other hand, it is not very probable that much can happen *without* them.

As a consequence, we see that the 'rainbow of new social movements' have brought new elements into politics in the last twenty or so years. It seems that movements of liberation spring up from experiences made not in the process of production directly, but in fields indirectly affected, not least by the experience of being kept out of wage labour. What becomes relevant as an experience of society is that of the regular, qualified, life-long work connected with wage labour becoming the 'privilege' of a limited core section of the labour force, whereas for the increasing 'margin' it is a make-do economy, demanding high versatility and, entrepreneurial qualities or virtuosity, in getting hold of means of subsistence without a clear-cut work/wage nexus or a reduction of personal needs and demands in exchange

---

[24] See Sim, Chapter 8 of this volume for further discussion of this.

for self-determined useful and less work. It seems that liberating movements can (if at all) rather be expected to grow out of the second type of experience, which in terms of social structure, is shared in a variety of social positions, that certainly do not correspond to the classical proletariat, but only parts of it, and that include formerly bourgeois positions, especially those of the 'cultural' and 'educated' bourgeoisie.

Thirdly, abolitionism brings in the stress on 'diversity' that has not been exactly in the centre of historical thinking of a Marxist kind but could be if the bourgeois concept of individuality is to be carried further and in a socialist direction. It seems that we have an intellectual challenge here to work out conceptions of historical development that do not depend on some central agency bringing about and controlling that development, but that on the contrary formulate the conditions of the maximum of possible decentralization. The market on the one hand and centralized, hierarchical, bureaucratic domination (controlled by checks and balances) on the other cannot be all the instruments of social coordination that we know and can think of. Perhaps we should think more about systems of mutual isolation and independence, with individuals moving freely between them, and less about independence and coordination. There are no recipes for this, of course. But the programme of 'negative reform' which says that we only have to take away means of domination and leave the rest to the autonomy of social inventiveness[25] or the idea of 'tribes' or 'communes' loosely connected or forming niches and subcultures[26] point the direction. But here again the main point to emerge is that conflicts and troubles cannot be got rid of by some perfectly functioning social machine, but have to be taken up as they come and be managed so that their consequences are not too harmful and, if possible, a gain in experience and social relations and a personal past. 'Diversity', I think, excludes some of the 'security' that is propagated today like never before — in a situation in which the most dangerous technical, social and international arrangements are brought about by the same politicians (and the social forces behind them) who declare the 'war on crime', so that we may be 'secure'. We obviously need much less of that kind of 'security'.

---

[25] See for example: Mathiesen, T (1974) *The Politics of Abolition,* Oxford: Martin Robertson
[26] See for example: Hulsman, L. (1986) 'Critical Criminology and the concept of crime', in *Contemporary Crises;* Christie, N. (1982) *Limits to Pain,* Oxford: Martin Robertson.

Bibliography

Auld, J., Dorn, N. and South, N. (1986) 'Irregular work, irregular pleasure: heroin in the 1980s' in Matthews, R. and Young, J. (1986) (eds.) *Confronting Crime* London: Sage

Box-Grainger, J. (1986) 'Sentencing rapists' in Matthews, R. and Young, J. (eds.) *Confronting Crime* London: Sage

Christie, N. (1982) *Limits to Pain* Oxford: Martin Robertson.

Foucault, M. (1977) *Discipline and Punish: The Birth of the Prison* London: Penguin

Gregory, J. (1986) 'Sex, class and crime: towards a non-sexist criminology' in Matthews, R. and Young, J. (eds.) *Confronting Crime* London: Sage

Hulsman, L. (1986) 'Critical Criminology and the concept of crime', in *Contemporary Crises,* Vol. 10, No. 1, pp. 63-80

Lea, J. and Young, J. (1984) *What is to be Done about Law and Order?* London: Pluto

Mathiesen, T (1974) *The Politics of Abolition,* Oxford: Martin Robertson

Matthews, R. (1986) 'Beyond Wolfenden: Prostitution, politics and the law' in Matthews, R. and Young, J. (eds.) *Confronting Crime* London: Sage

Phipps, A. (1986) 'Radical criminology and criminal victimisation: proposals for the development of theory and intervention' in Matthews, R. and Young, J. (eds.) *Confronting Crime* London: Sage

Pitts, J. (1986) 'Black young people and juvenile crime: some unanswered questions' in Matthews, R. and Young, J. (eds.) *Confronting Crime* London: Sage

Vargha, J. (1896) *Die Abschaffung der Strafknechtschaft* (The Abolition of the Serfdom of Punishment) *Volume 1: Studien zur Strafrechtsreform.* Berlin: Ulan Press

Young, J. (1986) 'The failure of criminology: the need for radical realism' in Matthews, R. and Young, J. (eds.) *Confronting Crime* London: Sage.

4.

The Necessity of Punishment in a Just Social Order: A Critical Appraisal

Willem de Haan

This paper was delivered at the European Group's 15th annual conference in Vienna and first published in Working Papers in European Criminology, Volume 9 'Justice & Ideology: Strategies for the 1990s' in 1989.

> There must indeed be some sort of ethical reward and ethical punishment, but they must reside in the action itself. (Ludwig Wittgenstein, *tractatus logico-philosophicus 6.422,* London 1922)

Introduction[1]

This paper is about justice and punishment or, more precisely, about their compatibility or incompatibility. To talk about justice and punishment is, of course, to talk about retribution. Justice demands that the guilty be punished and get their 'just desert'. However, retributive theories are not the main topic of this paper, even though it will be unavoidable to deal briefly with them. I will not present a critical discussion of current theories of punishment either. My topic will be slightly different; narrower in one sense, broader in another. In fact, the present paper begins where such discussions usually end, namely by addressing the future of punishment and, more specifically, the necessity of punishment in a just social order.

In the first part of this paper, I will locate the topic within current debates in critical criminology and the sociology of criminal law. I will argue that it is important to turn to relevant discussions in moral and political philosophy for answers to questions such as whether punishment is necessary, just and, therefore, fully justified in a just social order. In the next part of the paper, I will present one particular theory of a just social order[2] which is itself largely

---

[1] I wish to thank Rick Abel, Nils Christie, Stan Cohen, Kathy Davis, Derek Phillips and Joe Silvis for their helpful criticisms.
[2] Phillips, D. (1986) *Towards a Just Social Order,* Princeton: Princeton University Press

based on a specific theory of justice.[3] Together, they represent an extremely well-developed case for how punishment can be justified rationally and integrated into a conception of a just social order. In the third part, I will discuss some of the assumptions underlying their assertion that punishment is necessary, even in a just social order. In conclusion, I will make a few suggestions for how the case for penal abolition might be strengthened.

I.

Punishment

Punishment has, of course, always been morally problematic.

> Punishment, whatever else may be said of it, involves the intentional infliction of pain or suffering. For this reason punishment is a problem that must be confronted by all human beings concerned to be moral. To do something that intentionally increases human pain or suffering requires justification in a way in which many other things that we do to or with other persons do not. It is a special problem because the pain and suffering ... is intentionally imposed.[4]

A lot of ideological work goes into keeping punishment 'just'. Penal practices have always been despised by social movements, political groups and individual 'agitators' arguing, for instance, that 'the construction of a just system of criminal justice in an unjust society is a contradiction in terms'.[5] Moral philosophers have continued, however, to provide the 'punitive obsession' with a constant supply of 'new' justifications.[6]

There is a wider selection of theories on punishment available, all of which are variations on a theme or, rather two themes: retribution and deterrence. The possibilities are endless, albeit within the same basic frame of reference, for combining them within 'mixed' theories of punishment. However, just like in music, when a theme is played out too often, the music gets dull. So is it with evaluations of both traditional and more 'fashionable' justifications of

---

[3] Gerwirth, A. (1978) *Reason and morality,* Chicago: University of Chicago Press

[4] Wasserstrom, R. (1980) *Philosophy and Social Issues, Five Studies,* Notre Dame, Notre Dame University Press. p. 112

[5] *Struggle for Justice: A Report on crime and punishment in America, prepared for the American Friends Service Committee.* (1971) New York: Hill and Wang p.16

[6] Carlen, P. (1983) "On rights and powers" in Garland, D. & Young P. (eds) *The Power to Punish* London: Heinemann pp. 203-216

punishment which conclude *ad nauseam* that punishment in 'our societies' lacks moral justification.[7]

Common-sense

In spite of the apparent lack of moral justifications, liberals and radicals alike tend to accept punishment with reference to common-sense, *i.e.* either in a burst of 'realism' or on 'pragmatic' grounds.[8] Liberals only accept punishment half-heartedly 'under the circumstances' as a 'necessary evil'. A case in point is Andrew Von Hirsch. On the one hand, he views punishment as unavoidable, given the fact that 'our morality calls for a sanction that embodies blame ... that treats the acts as reprehensible and visits disapproval upon the actor for his conduct'.[9] On the other hand, however, he is still 'far from satisfied' with the current answers to the dilemma that 'the less equitable the legal and social arrangements which the state seeks to uphold, the more troublesome it becomes to argue that the state has the moral authority to censure criminal violators for their violations'.[10]

Surprisingly, radicals seem to have had less difficulty accepting punishment as part of political reality both in present and future society.[11] In fact, Greenberg has suggested that feelings of punitiveness towards criminals, although manipulated and confused, are nevertheless 'an authentic response to injury' and that, therefore, 'it may be important for socialists to espouse the general idea that punishment can sometimes be justified for a violation of the law'.[12] Clarke, also denies that 'from a Marxist point of view it is "unjustifiable" to punish for theft, vandalism, rape, murder, fraud, *etc.*'.[13] Explicitly referring to Von Hirsch's liberal ambiguity, Clarke argues that 'the dilemma is not the Marxist's, who has a practical revolutionary resolution' and consequently advocates 'constructing a "socialist" theory of punishment'.[14]

---

[7] Honderich, T. (1984) *Punishment: The Supposed Justifications, with a New Postscript,* Harmondsworth: Penguin Books. p.240

[8] Haan, W. de (1987a) 'Fuzzy Morals and Flakey Politics: The Coming Out of Critical criminology', *Journal of Law and Society,* No. 14 pp. 321-333

[9] Hirsch, A. von (1983) '"Neoclassicism", Proportionality, and the Rationale for Punishment: Thoughts on the Scandinavian debate', *Crime and Delinquency,* vol. 29, pp. 52-70. p. 64

[10] Ibid: 68-69 n.39

[11] See Steinert's discussion of left realism in chapter 3 of this volume.

[12] Greenberg, D. (1978) 'Reflections on the Justice debate', *Contemporary Crisis,* No. 7 pp. 313-327. p. 324.

[13] Clarke, D. (1982) 'Justifications for Punishment', *Contemporary Crisis,* No. 6, pp. 25-57. p. 53

[14] Ibid, p. 57 n.71

Abolitionism

An exception and, in part, a reaction to the tendency of considering punishment justified, if not 'in principle' at least, 'under the circumstances' is, of course, represented by the abolitionist persuasion. Abolitionism faces a twofold task: first it must engage in a 'politics of bad conscience', thereby making it as difficult as possible to justify punishment.[15] Second, it must show that there are other ways of dealing rationally, or at least *more* rationally, with crimes. Various proposals have already been made by abolitionists and others to decentralize or even completely dismantle the present penal system in order to create forms of 'informal', 'participatory', 'neighbourhood' or 'community' justice as additions to or replacements for the present criminal justice system. Unfortunately, such proposals have displayed shortcomings; many promises were left unfinished. In order to be more successful, these proposals need to be more concrete and empirical in one sense and more theoretical and utopian in another.[16] In this paper, I will, once again, take up the latter lead, as I am convinced that

> there is a need for more "Utopian" theory construction' and that 'the loose talk about legality, morality, justice ... needs to be related to classical and current attempts (Most notably those identified with Rawls 1971) to specify the abstract properties of a just system.[17]

The relevance of normative ('utopian') theorizing in moral and political philosophy will become even clearer when we return, very briefly, to the first task of abolitionism, namely making it as difficult as possible to justify punishment. To this end it will be worthwhile to take a closer look at the character of the moral claims on which the abolitionist position is based. Since this position has been formulated most articulately by Nils Christie, it is to his work that I will now turn.

Moral Rigorism

The perennial question of how to justify punishment has often been ignored or avoided by critical criminologists. A notable exception, however, is

---

[15] Haan, W. de (1987b) 'Abolitionism and the Politics of "Bad Conscience"', *The Howard Journal of Criminal Justice,* No. 26, pp.15-32. p. 28.
[16] Cohen, S. (1979) 'Guilt, Justice, and Tolerance: Some Old Concepts for a New Criminology', in D. Downes and P. Rock (eds.) *Deviant Interpretations,* Oxford: Martin Roberstson. p. 47.
[17] Ibid, p. 48

Nils Christie who has repeatedly scrutinized the various versions of the major theories of punishment and related them to the dominant schools of (neo-) classicism and (neo-)positivism in criminology. More specifically, he has decoded their 'hidden message' which, in the case of neo-classicism, is the 'denial of the legitimacy of a whole series of alternatives which should be taken into consideration'.[18]

Most relevant to the present discussion, however, is how he presents the case for penal abolitionism. He not only criticizes the 'supposed justifications' for punishment, but also and, more importantly, claims a moral position with regard to punishment, i.e. the intentional infliction of pain. His 'rigorist' position 'that it is right to strive for a reduction of man-inflicted pain on earth'[19] is put straightforwardly and, as always, with a personal touch, in the following statement:

> I can't imagine a position where I should strive for an increase of man-inflicted pain on earth. Nor can I see any good reason to believe that the recent level of pain infliction is just the right or natural one. And since the matter is important, and I feel compelled to make a choice, I see no other defensible position than to strive for pain reduction.[20]

The strength of this 'rigorist' position lies in its explicitly moral approach; the concomitant weakness is in its argumentation. Indeed, to say 'I see no other defensible position' is not the strongest argument in favour of one's own. Moreover, the claim that punishment has not been proved *right* is not the same as the claim that man-inflicted pain and hence punishment is *wrong*. To present this position as a matter of personal *choice* comes dangerously close to 'emotivism', i.e. there can be no rational standards of judgement other than individual, personal *tastes*.

In contrast to Christie, I will be arguing that it is quite all right to take a moral point of view, but that a stringent rational argumentation is possible and, is in fact, necessary to show why one position is morally superior to the other. In other words, I am also a moralist, but not a 'moral imperialist'.[21] As a 'moral rationalist' I view morality, i.e. the making and supporting of moral judgements, as a rational enterprise. It is my contention that it is right to consider punishment bad and wrong to consider it good or even acceptable as a 'necessary evil'. But, I also feel it is essential to point out *why* this is so.

---

[18] Christie, N. (1982) *Limits to Pain,* Oxford: Martin Robertson. pp. 4-5, emphasis removed.
[19] Ibid, p. 10
[20] Ibid, p. 11
[21] Ibid, p.10.

Moral Rationalism

It is important for a critical criminology to have a clear and well-founded conception not only of what a truly 'just' social order would be like, but also and more specifically, how much a just social order would be possible, *i.e.* how it could be enforced and maintained. To the abolitionist perspective, imagining a society without punishment seems particularly important, even vital. The perspective of penal abolition only makes sense if it implies that a social order without institutionalised state-inflicted punishment can be conceived. Since its fate 'depends on the condition of … the future society "without the penal law"', we should turn to moral and political philosophy for the sort of rational argumentation on which the abolitionist perspective might be based.[22]

This requires not only making the principles on which the abolitionist perspective is based explicit, but also rationally justifying them as against other claims such as, for example, that our morality demands that the guilty be punished. It should be argued more stringently why punishment can never be justified – not only in the present circumstances, but, in principal, never ever. This might be attempted by showing that punishment is incompatible with notions of equality or justice, thereby indicating the need for more "utopian", *i.e.* normative theory construction.

Analytical Justification

There is yet one more reason why it is maybe worthwhile or even necessary to turn to moral and political philosophy. This reason is delivered by moral philosophy itself, as we see when we take a look at the results of recent assessments of traditional and current theories of punishment by moral philosophers.

Like jurisprudential scholarship, philosophical reflection of punishment has largely led a life of its own. However, there is a tendency to justify punishment 'analytically' rather than intuitively or in utilitarian terms. It is increasingly stressed that any specific theory of punishment should be interpreted within the broader context of political and social analysis.[23]

> 'Analytically' speaking, the question of whether punishment is right or wrong is irrevocably located within political philosophy:

[22] Smaus, G. (1986) 'Gesellschaftsmodell in der abolitionistischen Bewegung', *Kriminologisches Journal,* Vol. 188, pp. 1-18. p. 18

[23] Plant, R. (1980) 'Justice, Punishment and the State', in A, Bottoms and R. Preston (eds.), *The Coming Penal Crisis: A criminological and theological exploration,* Scottish Academic Press, pp. 53-70. p. 64

whatever the answer is, it must be part of a conclusion drawn from … the fundamental principle, certainly of a moral kind, by which societies are to be judged, and by which societies ought to be guided.[24]

This 'Postscript' – like most similar discussions – ends by turning to moral and political philosophy for answers to questions concerning whether punishment will be necessary, just and, therefore, fully justified under the conditions of a just social order. And this is where the present paper begins.

II

Normative Theory

Since the publication of Rawl's *A Theory of Justice* in 1971, there has been an increasing number of publications sharing an interest in providing adequate rational justification for specified moral principles that can be used to decide on the moral rightness of an act, the justice of social institutions such as the legal system, the criminal law or legal punishment, or of the social order as a whole.

For obvious reasons, I cannot give the reader a *'tour d'horizon'* of moral and political philosophy or a discussion of their major issues. Even a comparative evaluation of the various theories of justice in terms of their conceptions of a just social order and its enforcement is beyond the scope of this paper. Fortunately, however, this is just what has been done by the sociologist Derek Phillips in a recent book[25], *Toward a Just Social Order*, in which an attempt is made to locate the principals required for regulating a just social order as opposed to a social order resting on coercion, fear, ignorance, or other factors which can be viewed as undercutting its moral justifiability.[26]

Phillips draws on normative theorizing in moral and political philosophy directed at justifying such principals and at specifying the kinds of social political and economic arrangements that 'justice' requires. In particular, he works his way through a whole series of theories of justice (Rawls, Nozick, Habermans, and Gewirth, in contrast to MacIntyre, Sullivan, and Walzer) as well as theories of law (Kelsen, Hart, Fuller, and Dworkin) in an attempt not only to locate the justifiable principles for a just social order, but also to

---

[24] Honderich,(1984) p. 239
[25] Editors' note: recent at the time of this paper's original publication in 1989
[26] Phillips, (1986) p. 6

assess the moral standing of a legal system that would be in accord with them. As a result of this *'tour de force'* Phillips comes to the conclusion that:

> Gewrith has provided all that is required in the way of rational justification for the rights ... which should − normatively speaking − regulate the just social order.[27]

Phillips considers Gewirth's theory of justice 'superior' to other theories which attempt to rationally justify a set of principles for structuring just social relationships and institutional arrangements. Gewirth's theory is attractive, not only because it is logically stringent and avoids problems encountered in other theories of justice, but also because its focus on human action is in line with and, in fact, goes beyond the sociological tradition.[28]

Last but not least, what makes Gewirth's theory of justice particularly attractive with regard to the present paper is that it is so much more explicit on the issues of law enforcement and the justification of punishment than the theories of either Rawls of Habermas. In short, Gewirth's theory represents a particularly strong case for how punishment can be seen as fully compatible with justice.

Before going into the issue of criminal law and legal punishment specifically, let me first summarize how Gewirth derives his principles of morality and justice. I will then show how Phillips bases his conception of a just social order on these principles and how he comes to conclude that in such a social order, sentencing a criminal to prison and thus subjecting him/her to coercion and pain 'is morally justified' on the basis of his having violated one or another law that is intended to protect 'everyone's rights to freedom and well-being'.

I will review this dual theory of Gewirth and Phillips not so much for their conclusion, which obviously contradicts basic abolitionist beliefs. What is of particular interest to the present paper is the way this conclusion is reached. It is from this that abolitionism has something to learn.

Generic Consistency

Give that moral principles have strong implications for what are considered 'right' modes of behaviour or 'just' institutional arrangements, it becomes important whether or not these principles are adequately justified.

---

[27] Ibid, p.114
[28] Ibid, p. 101

Unfortunately there is no agreement among moral philosophers with regard to how moral principles should be justified 'correctly'.

Some conceive of moral principles as being obvious in and of themselves and, therefore, not in need of further justification. Others would argue that moral principles are sufficiently justified when, in fact, they underlie the morality of a society. Still others demand that moral principles be rationally justified, *i.e.* established on the basis of logically consistent arguments. Even though numerous attempts have already been made, no such project has ever been successful.

Gewirth's theory of justice belongs to the latter type and represents yet another, albeit more rigorous and logically stringent, attempt at rational justification of a moral principle. His major breakthrough is the connection between human action and morality as 'much closer and more substantive that has hitherto been thought', which allows for 'the logical derivation of a substantial normative moral principle for the nature of human action'.[29] This supreme moral 'Principle of Generic Consistency' (PGC) reads: 'Act in accord with the generic rights of your recipients as well as of yourself'.

The major strength of Gewirth's theory is, therefore, that both the form and content of his supreme moral principle are *logically* necessary. He not only shows how moral principles can be established on the basis of logical reasoning, but he also points out *which* moral rights can be justified by logical necessity and, therefore, shown to be morally superior. Moreover, he does this without recourse to thought experiments or hypothetical models such as Rawls' 'original position' and Habermas' 'ideal speech situation'.

The definitive justification of moral principles and rights is provided by applying reason, *i.e.* the canons of deductive and inductive logic, to the concept of action. He locates his 'supreme principle of morality' in the 'normative structure of human action' and subsequently shows how substantive moral rights claims can be logically derived from nature, *i.e.* the 'generic features' of human action. His main thesis is:

> that every agent, by the fact of engaging in action, is logically committed to the acceptance of certain evaluative and deontic judgments and ultimately of a supreme moral principle, the Principle of General Consistency, which requires that he respect his recipients' necessary conditions of action.[30]

Taken together, these rights to freedom and well-being which the PGC makes mandatory for all rational agents, guarantee:

---

[29] Gewirth,(1978) p.x
[30] Ibid.

that each person have rational autonomy in the sense of being a self-controlling, self-developing agent who can relate to other persons on the basis of mutual respect and cooperation, in contrast to being a dependent, passive recipient of the agency of others.[31]

A Just Social Order

According to Phillips, these rights, having received a rational foundation based strictly on systematic logical reasoning, should be declared as the 'first principles' of a just social order. Such a just social order would be 'regulated by two fundamental moral principles – the rights to freedom and well-being – and by the institutional arrangements to which they give rise'.[32] More precisely, a social order will be just 'if and only if (1) people recognise and respect everyone's generic rights to freedom and well-being, and (2) their actions are guided by this conception of justice'.[33]

Having defined the just social order in terms of its first moral principles, Phillips turns to the issues of moral learning, socialisation and social control, *i.e.* the prevention of deviance as well as its containment and control. In particular, he deals with questions like whether we can rationally justify the legitimate authority of a legal system that helps to regulate the just social order as well as the moral obligation of all citizens to obey the law.

It is in this context that the questions which are central to the present paper will also be 'analytically' located: is state-inflicted pain at all compatible with justice? Can legal punishment be just and, therefore, justifiable in a just social order? Phillips doesn't seem to have any doubts about the answer: 'Since the equality of rights is inherently morally justifiable, so is the system of criminal law that defends these rights'.[34]

For the critical criminologist or sociologist of criminal law, this conclusion leave a few questions open to debate.[35] At the very least, we would have expected that a discussion about the necessity of punishment in a just social order be included. This is not simply because the possibility of a just social order without punishment is conceivable, at least in principle, but it is also

---

[31] Ibid, p. 5

[32] Phillips, (1986) p. 115

[33] Ibid, p. 184

[34] Ibid, p. 325

[35] Also for the moral philosopher, of course. It is not the purpose of this paper, however, to review the specific philosophical theories of punishment (see Honderich). Instead, I am concentrating on how punishment is justified 'analytically' in the context of a conception of a just society or a just social order.

because there are developments in contemporary society which are moving away from punishment as a major form of social control.

This would suggest that opportunities for creating and operating other forms of social control than formal legal control as discussed in current debates on 'the politics of informal social control'[36] should be taken in to account in any treatment of social control in a just social order or, in Gewirth's words, of what is to be done to protect the generic rights freedom and well-being 'in all actual or possible *empirical* situations'.[37]

Since Phillips, whenever he talks about punishment, draws extensively on Gewirth's theory of justice, we may do well to go back to Gewirth and take a closer look at his position regarding the issue of the compatibility or incompatibility of justice and punishment.

The Static Phase

Obviously, every person values his or her freedom and well-being and wants them to be defended against attacks by others. It is also evident that people's rights are protected only if other persons either refrain from infringing upon them of their own volition or are prevented from doing so by others. The question arises, however, concerning what sort of institutional arrangements will be needed for that purpose. More specifically, we may ask whether these arrangements will necessarily include provisions for punishment.

The answer can, once again, be found in the PGC where everyone must act in accordance with his or her generic rights to freedom and well-being. Applying the supreme principle 'indirectly' to social rules and institutions, Gewirth argues that they must be 'instrumentally' justified. A distinction is made, however, between a 'static' and a 'dynamic' phase, depending on whether or not equality in terms of generic rights already exists. In the static phase, it is assumed that persons are equal in their effective possession of the generic rights. In the dynamic phase, dispositional inequalities in well-being based on institutional sources first have to be removed by redistributive justice in order to achieve a situation in which the equality of generic rights exists.

For the purpose of the present discussion concerning the necessity of punishment in a just social order, it suffices to concentrate on the 'static' phase. In this situation, social rules, and institutions in general, are 'instrumentally' justified by the PGC insofar as they are required to maintain,

---

[36] Cohen. (1979)
[37] Gerwith, (1978) p. 292, emphasis added.

i.e. protect and restore, the equality of generic rights among persons. This applies to criminal law as well.

Criminal Law

The rules of criminal law are justified 'in that they serve to uphold in certain ways the rights of all persons to such basic goods as life, liberty, and physical integrity'.[38] In dealing with the relation of criminal law to the PGC, Gewirth differentiates between the content of criminal law and the enforcement provisions in the form of what he calls the 'minimal state', *i.e.* institutional arrangements to enforce the rules and rectify violations, such as a police force to apprehend and arrest suspects, courts to try them and sentence the guilty, and a system of penalties.

The content of the rules of criminal law is largely, if not entirely, the same as that of the most basic part of the PGC. By virtue of this instrumental relation to the supreme moral principle, the rules of the criminal law have a stringent logical status. Since it is self-contradictory for any agent to deny the obligatoriness of the supreme principle, it is also self-contradictory for him or her to deny the obligatoriness of the rules of the criminal law.

The rules of criminal law are, however, intended not only to prohibit, but also to prevent people from infringing upon each other's generic rights. With regard to enforcement provisions, *i.e.* the threat and application of punishment for violators of the rules, the instrumental justification of the criminal law 'is not logical but causal: the functioning of the criminal law is a necessary means to the end of persons' obeying the PGC'.[39] In other words, 'to say that the criminal law is required to bring about the equality of generic rights prescribed by the PGC is, in part, to make an empirical, contingent statement'.[40]

Nevertheless, Gewirth argues that insofar as 'enforcement of the rules through punishment is causally required for protecting the PGC's equality of generic rights... the obligatoriness of the enforcement must also rationally be granted'.[41] The moral correctness of this conclusion is neither optional, nor empirical or contingent, but rational and necessary. Consequently, 'since agents logically must consent to accept the rules of the criminal law, these rules and the minimal state have a consensual basis'.[42]

---

[38] Ibid, p.294
[39] Ibid, p. 295
[40] Ibid.
[41] Ibid, p. 300
[42] Ibid, p. 303

The Justice of Punishment

With regard to punishment, Gewirth argues, specifically that 'if one person voluntarily and purposively kills, kidnaps, physically assaults, or defames another, then in that transaction the former sets up an occurrent inequality between himself and his recipient'[43] and that the criminal law 'provides punishments that rectify this inequality'.[44]   Therefore, the criminal law is justified 'by providing for enforcement of the PGC's requirements through the threat and application of punishment'[45] and 'the punishment prescribed by the criminal law is justified as a way of restoring the equality by redressing the previously disturbed balance'.[46]   Finally, Gewirth refers to a 'conceptual relationship whereby punishment is intended to restore the PGC's equality of generic rights'.[47]

Thus, punishment is justified by virtue of its instrumental relationship to the PGC.   This instrumental relationship is, however, a duel one: a simultaneously backward- and forward-looking relationship.   On the one hand, punishment as prescribed by criminal law restores the equal distribution of generic rights by redressing situations disturbed by a previous infringement of these rights.   These situations are morally wrong in that they violate the equality of generic rights which the PGC makes mandatory for all actions and institutions.   On the other hand, punishment is also justified by it being a deterrent which helps to ensure that people abide by the PGC.

Punishment is accepted as legitimate, partly due to its deterrent effect, but 'only insofar as punishment is justified by its serving to restore the PGC's equality of generic rights through being inflicted on persons who infringed the equality'.[48]   Thus, ultimately, the utilitarian aspect of punishment is subordinated to the retributivist dimension.

Consequentialism and Retributivism

Gewirth's construction may seem rather complex.   One reason is that he draws upon a 'mixed' theory of punishment which combines elements of retribution as well as deterrence theories of punishment, trying to compensate for the weaknesses in the latter by using particular strengths of the former.   He wishes to avoid certain difficulties inherent in utilitarian

---

[43] Ibid, p. 294
[44] Ibid.
[45] Ibid, p. 295
[46] Ibid, p. 297
[47] Ibid, p. 299
[48] Ibid, p. 299

theories which justify punishment in terms of the ends to be achieved, *i.e.* protection of society or prevention of crime.

One important problem in these 'consequentialist' theories is that the rights of individuals are subordinated to the system's goal. Justifying the threat and application of punishment as providing enforcement of the PGC's requirements runs the risk that some persons will suffer for the protection of others. They become merely means toward an end, albeit a justifiable one.

Gewirth defends his theory against this critique by pointing to the fact that the end to which criminal law is instrumental is not simply a utilitarian goal, like control and prevention of crime, but rather the maintenance of the equality of generic rights. As this distributive end is morally justified by the PGC, it can itself, in turn, justify interventions intended to protect, restore or re-instate that same equality of generic rights.

Although Gewirth devotes some attention to the shortcomings of consequentialism and defends his theory against such critiques, he still seems to ignore the weaknesses of retributivism, which is after all the other side of the coin. This is not unimportant, since it stresses the backward-looking, retributive side, giving it priority over the forward-looking, deterrent aspect.

This construction is understandable as retributivism – at least in moral philosophy – and has always enjoyed a much better reputation than utilitarian theories. According to Murphy, retributivism is 'the only morally defensible theory of punishment', despite its being largely inapplicable to modern societies. Nevertheless, 'we have the moral right to punish under the condition that we have restructured society in such a way that criminals genuinely are autonomous and that they do benefit in the requisite sense from the rule of law'.[49]

In agreement with Murphy, Wasserstrom holds that strong retributivist theories are what a justification of punishment requires but, unlike Murphy, he concludes that such theories do not establish a sufficiently sound set of moral arguments, which are unambiguous and persuasive enough to provide the basis for a general justification of punishment.[50] According to Wasserstrom, whether it is a right to punish people, and if so, for what reasons, are still open questions, both within philosophical thought as well as in society at large. Gewirth's solution to the problem of justifying punishment is to show that punishment is logically necessary in a just social order, *i.e.* rationally justifiable. It is to this solution that I will now be turning.

---

[49] Murphy, J. (1980)'Marxism and Retribution' in M. Cohen, T. Nagel and T. Scanlon (eds.), *Marx, justice and History*, Princeton: Princeton University Press, pp. 158-184. p. 162
[50] Wasserstrom (1980)

III

Introduction

Evidently, Gewirth's theory of justice offers one of the most, if not *the* most, rational justifications for the necessity of punishment in a just society that one can imagine. For this reason it seems to 'embody' a perfect 'sparring partner' for the abolitionist wishing to shape up in a 'realistic' training session. This is exactly what I intend to do in the remainder of this paper. Before the gong sounds for the first round, I wish to indicate, however, that I do not intend to challenge the logical correctness of Gewirth's rational justification for the PGC. Nor will I be discussing Phillips's conception of a just social order in any detail. The topic of the present paper does not concern principles upon which a just social order should be based, *i.e.* a Principle of Equality (Honderich), Generic Consistency (Gewirth), Justice as Fairness (Rawls) or any other abstract principle for that matter.[51] I will concentrate instead upon the question of *how* punishment as a social institution is currently being integrated in theories of justice and, more generally, of a just social order, thereby making it justifiable as being necessary, both logically and empirically speaking.

I will now discuss various aspects of the instrumental relationship with the PGC by which criminal law and punishment are justified. As we have seen, this instrumental relationship is a twofold one: on the one hand, it is conceptual and logical, on the other, it is empirical and causal. I will first discuss whether there is, indeed, a conceptual relation between the PGC and punishment and, thereby, making punishment a logical necessity in a just social order. Next I will discuss the causal-empirical relationship involved in the justification of punishment. This will be done in terms of means and ends, intended and unintended consequences, and a 'special problem'. Finally, I will take a look at the issue of rational justification. The pros and cons of the

---

[51] In this respect recent feminist critiques of dominant theories of (social) justice (Benhabib; Olkin; Young) are highly relevant, even though, once again, little is said about the justification of punishment. In her critique of the (masculine) 'Portia' model of rights and justice, Heidensohn briefly touches on the subject. However, the intriguing question concerning whether punishment is, on principle, compatible with the (feminine) 'Persophone' model of responsibility and care remains unanswered, awaiting further research. Behabib, S. (1987) 'The Generalized and the Concrete Other: The Kohlber-Gilligan Controversy and Feminist Theory', in S. Behabib & D. Cornell (eds.), *Feminism as critique,* Oxford: Polity Press, pp. 77-95; Okin, S. (1987) 'Justice and Gender', *Philosophy and Public Affairs,* no. 16, pp. 42-72; Young, I. (1987) 'Impartiality and the Civic Public: Some implications of feminist Critiques of Moral and Political Theory', in S. Behabib and D. Cornell (eds.) *Feminism as Critique,* Cambridge: Polity Press, pp. 57-76; Heidensohn, F. (1986) 'Models of Justice: Portia or Persephone? Some Thoughts on Equality, Fairness and gender in the fiels of Criminal Justice', *International Journal of the Sociology of Law,* No. 14, pp, 287-298.

type of rational justification employed by Gerwirth will be discussed and, finally, some conclusions for the abolitionist project will be drawn.

Rectification

My first point concerns what Gewirth calls the 'equalizing function' of punishment, *i.e.* the claim that punishment is intended to 'restore' the PGC's equality of rights by 'redressing' the previously disturbed balance, thereby 'rectifying' this inequality.[52]

This comes close to the retributivist idea that justice requires that the guilty be punished because burdens have been unfairly assumed *vis a vis* the criminal by law-abiding citizens and benefits have been unfairly appropriated by the criminal *vis a vis* these same law-abiding citizens. Thus, the wrong-doer has obtained a benefit to which he or she is not entitled by virtue of not restraining from acting on inclinations and desires as most other people have done. In punishing him or her, that benefit is taken away, thereby restoring the social equilibrium which existed prior to the offence.

It is worth noting that Gewirth refers to punishment strictly with regard to an agent and his or her recipient and not to some general interest or rule of law with regards to society at large. An exception, of course, is the PGC itself and the equality of generic rights it requires. The question arises concerning how, in fact, punishment may rectify, redress, restore or equalize. Can punishment as means ever be consistent with the end of maintaining a just social order as defined by the PGC? Gewirth clearly sees punishment as being 'in accord' with justice since punishment 'expresses' the equality of generic rights. As a means to the end of protecting the equality of rights, punishment 'embodies distinctive features of the result'.[53]

However, it can and, in fact, has been argued to the contrary that, in general punishment, and

> even punishment for obvious and serious wrong-doing, also produces a kind of greater disequilibrium. Where there was previously the unhappiness, pain, suffering, or deprivation caused by the wrong doing, there is now, after the punishment, the addition deprivation that is the punishment.[54]

Thus, it is not unproblematic to view punishment as restoring the equality of rights or to regard it as required by justice, particularly given that this

---

[52] Gerwirth, (1978) p. 294.

[53] Ibid, p. 296

[54] Wasserstrom, (1980) p. 146

'balance' depends upon the intentional production of additional suffering and pain. The question arises concerning how one person's rights can be restored by inflicting pain on someone else? In other words how can equality of rights be restored by the means of punishment which itself creates inequality? Moreover, in many, if not most cases, the removal of benefit through punishment is, at best, metaphorical. If restoring the social equilibrium of equality of basic rights is the real goal, redress by compensation or restitution to the victim by the wrong-doer, not punishment, appears to be the more natural and direct way to restore the balance in respect to wrongful appropriation of something that belonged to the victim of the crime. In short, it is not easy to see how punishment 'expresses' or 'embodies' justice as opposed to compensation or restitution.

Conceptual Relation

My second point concerns the conceptual relation involved in punishment. As we have seen, it has been suggested that there is an 'internal' conceptual relationship between punishment and the PGC and that, therefore, there is a logical necessity for justice in a just social order. Gerwith regards the PGC as 'requiring' agents to act in accordance with their recipients' rights. It has been noted, however, that the idea of a 'requirement' is not strong and certainly not identical to the ideal of a legal 'must' as in the rule of criminal law. For this reason we can understand the idea of something being required, and in that sense being different from a request or, more generally, what is optional, without the idea of punishment being attached. More importantly, however, I would argue that, if there is a conceptual relationship involved in punishment, it would be "through" the criminal law. To say that punishment is conceptually related to the PGC presupposes that punishment is conceptually related to criminal law.

On the contrary, I would argue that there is no such internal, conceptual relation. In fact, we can distinguish clearly the rule prohibiting certain behaviour from the provision for penalties to be exacted if the rule is broken, and suppose the first to exist without the latter.[55]

Gewirth can only conceive of such a relation because he identifies law enforcement with one specific form of sanctioning lawbreakers, *i.e.* punishment. Sanctions, however, should not be immediately identified with punishment because sanction and punishment can mean different things.

---

[55] Hart, H. (1961) *The Concept of Law,* Oxford:Clarendon Press p. 125

Moreover, as Hirst has recently argued, there is 'no intrinsic relation between sanction and any of the definite means by which it has been represented'.[56]

Taken together these remarks should suffice, at least provisionally, for reaching the conclusion that no internal conceptual relationship between punishment and the PGC, as well as the equality of generic rights to freedom and well-being it requires, exists. However, it seems reasonable to assume that there is no *logical* necessity for punishment in a just social order. This does not, of course, exclude the *empirical* necessity for punishment and it is to this matter that I will now turn.

Causal Relation

As we have seen, Gewirth also conceives of an empirical, *causal* relationship between punishment and the PGC. In the conceptual relationship the PGC is 'embodied' and 're-stored', in the causal, empirical relationship it is 'protected'. Empirically speaking, 'the functioning of the criminal law is a necessary means to the end of persons' obeying the PGC'.[57] And since

> punishment and the threat thereof are *intended* to bring about that persons refrain from inflicting on others the basic and serious harms the PGC prohibits, punishment and the rules that provide for it are also justified as *having* a deterrent effect.[58]

My first remark concerns the contingency of the relationship involved, *i.e.* the causal, empirical relationship between criminal punishment and the equality of rights. This contingency is, in fact, reflected in Gewirth's formulations. On the one hand, punishment and the threat thereof are seen as *intended* in order to enforce compliance; on the other hand, punishment is justified as *having* a deterrent effect. Intentions are, as we all know, no guarantee that the intended result will be achieved. In practice, there may be a mixture of intended and unintended results, whereby the unintended consequences may either be positive, *i.e.* reinforcing, or negative, or, weakening the intended result. From deterrence research, we also are familiar with the fact that the deterrent effects of punishment are, at best, a 'mixed bag'. Empirically speaking, the causal relationship is contingent indeed. This is even more so as the empirical contingency involved is also 'aggravated' by a 'special problem'.

---

[56] Hirst, P. (1985) 'Socialist Legality', *Economy and Society,* Vol. 14 pp. 113-127. p. 125
[57] Gewirth, (1978) p. 295
[58] Ibid, p. 299; emphasis added

This 'special problem', as Wasserstrom has called it, is created by the fact that we are talking about the empirical necessity of punishment in a non-empirical just social order. Consequently, we are making assumptions in regard to human behaviour under hypothetical conditions. Grounding such assumptions would demand a theory of human nature describing human beings as they would be likely to behave in a just social order.

> Thus, what is needed is both a plausible theory of human nature, of the ways persons would be disposed to behave within a reasonably just (or at least not seriously unjust) society, and a plausible description of the basic institutional structure of such a society. The two issues are surely related and a part of any larger, more comprehensive theory of a just society.[59]

No such theory of human nature is systematically included in Gewirth's account of the necessity of punishment in a just society, structured according to the PGC. In fact, the empirical necessity of punishment remains empirically contingent, notably since we cannot transfer results of deterrence research – assuming for the moment they were unambiguous – to the conditions of a just society. The 'relation of requirement' involved seems to be intentional, rather than causal. This means, to quote Wasserstrom once again,

> to return, perhaps to the fairly plausible intuition with which retributivism brings – that serious crimes, serious culpable behaviour, deserves to be punished – but it is not yet to give a generally applicable series of reasons for thinking that intuition defensible.[60]

Rational Justification

How does what has been said so far bear upon the rational justification which Gewirth offers for punishment in a just social order? As we have seen, he claims that the rules of criminal law have a 'stringent logical status' by virtue of their instrumental relation to the PGC. With regard to punishment, he adds that 'insofar as enforcement of the rules through punishment is causally required ... enforcement must also rationally be granted'.[61] The question arises concerning the precise 'status' of punishment or, put somewhat differently, what exactly does this supposed causal relation

---

[59] Wasserstrom, (1980) pp. 150-151, n. 39
[60] Ibid, p. 146.
[61] Gerwirth,(1978) p. 300.

provided by Gewirth add to or subtract from the rational justification of punishment within the 'static phase' Gewirth claims to provide?

Gewirth's answer to these questions is that the causal, empirical relation can be defined 'within the limits of' and 'subordinate to' the conceptual relation. More specifically, he asserts that punishment is justified in part by its having a causal, deterrent effect, but that this justification holds 'only insofar' as punishment is justified by its serving to restore the PGC's equality of rights. One way of making sense of this would be to consider the conceptual relation as necessary condition. In that case, we would need to say 'if' rather than 'insofar', which assumes degrees of validity rather than a dichotomy. Another way of making sense of this is to focus on the fact that Gewirth is intending to provide a *rational* justification for punishment. Since he defines 'rationality' in terms of logic, we could conclude that justification of punishment is only warranted in terms of strict logical necessity. Gewirth, however, assures us that insofar as enforcement through punishment is causally required, it must also rationally be granted. I am afraid we may have to admit that Gewirth is a bit ambiguous on this point.

Another aspect of the rational justification provided by Gewirth concerns 'intentionality' of criminal punishment. According to Gewirth, punishment and the threat thereof are intended to ensure that people refrain from infringing upon each other's rights. This also raises a few questions. Given the fact that intended actions can, and often do have unintended consequences, how would a rational agent account for them? How would a rational agent justify punishment – indeed, rationally – as a social institution integrated in a just social order, given that 'the whole quality of life in a society … is influenced by the existence of a central practice of an authoritarian and repressive nature' which is what punishment inherently is.[62] Would a rational agent consider punishment rationally justified irrespective of any causality consideration, *i.e.* ignoring its impacts even if they turn out to be counterproductive? It seems clear that such an attitude can hardly be presented as 'rational'.

Gerwirth's approach is not particularly sensitive to such unintended consequences of punishment in a just society. The moral aspect of such consequences, however, creates a demand for additional justification. Additional justification is needed in order to justify a just social order with punishment against a just social order without punishment or, more specifically, enforcement through punishment as against enforcement through non-punitive forms of sanction.

---

[62] Honderich, (1984) p. 12

Hidden Message

The strength of Gewirth's theory is also its weakness, the former being the logical stringency of the justification provided, whereas the latter is the price to be paid for employing a minimalist definition of rationality. This definition ignores other, possibly more 'reasonable', reactions to problematic situations and behaviours. In this respect Gewirth's and, for that matter, Phillips' theories proliferate the hidden message decoded by Christie in the neo-classical approach; namely, the implicit 'denial of a whole series of alternatives which should be taken into consideration'.[63] Christie refers to 'non-reaction', 'forgiveness', and the like. However, conceptions for alternative reactions on behalf of the offender are also in order.

As previously mentioned, human behaviour under the conditions of justice are hard to predict. Similarly, the perceptions of the seriousness of infringements of others' generic rights would also vary. Therefore, I see no reason – either conceptually or empirically – to exclude the possibility that under such conditions the influence or effect of other forms of informal (or formal) social control would be very different. Under these conditions, even self-restraint might evolve to unknown levels. In that case, the 'punishment' for doing something wrong would be having to live with the memory of it.

Ironically, there is a tendency, in Gewirth's, but particularly in Phillips' approach, to allow, albeit reluctantly, for a just social order without the necessity of punishment. Gewirth, speculating about a hypothetical, future situation using the language of the past, can only admit that punishment and the whole apparatus of the criminal law are 'necessary evils' and that 'it would be far better if the evil of inflicting basic and other harms had not occurred so that its rectification was unnecessary'.[64] Phillips, however, allows for the possibility that the use of punishment in such a social order would be 'minimized'. He argues sociologically that a legal system whose legitimate authority is rationally justifiable creates more reliable conformity and that, therefore, 'the need for the legal system and its apparatus to maintain means of coercion in constant readiness is minimized'.[65] What holds for means of coercion in general would certainly hold for punishment in particular. Most aptly, however, Murphy has formulated the 'withering away' of punishment in an elegant paradox. He virtually says that making justifications of punishment possible is, in fact, making punishment unnecessary and, hence, enabling its disappearance.[66]

---

[63] Christie, (1982) p. 45
[64] Gewirth, (1978) p. 299
[65] Phillips, (1986) p. 248.
[66] A case in point is Campbell (1983) who assumes that socialism will produce that 'revolution in

In summary, I would like to say that the rational justification of punishment in a just social order as provided by Gewirth should be taken as a justification of law enforcement by sanction rather than punishment. *Prima facie* punishment in a just social order seems neither logically nor empirically necessary. Moreover, as means, it is not 'in the spirit' of the end. It is incompatible with the notion of justice as it involves additional suffering instead of truly compensating for loss, suffering and pain. Given the potential – logically and empirically – for other ways of dealing more reasonably with wrong-doings, punishment in a just social order cannot *prima facie* be considered rationally justified.

Conclusion

My point of departure for this paper was a very simple one. I wanted to take a plunge into moral and political philosophy, hoping to bring up a few effective arguments which could provide the abolitionist point of view with a more solid foundation. I was motivated by a certain uneasiness with the way the sympathetic abolitionist intention, *i.e.* limiting and ultimately abolishing human suffering and pain, is being defended. It seemed to me that, in general, the abolitionists too easily assumed that theirs is and has to be the morally superior point of view.

I began the present paper by pointing to the need for normative, 'utopian' theory construction and the necessity for critical, abolitionist criminologists and sociologists of criminal law to turn the normative theorising in moral and political philosophy for more grounded accounts of the just social order they have in mind. As we have seen, moral and political philosophy does not provide us with the ready-made building blocks for a more solid foundation of the abolitionist point of view which I had been hoping to find. On the contrary, I found that if punishment may ever be fully justified, it will be under the very conditions of justice in a just social order. Obviously this runs against the abolitionist intuition. Nevertheless, it should not be concluded that normative theory is, therefore, of no use to the abolitionist. Rather it is my contention that on the basis of a critical reception of results of recent work in moral and political philosophy, it is possible to provide abolitionism with a more solid theoretical grounding which it lacks by arguing more convincingly that there is no necessity and no justification for punishment, particularly in a just social order. In other words, punishment is incompatible with justice.

---

human motivation' which makes uncoerced obedience to social and legal rules possible.

The points I have tried to make are that there is no intrinsic, conceptual relation between criminal law and punishment; that law enforcement (coercion) and punishment should be differentiated; that there is no conceptual relationship between criminal justice and the PGC and that, therefore, there is no logical necessity for punishment in a just social order. Furthermore, I have argued that there can be no empirical necessity for punishment in a just social order and that, therefore, punishment in a just social order cannot be rationally justified.

Of course, I have raised rather than 'made' these points. They can, in fact, be no more than suggestions for lines along the normative, 'utopian' theory construction might proceed for the development of the abolitionist project. It has not been my intention to claim that all criminologists should now engage in normative theorizing. What I do want to say, however, is that it may be important for critical criminologists, and certainly for abolitionists, to be at least aware of developments in these fields of moral and political philosophy, in order to learn how particular moral positions can be strengthened by systematic reasoning. We can learn from normative theory how to avoid the position of just having to *assume* that we are arguing from a morally superior point of view without being able to bring up the rational arguments for such a claim.

The moral claim that it is wrong to punish persons in principle, not only in an unjust but also in a just society can and has to be better grounded in normative theory. It is one thing to say that it has not been convincingly argued that punishment is right, *i.e.* that it remains an open question whether punishment can be justified at all. It is another thing, however, to conclude that if punishment is not right, it must, therefore be wrong. Yet I think this is the task which lies ahead for the abolitionist.[67] On a more encouraging note, let us remember that growth of knowledge is achieved by conjectures and refutations, *i.e.* not by proving that an idea is right, but by proving that it was wrong. When viewed in this way, abolitionism remains a most promising perspective.

---

[67] Unlike Nils Christie, who argues that those advocating the higher value of reduction of pain should refuse to take this 'burden of proof' on their shoulders. I think this is exactly the task which lies ahead of us as abolitionists.

Bibliography

Bean, P. (1981) *Punishment: A Philosophical and Criminological Inquiry,* Oxford: Martin Robertson

Behabib, S. (1987) 'The Generalized and the Concrete Other: The Kohlber-Gilligan Controversy and Feminist Theory', in S. Behabib & D. Cornell (eds.), *Feminism as Critique,* Cambridge: Polity Press, pp. 77-95

Carlen, P. (1983) 'On rights and powers' in Garland, D. & Young P. (eds) *The Power to Punish* London: Heinemann pp. 203-216

Chapman D. (1987) 'The "Ballad of Reading Gaol"' in Blad J.R., van Mastrigt H., Uildriks N. (eds.), *The Criminal Justice System as a Social Problem: an Abolitionist Perspective,* Liber Amicorum Louk Hulsman, Rotterdam: Erasmus Universiteit.

Christie, N. (1982) *Limits to Pain,* Oxford: Martin Robertson.

Clarke, D. (1982) 'Justifications for Punishment', *Contemporary Crisis,* No. 6, pp. 25-57

Cohen, S. (1979) 'Guilt, Justice, and Tolerance: Some Old Concepts for a New Criminology', in D. Downes and P. Rock (eds.) *Deviant Interpretations,* Oxford: Martin Roberstson

Elias, N. (1978) *The Civilising Process,* Oxford, Blackwell

Gerwirth, A. (1978) *Reason and morality,* Chicago: University of Chicago Press

Greenberg, D. (1978) 'Reflections on the Justice debate', *Contemporary Crisis,* No. 7 pp. 313-327

Haan, W. de (1987a) 'Fuzzy Morals and Flakey Politics: The Coming Out of Critical criminology', *Journal of Law and Society,* No. 14 pp. 321-333

Haan, W. de (1987b) 'Abolitionism and the Politics of "Bad Conscience"', *The Howard Journal of Criminal Justice,* No. 26, pp.15-32

Hart, H. (1961) *The Concept of Law,* Oxford: Clarendon Press

Heidensohn, F. (1986) 'Models of Justice: Portia or Persephone? Some Thoughts on Equality, Fairness and gender in the fiels of Criminal Justice', *International Journal of the Sociology of Law,* No. 14, pp, 287-298

Hirsch, A. von (1983) '"Neoclassicism", Proportionality, and the Rationale for Punishment: Thoughts on the Scandinavian debate', *Crime and Delinquency,* vol. 29, pp. 52-70

Hirst, P. (1985) 'Socialist Legality', *Economy and Society,* Vol. 14 pp. 113-127

Honderich, T. (1984) *Punishment: The Supposed Justifications, with a New Postscript,* Harmondsworth: Penguin Books

Okin, S. (1987) 'Justice and Gender', *Philosophy and Public Affairs,* no. 16, pp. 42-72

Phillips, D. (1986) *Towards a Just Social Order,* Princeton: Princeton University Press

Plant, R. (1980) 'Justice, Punishment and the State', in A, Bottoms and R. Preston (eds.), *The Coming Penal Crisis: A criminological and theological exploration,* Scottish Academic Press, pp. 53-70

Murphy, J. (1980)'Marxism and Retribution' in M. Cohen, T. Nagel and T. Scanlon (eds.), *Marx, justice and History,* Princeton: Princeton University Press, pp. 158-184

Rawls, J. (1971) *A Theory of justice,* Cambridge, Mass.: Harvard university Press

Smaus, G. (1986) 'Gesellschaftsmodell in der abolitionistischen Bewegung', *Kriminologisches Journal,* Vol. 188, pp. 1-18

Spitzer, S. (1982) 'The Dialectics of Formal and Informal Control', in R. Abel (ed.) *The Politics of Informal justice, Vol. 1,* New York: Academic Press, pp 167-205

Struggle for Justice: A Report on crime and punishment in America, prepared for the American Friends Service Committee. (1971) New York: Hill and Wang

Swaaningen, R. van (1986) 'What is abolitionism' in H.Bianchi and R, van Swaaningen (eds.), *Abolitionism: Towards a Non-Repressive Approach to Crime,* Amsterdam: Free University Press, pp. 9-21

Wasserstrom, R. (1980) *Philosophy and Social Issues, Five Studies,* Notre Dame, Notre Dame University Press

Young, I. (1981) 'Towards a Critical Theory of Justice', *Social Theory and Social Practice,* No. 7 pp. 279-302

Young, I. (1987) 'Impartiality and the Civic Public: Some implications of feminist Critiques of Moral and Political Theory', in S. Behabib and D. Cornell (eds.) *Feminism as Critique,* Cambridge: Polity Press, pp. 57-76

5.

Dissolution and Expansion

Sebastian Scheerer

This paper was delivered at the European Group's 13th annual conference in Hamburg and first published in Working Papers in European Criminology, Volume 7 'The Expansion of European Prison Systems' in 1986.

Introduction

No reason to blame it on Michel Foucault or Andrew Scull, although their works probably did exert the decisive influence on a radical belief system which is now about to crumble.[1] At the centre of this belief system stood the idea that visible repression and with it prisons were on their way out, historically speaking, and that so- called 'soft' kinds of control would take over. The belief did not go as far as to assert that *all* prisons would be replaced by political intimidation, surveillance, and so on, but the bulk of control would be achieved by the much more subtle ways that reigned in the Foucaultian universe. While the times of the 'Great Incarceration' were nearing their end, 'decarceration' would reign the day and just a small number of high security prisons would keep 'the Dangerous Few' away from society. The days of this belief system were the days of diversion, of reduced numbers of prison inmates, of the closing of local jails and the modernisation of social control.

To all of those who believed in the end of imprisonment, the developments of the last few years must have come as a surprise. All of a sudden new and additional prisons are being planned, constructed and filled up with people wherever one looks in Europe or the United States. Not decarceration but overcrowding is the key word in the hallways of the criminal justice system. In West Germany for example there was a sharp rise in prison inmates (not counting pre-trial detainees) between 1971 and 1984, from about 33,000 to 48,000 people. While in 1972 there used to be 69

---

[1] Foucault, M. (1977) *Discipline and Punish: The Birth of the Prison*, London: Penguin; Scull, A.T. (1977) *Decarceration: Community treatment and the Deviant,* Englewood Cliffs, N.J.: Prentice- Hall

prisoners to each 100,000 of the population, there were 114 in 1984. Quite contrary to an assumption held by some radical criminologists that saw prisons' use decline, in West Germans currently[2] no less than 10,000 additional prison places are either planned or being built.

Overcrowding is not connected with a more frequent use of unconditional imprisonment by the judiciary. The number of persons actually sent to prison each year is on a steady decrease (and may justify some of the criminological assumptions about the end of the prison era in the long run). What is increasing – and responsible for overcrowding – is the length of sentences handed out to offenders. As a first differentiation one should therefore keep in mind that overcrowding in the Federal Republic of Germany is not a result of more people being actually sent to prison, but a result of a sharp *increase in longer sentences*, especially those between two and fifteen years.[3] Secondly, one would have to look at the kind of crimes that attract these very harsh sentences, and one would find drug and drug-related offences, rape and robbery. A complicated network of conditions, on the etiological as well as the societal reaction side, would be necessary to find out something of the reasons for this, the argument would have to lead all the way to socio-structural and economic changes in the last decades. A solid beginning though has been made.[4]

Thirdly, one would need a deeper understanding of *long-term transformations* within relatively autonomous fields – or 'autopotetic subsystems' – such as the criminal law, which evidently have something to do with what is going on in terms of prisons and their populations. What I should like to do on the following pages is to sketch some dimensions of this larger context using the – admittedly pale – notions of *expansion* and *dissolution*. While the latter evidently reminds us of Max Weber's critique of anti-formal tendencies in modern law,[5] as well as of the recurrent theme that 'law be dead',[6] the notion of expansion may sound familiar because of its closeness to topics like 'legal explosion' or 'juridification'. The original contribution this paper could make to our understanding of the rapid changes in the field of prisons and the criminal justice system thus lies in the description of some interrelations. Although examples given all relate to the German experience,

---

[2] Editors' Note: 1986
[3] Vos, M. (1985b) 'Verwahrvollzug-Behandlungsvollzug' der strafrechthche Gebrauch der Freiheitsstrafe im Zuge ihrer veranderten Anspruche Zugleich eine Kntik der Kurzstrafenkntic', in U O Sievering (ed) *Behandlungsvollzug Zwischenstufe oder Sackgasse*, Arnoldshamer Text,
[4] See: Steinert, H. (1984) 'Was ist eigentlich aus der 'Neuen Kriminologie' geworder? Einige Thesen, um die Suche zu onentieren, *KrimJ* 16, pp 86-89.
[5] Weber, M. (1969) *Max Weber on Law and Society 3rd edition* [edited with an introduction and annotations by M Rheinstein], Cambridge, Mass: Harvard University Press
[6] Rostow, E.V. (ed) (1971) *Is Law Dead*, New York, Simon and Schuster

there seems reason to believe that the developments shown are by no means confined to the Federal Republic, and that similarities to any other countries would not be purely coincidental.

Dominant tendencies

> Our ability to identify areas in which the penetration of law has diminished as well as areas where it has increased suggests that we not use terms such as "evolution", which imply uni-directionality, nor such loaded words as "progress" for the sorts of legal change that we observe in our lifetime. We should more modestly talk of "tendencies". Among other advantages, this would encourage us to search more seriously for "counter-tendencies" and to weigh these in relation to what might be considered "main" tendencies.[7]

Many such 'tendencies' have been postulated. Many of them are normative and evolutionist, but see themselves as descriptive of reality. Many of them seem as artificial as the most twisted works of scholasticism. These shall not be repeated nor refuted. Just two tendencies shall be featured dissolution of formal rationality and expansion of a weaker kind of law which much resembles the circular letters of a middle-echelon police administration.

Dissolution

Law is in a process of dissolution. 'What the law says' is becoming ever more unclear to ever more people, high-ranking jurists included. Cases cannot be solved anymore by mere logical deduction (subsumption of a case under a law). There are two evident reasons for this. Firstly, the law is so vague that every case becomes a hard case. Secondly, there is ever less internal coherence within the body of law, so a systematic reasoning which would rule out one interpretation and allow another is becoming ever more difficult and/or wilful. More and more cases are not decided through the law, but 'decided' by consideration.[8] If 'law' is a normative regulation of societal interactions of enforceable character, and if this regulation is one of general and abstract sentences, so that every decision of a concrete case consists in the 'application' of an abstract rule of law to a concrete fact situation, by means of legal logic the abstract rules of the positive law can be made to yield

---

[7] Blankenburg, E. (1984) 'The Poverty of Evolutionism', *Law and Society Review*, p. 278
[8] See Ladeur, K–H. (1984) *'Abwagung' - Ein neues Paradigma* Ffm

the decision for every concrete fact situation. Consequently, if the positive law constitutes a 'gapless' system of rules which are at least latently contained in it or at least the law is to be treated for the purposes of legal practice as if it were such a 'gapless' system every instance of social conduct can and must be conceived as constituting either obedience to, or violation of rules of law – then law must indeed already be counted among the deceased.[9] And there are good reasons not to water the concept of law down to denote just any 'secondary rule', in the sense of H. L. A. Hart (which neither resolves the question whether or not 'primitive societies' were in possession of law nor that of how to prevent implicit ideologies of 'progress' to be incorporated in legal theory). The 'rule of law' would cease to be a 'rule' if law were just a number of regulations of a vague and wilful character, because the very element that is signified by the word 'rule' – that is, in real terms the relative autonomy of the legal sphere – would have been reduced to virtually nothing.

I do not intend to answer the open question of whether we have to suppose a 'first death' of law or whether we are witnessing just one phase in a cyclic movement of formalisation, materialisation, and formalisation and materialisation again. But I should like to show just how this process came about in the field of criminal law.

Criminal law and the rule of law

In criminal law the rule of law (in its continental version of 'formal rationality') expressed itself in the ideas that crimes should be defined by (a) general rules, (b) precise in their wording, and impossible to circumvent or enlarge in their scope by means of (c) analogy or (d) retroactivity.

Marxen called attention to the fact that the notion of 'liberal criminal law' included a scholarly habit of mind (connected with a more than formal respect for the aims of the law and a corresponding seriousness in the treatment of legal questions), and a deep distrust of expanding state powers (fearing that the protection by the law could suddenly reveal itself as a repression of freedom), these two are prerequisites for the build-up of a certain professional 'autonomy' of jurisprudence and criminal justice systems in the face of political power-holders.[10] A closer look at the kind of criminal law these jurists propagated shows that these 'liberal' ideals of the rule of law – once cornerstones of a certain distance the law could hold towards political powers – have vanished the concept of crime which was systematically elaborated with an emphasis on outer, visible elements in order to free it

---

[9] Luhmann, N. (1981) 'Rechtszwang und politische Gewalt', in ibid, *Ausdifferenzierung des Rechts*, Frankfurt a M, 1981 154-172,

[10] Marxen, K. (1975) *Der Kampf gegen das liber ale Strafrechtr*, Berlin, p. 265.

from arbitrariness and subjectivity of the judges;[11] a concept of punishment adequate to the seriousness of the intervention into the individual's sphere of freedom, that is, one with a high level of need of justification, with restrictive requirements as for the length of imprisonment (refusal of indeterminate sentencing); a concept of guilt that corresponds with a 'heroic' rather than an empirical idea of subjectivity and responsibility;[12] and finally, a strict method which stresses the difference between *de lege lata* and *de lege ferenda* arguments, between interpretation and analogy, and between a formal and a material concept of crime.[13]

All this was meant to secure the 'relative autonomy' of the law, that is, the rule of law. Thus, liberal criminal law - its formal rationality at least - was a prerequisite of the rule of law. It may be remembered that this type of criminal law is deeply different from today's style in that it had sharp edges, was at some distance from society (and wanted to secure the very basis of social life). It was a type of criminal law that stressed the fact that it was legal, not political, which saw itself as not being subject to fashion or to social change. It was a type of law that was tough but not brutal, that was emphatically public, not private, law, that searched for distance from police and administration laws by dispersing the aura of a rational, non-theological metaphysics, one which - following Immanuel Kant - stressed the idea of non-functional justice.[14]

Two types of criticism and their common denominator

There used to be two kinds of argument against 'autonomous law', as Nonet and Selznick call it.[15] One came from the political right, the other from the political left and progressives.

a) Critique 'from the right'

Authoritarian criminal policy in the 1930s used to attack the criminal law for its political self-restraint and insistence on clear-cut 'borders' between legal and illegal behaviour; its formal concepts of equality and liberty (which deliberately ignored special personal ties, that is, clientele systems and personal idiosyncrasies), closely connected with a formal idea of 'freedom' which is not immediately material and the impression of the state's weakness

---

[11] Ibid, p. 268.
[12] Ibid, p. 267.
[13] Ibid, p. 268
[14] Naucke, W. (1984) 'Vom vordringen des Polizeigedankens', *Ms* p.214
[15] Nonet, P. and Selznick, P. (1978) *Law and society in transition: Toward responsive law* London: Octagon Books

which went with it; its rigid system and abstract concepts which systematically filtered a small number of 'relevant' factors from a heap of 'irrelevant' ones and its restricted field of activity.[16]

b) Critique 'from the left'
The critique of the rule of law as a rule of veiled class interests (or the change in background conditions of the law's legitimation) and the inability of liberal law to provide for material justice or even consider material inequality in its reasoning stood in the centre of progressive nineteenth century criticism of the rule of law, which, in jurisprudence, culminated in the reform postulates of the 'modern school's' Marburg Programme of 1882. Although the political perspective of progressives was distinctly different from that of the political right, it is interesting to note that right and left formed a 'negative coalition' against (the rule of) law in that they fought its abstractness, the rigidity of its concepts, its disregard for material justice and its emphasis on individual liberties.

c) The common denominator
Both criticisms shifted the (theoretical) bearer of subjectivity from the demystified individual to the (mystified) system/state. This small operation of trading a metaphysical for a 'realistic' theory of law – an operation, by the way, which was reproduced later by the sociology of law of Niklas Luhmann – did make the whole difference.[17] From a bi-polar equilibrium, law moved to a one-dimensional functionality in terms of the state administration's requirements. A neglect – historically explainable, but out of today's perspective, regrettable – of the state question had paved the way.[18]

The basic new idea that was contained in both criticisms of the rule of law was that *criminal law should start making sense*. That is, it should not be allowed to hide behind unintelligible metaphysical phrases but forced to justify itself with reference to its *empirical consequences*. This meant that the law should not only vaguely be 'just', but first of all *useful in the defence of the state and society*. In these goals, differentiations would only be allowed in terms of technical differences, for instance, between those who could be re-socialised and others who could not. Offenders should be helped, if possible, but not in a way that could bar the effectiveness of general deterrence.

---

[16] Marxen, (1975) p.269
[17] Luhmann, N. (1972) *Rechtssoziologie*, Reinbek,
[18] Marxen, (1975) p. 274

Findings

What makes Max Weber's sociology so attractive is, among other things, his refusal to see the world only through the eyes of 'social actors' intentions, and to show instead the paradoxical relationship which often occurs between input in terms of intentions and outcome in terms of social effect. A look at the outcome of the last modernisation crisis of criminal law can only reaffirm the necessity to continue this tradition of his.

> a) The idea of 'man', 'human nature' and the like - once almost preposterously inflated by metaphysical philosophy - has been deflated to match the human individual's life size. Modest and sympathetic as this modern trend may seem, it nevertheless *denies autonomy*, which in the context of criminal law implies that a person's expressions and desires are not seen as (sensible) actions but as (indifferent) behaviour. The effects of this change in attitude are most clearly visible where re-socialisation of the offender is seen as a challenge for *treatment* techniques. The persons in question are seen and treated as *objects* whose intentions and constitutional rights are near to irrelevant. While these constitutional borders - which were of so much concern to the rule of law - are being blurred, another border becomes more distinct. The more the rehabilitative ideal was believed to be developing adequate techniques, the more the clients became 'defective' and 'irresponsible', thus widening the gulf between 'experts' and 'normals' on the one hand and 'offenders' who were more or less 'irresponsible' on the other.

> b) Aims of punishment, once formulated in the Judaeo-Christian tradition of sin and redemption, and somewhat more sublimely repeated by idealist philosophy, were to be made relevant to society (re-socialisation) and accountable for their empirical consequences. As a first step, special prevention was formulated as an empirical concept and revalued against the old ideals. What had been overlooked (or tacitly approved) was that the point of orientation was not the individual anymore, but 'society' and that meant in the remarkable blindness of late-nineteenth century jurists, the 'state' too. The movement from special to general prevention and to 'positive general prevention' corresponds to the development of system theory, no wonder, at last, that positive general prevention seems to

have rediscovered an old but hidden truth in the so-called absolute theories of punishment (which had never been so 'absolute' as they have been depicted by their enemies). But what does the shift of subjectivity from the individual to the system mean.[19] For one thing, the shift only made explicit what had always been the case by expressing the *common but hidden instrumental aims* that had also been behind metaphysical reasoning. But on the other side, the shift meant a desublimation that used empirical reality to reaffirm the status quo and to take (cynical) instrumentalism to its extremes by indiscriminately using all kinds of interventions for all kinds of offences.[20] The overall effect of this is that, in the face of the system's imperatives, those individuals and groups who keep insisting on the utility value of politics (and their actions), that is, those who just do not accept the inbuilt irrationality of the political exchange processes are being defined as disturbers.

c) In legislative politics, this shift towards 'the system' threatened to revise the traditional boundaries between 'the individual' and 'the state', if not to wipe these boundaries away (especially in the criminal law, which has no interest groups on the side of the people most affected by it). While at the turn of the century the idea of the individual was a strong remnant of idealist philosophy, it decayed progressively until 1945 in Germany, with its practical annihilation. Re-established in a reaction to the Third Reich, the functional imperatives of a modernising society could not be suppressed for very long, and the idea of individual rights experienced serious setbacks at the occasion of 'moral panics' (drugs) and 'security crises' (terrorism) after the end of the reconstruction boom. Since then, 'the function of' is increasingly said to require losses of liberty.[21]

d) In terms of sanctions, the shift leads to an *amalgamation* of help and punishment and other interventions whose character is not so clear. This amalgamation is designed to go much deeper into the identity of the sanctioned persons, and is certainly experienced as a more severe intervention than traditional

---

[19]   Barrata, A. (1984) 'Integration-Pravention' *KrimJ,;* Smaus, G. (1985) 'Technokratische Legitimierungen', *ZfRechtssoziologie.*
[20] Naucke, W. (1985) *Die Wechselwirkung swischen Strafziel und Verbrechensbegriff,* Stuttgart
[21] Preus, U K (1985) *Die Internalisierung des Subjekts,* Ffm

interventions used to be. This phenomenon is made even more acute by the fact that psychological and technical progress has been made over the last decades and was readily employed in corrections, at least in those vanguard areas of the control system which were also leading the way in terms of legislation and theory.

e) The loss of respect for the individual - or its transportation into the state, which now has the burden of seeing to it that individual freedom can be realised[22] - and the corresponding end of metaphysics in criminal law[23] - led to what may be called a loss of 'auratic' qualities of criminal law which not only used to enhance acceptance of it (that is, the dimension of legitimation), but also secured a relative authonomy. This gone, there begins the *administrativation* of criminal law,[24] that is, the loss of criminal law's *differentia specifica* with regard to general administration and the police in general.

f) Finally, the same phenomenon creates hegemonial powers for all executive branches - in theory and implementation - at the loss of the dominant role of the judge. A reformulation of the classical concept of class justice - which has not been achieved yet - would bring this out in the open.

Expansion

The driving force behind the very establishment of the criminal justice system was the centralised powers' interest to demonstrate their superior might in a form that had as little disintegrating effect as possible on society. The very emergence of notions such as 'crime' (out of something that resembled tort) and public penal law (out of egalitarian societal ways of handling transgressions) is indeed an offspring of the emergence of centralised political institutions. Two elements legitimising the law since its beginning were its ability to put an end to feuds, that is, to prevent conflicts from leading to bloodshed and bloodshed from leading to mutual extermination of lineages, and the belief that the law was binding with regard not only to those subjected to political domination but also with regard to the power-holders themselves. This is not to say that legal institutions developed

---

[22] Preus; Cobler, S. (1979) 'Grundrechtsterror', *Kursbuch* 59, Berlin
[23] Naucke, W. (1984) 'Vom vordringen des Polizeigedankens', *Ms*
[24] Hassemer, W. (1984) *Il bene giuridico Dei dehtti e delle pene,*

by mere consent of the governed. To the people, the violent core of 'universally binding law' had always been obvious and the very relative inclination of the powerful to go by the law as well. From the Franconian Kings (500 A.D.) to the Penal Code (1871 A.D.) nothing went smoothly, and all was struggle between those forces which finally succeeded in the expropriation of societal conflict and rituals and those who defended autonomous social controls.

It is useful to remember that the modern state's jurisdiction performed its largest leap forward not so long ago. In Prussia for example the autonomous local jurisdictions over petty and 'normal' offences were absorbed by state institutions between 1848 and 1854 only, resulting in the doubling of the number of those who received criminal punishment. Procedural laws after 1848 were all derogatory of the idea of prosecutorial discretion and consequently resulted in the 'legality principle', which drove up criminal statistics even further. The expansion of state interventions and a growing bureaucracy finally initiated another drive towards expanding social control through penal law while at the same time modernising it. The much deplored crisis of over-criminalisation is but a continuation and a superficial expression of this age-old process, in which the liberal interlude of the late sixties and early seventies was but comparable to the loss of speed during a shift of gears in a self-propelling course of modernisation. What looked like decriminalisation - the deletion of the legislation of morality, crimes without victims - can also be interpreted as clean-up, designed to assure the swift functioning of a new understanding of criminal law.

Dissolution does not equal the immediate 'death of law'. In fact, there is plenty of evidence for an expansion of the reach of law into areas with hitherto slight or no legal regulation at all. As Habermas has pointed out, this phenomenon of the colonisation of life-worlds by means of juridification is not due to the malice of rulers or classes, but rather to serious attempts – especially of the working class – to 'constitutionalise' the economic and social areas of life as well as in foregoing periods of political sphere.[25] Juridification of the educational system as well as of the family were the most progressed forms of this attempt, while juridification of industrial relations and of corrections can be seen as some of the older attempts.

Some of the outstanding expressions of this tendency have been mentioned in the passage on dissolution – proof of the fact that both tendencies are mutually supportive. We just have to recall that administration expresses itself in:

---

[25] Habermas, J. (1981) *Theorie des kommunikativen Handelns,* Ffm p. 527

a)   the loss of limitations to the number of legally protected interests (decay of a critical theory of the aims of criminal law, and especially of legally protected interests),

b)   the construction of ever more supra-personal, systemic objects of protection through the criminal law (for example, soil, air, water, health of the population, trust in the functioning of the economic order, *etc.*),

c)   which in turn leads to an overflow of criminal law into special areas of administrative law, which endangers the connection between the general and the specific parts of criminal law,

d)   vague and 'general', instead of restrictive and precise legislation, which naturally encompasses more social phenomena than the older types of law,

e)   and leads to a – paradoxical – lessening of social effectiveness of the law, which in turn has to rely to a higher degree on the monetary symbolic effect of the act of legislation itself – which calls for a repetition of these kinds of symbolic acts at an ever fast pace.

In terms of criminal law it would be necessary to have a look at the number of persons touched by it in relation to earlier times. As we have seen, a point of reference of about 150 years ago as well as one dated some 100 years ago would hardly lead to findings of Durkheim's 'humanisation' thesis. It would rather support the idea that social control, by dissolving but ever expanding criminal law, was spreading at the pace of state penetration. If we take a shorter period of time, it would be advisable to compare today's situation with the point in time when the last decriminalisation offensive was beginning to show effects, that is, around 1970/71. Since 1971 the prison population in West Germany has risen by 32%, moreover, one would have to consider the increase (of 159%) of people under probation, as well as those who are doing time in pseudo-private institutions such as diversionist homes, enforced drug therapy, *etc.* - no doubt that any such comparison would find a significant increase in the extension of the populations controlled by the administration of justice.

Alternatives

Are there counter-tendencies against pathological over-criminalisation?

The general theory of law

The focus of all discussions in the realm of the general theory of law is the crisis of instrumentalism and the idea that there must be models of 'post regulatory law'.[26] It is not worthwhile to delineate the postulates that have been accumulated so far in this context. But the quintessential message of this discussion is worth stating. It reads that dysfunctions of legal regulation are due to the hubris of the political sphere that all kinds of social processes could be directly rearranged through law. The new law, according to the bulk of modern sociologists of law, should recognise its limits. It should be aware of the fact that transgressions of its actual capacity will render law irrelevant to society, or noxious, or be destructive to the legal system itself. Positively speaking, all that law can do is to trigger processes of self-regulation, the direction and effects of which cannot be told in advance. A new carefulness is at the heart of the most acclaimed recommendations.[27]

This idea of 'reflexive law' and its solutions to over-regulation has attracted numerous criticisms concerning its theoretical status and validity.[28] What is interesting in our context is the fact that the most advanced areas of discourse on law are themselves defining the reach of law as a problem in itself. That is, the whole discussion on juridification and what can be done about it is part of a counter-tendency.

Discourse on criminal policy

The same holds true for much of the present discourse on criminal policy. Prisons and punishment are under constant attack, and even if it is true that corrections have for a long time been moving from the heart of the cities and from the pride of respectable citizens to the outskirts of town, that occidental societies seem to have developed a 'culture of shame' in this respect for quite some time, these attacks have gained a new momentum during recent years. 'Diversion' is a key concept of an aggressive new tendency to cut down regular punishment in favour of informal, nonjuridical, if possible, conflict resolution.

---

[26] Teubner, G. (1985) 'Verrechthchung ' in Zacher u a *Verrechthching,* Ffm,

[27] Ibid, p. 316

[28] Blankenburg, E. (1984) 'The Poverty of Evolutionism', *Law and Society Review,*

The whole discussion of 'informal justice',[29] the blurry lines between diversionism and 'real' abolitionism[30] is not only overshadowed by the often paradoxical relation between intention and outcome. The problem lies in a lack of differentiation between:

a)   the prisons and the criminal justice system,
b)   the law in its relative autonomy,
c)   the state as the authority for conflict resolution.

Regarding a) the bulk of diversionist literature is anti-prisons, but not wholeheartedly anti-criminal law, because their 'alternatives to prison' depend on the criminal law as the institution that sends them clients. More radical diversionist literature is against prisons and against the criminal law (or criminal justice system) as far as their expansion is concerned. But they propagate the dissolution of criminal law in its formal rationality and they support the idea of a state-sponsored system of modernised interventions.

Regarding b) the orientation along the lines of a 'classical' penal law goes along with diversionism in as far as the opposition towards expansionist tendencies is concerned, and also with regard to the legitimacy of the state operating the system, but they refuse to find any attraction in the idea of dissolving the formal rationality. They are more consequential than diversionists in as far as they do not simply oppose the expansion of the prison system, but these diversionist expansions as well.

Regarding c) the abolitionists' stricto sensu oppose all three, that is, the expansion of the prison system, the dissolution of relative autonomy and the state's ideas about conflict resolution and symbolic affirmation of normative order. The questions that remain pertain to the very basic concepts of law and the state, as well as human nature.

Real-life counter-tendencies

Many of the critiques of over-regulation and over-criminalisation are themselves being subject to the criticism that it is 'naive' to believe that arbitrary de-regulation of any social areas are possible. Teubner, to cite just one example, asserts that the only serious discussion he can imagine of the topic is 'how to soften dysfunctional consequences of juridification'.[31] Others

---

[29] Abel, R. (ed) (1982) *The politics of informal Justice*, New York: Academic Press; Cain, M. (1985) 'Beyond Informal Justice', in Matthews, R. (ed) (1988*) Informal Justice* London: Sage
[30] Hulsman, L. (1986) 'Critical Criminology and the concept of crime', in *Contemporary Crises;* Naucke, W. (1985) *Die Wechselwirkung swischen Strafziel und Verbrechensbegriff,* Stuttgart
[31] Teubner, (1985) p. 313

would second his motion in the field of criminal law and criminal policy. This raises the question of the status of abolitionist thinking. Is it and does it have to be just a whim? Some of the arguments that are being advanced by abolitionists seem to fit pre-state 'regulated anarchy'[32] better than modern industrialised states. On the other hand, the very fact that abolitionism is being defended by not so few scholars in some European countries could show that the existence of this discourse is in itself a social fact and that it must have more than simply personal reasons.

The explanation has been put forward that abolitionism is a 'reflex' of real-life processes such as the division of society and the labour market along the lines of 'absorbed' and 'alternative' spheres, or others.[33] In the alternative spheres, it is true, some kinds of 'informal justice' are being practiced which bear little similarity to anything that could be called 'informalism from above'. The decisive difference between these kinds of informalism lies in the question of the state and/or autonomy. Nils Christie has shown some of the conditions under which a new kind of 'autonomous' and more civilised kind of conflict resolution *is being practiced* at this time.[34] Implicit in this is the demand to make punishment a mere conflict resolution again, that is, to take the state's self-interest out of the criminal justice system.

It is true that juridification is part of a larger historical tendency and cannot be reversed by mere wishful thinking, or by political decisions taken from the administrative point of view. But for scholars it is certainly possible not to close their eyes in the face of actual turns in historical movements and of their legal or anti-legal consequences.

Bibliography

Abel, R. (ed) (1982) *The politics of informal justice*, New York: Academic Press

Barrata, A. (1984) 'Integration-Pravention' *KrimJ,*

Blankenburg, E. (1984) The Poverty of Evolutionism', *Law and Society Review,*

Cain, M. (1985) 'Beyond Informal Justice', in Matthews, R. (ed) (1988*) Informal Justice* London: Sage

Christie, N. (1981) *The Limits to Pain*, Oxford: Martin Robertson

Cobler, S. (1979) 'Grundrechtsterror', *Kursbuch* 59, Berlin

Foucault, M. (1977) *Discipline and Punish: The Birth of the Prison*, London: Penguin

---

[32] Weber, M. (1969) *Max Weber on Law and Society 3rd edition* [edited with an introduction and annotations by M Rheinstein], Cambridge, Mass: Harvard University Press

[33] Steinert (1984)

[34] Christie, N. (1981) *The Limits to Pain*, Oxford: Martin Robertson

Habermas, J. (1981) *Theorie des kommunikativen Handelns,* Ffm

Hassemer, W. (1984) *Il bene giuridico Dei dehtti e delle pene,*

Hulsman, L. (1986) 'Critical Criminology and the concept of crime', in
   Contemporary Crises Vol. 10, No. 1, pp.63-80

Ladeur, K –H. (1984) *'Abwagung' - Ein neues Paradigma* Ffm

Luhmann, N. (1972) *Rechtssoziologie,* Reinbek,

Luhmann, N. (1981) 'Rechtszwang und politische Gewalt', in ibid,
   Ausdifferenzierung des Rechts, Frankfurt a M, 1981 154-172,

Marxen, K. (1975) *Der Kampf gegen das liber ale Strafrechtr,* Berlin,

Naucke, W. (1984) 'Vom vordringen des Polizeigedankens', *Ms*

Naucke, W. (1985) *Die Wechselwirkung swischen Strafziel und Verbrechensbegriff,*
   Stuttgart

Nonet, P. and Selznick, P. (1978) *Law and society in transition: Toward responsive
   law* London: Octagon Books

Preus, U K (1985*) Die Internalisierung des Subjekts,* Ffm

Rostow, E.V. (ed) (1971) *Is Law Dead,* New York, Simon and Schuster

Scull, A.T. (1977) *Decarceration: Community treatment and the Deviant,*
   Englewood Cliffs, N.J.: Prentice- Hall

Smaus, G. (1985) 'Technokratische Legitimierungen', *ZfRechtssoziologie,*

Steinert, H. (1984) 'Was ist eigentlich aus der 'Neuen Kriminologie' geworder?
   Einige Thesen, um die Suche zu onentieren, *KrimJ* 16, pp 86-89.

Teubner, G. (1985) 'Verrechthchung ' in Zacher u a *Verrechthching,* Ffm,

Vos, M. (1985a) in Kerner et al, (eds), *Diversion,* Heidelberg, 'Verwahrvollzug -
   Behandlungsvollzug', *Ms*

Vos, M. (1985b) 'Verwahrvollzug-Behandlungsvollzug' der strafrechthche
   Gebrauch der Freiheitsstrafe im Zuge ihrer veranderten Anspruche Zugleich
   eine Kntik der Kurzstrafenkntic', in U O Sievering (ed) *Behandlungsvollzug
   Zwischenstufe oder Sackgusse,* Arnoldshamer Text,

Weber, M. (1969) *Max Weber on Law and Society 3rd edition* [edited with an
   introduction and annotations by M Rheinstein], Cambridge, Mass: Harvard
   University Press

Section B:

Exposing and resisting criminal justice's harms

6.

Mental and Social Sequelae of Isolation: The evidence of deprivation experiments and of pre-trial detention in Denmark

Ida Koch

This paper was delivered at the European Group's 13th annual conference in Hamburg and first published in Working Papers in European Criminology, Volume 7 'The Expansion of European Prison Systems' in 1986.

Isolation and sensory deprivation

Isolation means a total deprivation or considerable reduction of normal sensory stimuli and of perceptual and physical possibilities of action. Isolation further includes a total deprivation or considerable reduction of social contact. Prisoners in isolation are thus in an abnormal situation, which, in terms of quality as well as quantity, differs from everyday situations such as loneliness, boredom or monotony. In the last century, prison sentences in Europe were served in solitary cells in so-called cellular prisons. The idea was that the reformation of the reprehensible individual could take place, for example through biblical studies and solitary confinement. However, prison authorities soon realised that the prisoners suffered considerable mental stress as a result of being isolated and developed in an 'undesirable' direction. Many went mad and became unruly. Today these observations are consciously utilised in certain countries where isolation is used as a means of punishment or of obtaining confessions, information, *etc.* Isolation used in this way as a form of torture is known from the countries of the Third World, such as Chile and Mexico. But this form of torture is also found in Europe, for example, in West Germany,[1] Spain[2] and Northern Ireland.[3]

Scientific research on sensory and social deprivation and its consequences

---

[1] Jensen, P. (1978) J *De forfulgtes psvkologi* Bo Cavefores,

[2] Forest, E. (1977) *Tortur i Spanien*, Gyldenal

[3] McGuffin, J. (1974) *Guineapigs,* Harmondsworth: Penguin

really got underway in the 1950s. The most famous names in this line of research are Hebb, Sollomon, Goldberger and Grunewald.[4] The scientific design varies somewhat from study to study, but the purpose is identical to examine the mental, intellectual, somatic, neurological and social sequelae to various degrees of experimentally induced deprivation. The experiments involve either a total deprivation of sensory and social stimuli or a very considerable reduction of such stimuli.[5]

The following summary can be given of the results of the experiments of Hebb and Goldberger.[6] Developmental psychology has shown that the child's normal development is dependent upon adequate stimulation of the subject. Similarly, the adult personality and intellectual health and level of functioning depend on adequate sensory and social stimulation and contact. Permanent contact with a structured reality is a necessity for intellectual functioning. If this does not take place, primary impulses (in the Freudian sense) will dominate the subject's consciousness and hallucinations and a sense of depersonalisation will occur. The above-mentioned researchers unanimously demonstrate a symptomatology of isolation which shows that the level of functioning of adult, well-balanced and healthy persons changes under deprivation. The perception of identity of the person's changes and mental disorders of a depressive and psychotic character are normal.

The most commonly described disorders are problems of concentration and thought disturbances. Organised and meaningful mental activity is rendered difficult or impossible. The rhythm of sleep is interrupted and it is impossible to distinguish between sleep and being awake. Similarly, the subjects in the experiments find it difficult to distinguish between reality and fantasy/dream. Their emotional control fails and lability is widespread. Hallucinations and pseudo-hallucinations may be induced after a few hours in the experiments. They are usually accompanied by violent attacks of anxiety and a sense of disintegration of identity. The results of the above-mentioned experiments are in agreement with a less extensive study of isolated patients with contagious diseases.[7] The degree of sensory and social deprivation of these patients is far from that of the persons in the experiments.

---

[4] Hebb, D. O. (1964) *Psykologi - pa biologisk grund*, Gleerup; Sollomon, P. and Kubzarisky, P. E. (1961) *Sensory deprivation*, Cambridge, Massachusetts: Harvard University Press; Goldberger, L. and Holt, R. R. (1958), 'Experimental interference with reality contact (perceptual isolation) methods and group results', *Journal of nervous and mental disease,* 127 (2); Grunewald, K. (1967) 'Sensorisk Hamning vid isolenng\ *Nordisk tidsskrift for kriminalvideriskab.*

[5] See Jensen, P. (1978) J *De forfulgtes psvkologi* Bo Cavefores, for a survey of the results of deprivation research.

[6] Hebb; Goldberger and Holt.

[7] Nielsen, B. (1981) 'Aspekter i den psykiske pleje af isolationspatienter', *Sygeplejersken - tidsskrift for sygeplejersker,* 40, (Tillaeg Perspektiv)

Nevertheless, these patients suffered from a large number of the experimentally induced symptoms of isolation. Social isolation seems especially liable to give rise to the symptoms. This is in agreement with Grunewald's conclusion, which points out that social deprivation is probably the part of the isolation complex which has the most violent consequences, as the symptoms of isolation can also be seen in cases where a certain perceptual and sensorily varied field of stimulation is present.[8] There is a step from the above mentioned experimental designs in deprivation research to the specific situation of isolation experienced by pre-trial detainees in solitary confinement in Danish prisons and jails which I describe below.

Solitary confinement of pre-trial detainees

In spite of differences as to quality and quantity, all experience seems to indicate that the degree of sensory and social deprivation to which pre-trial detainees are subjected when kept in solitary confinement is sufficient to induce the symptoms and disorders known from the experiments. This appears, objectively as well as subjectively, from fully identical descriptions which the persons in the experiments and the detainees offer, and which researchers and others can ascertain. As a natural consequence of the somewhat lesser degree of total deprivation of the detainees (they are not in sound- and light-proof rooms, have a certain, very limited social contact, and so on), the symptoms occur somewhat later than in the experimental situations, that is, not after a few hours, but rather after days or weeks. The most widely used form of isolation in Danish court practice concerns persons who are held in custody while a criminal case is being investigated. No judgment has been given against these persons and therefore, in principle, according to the law they are innocent. The reason given by the police for requesting that a suspect be held in custody is almost always the risk that, if the accused was released, s/he might prevent or obstruct the investigation of the case. The reasons for further requesting that the detainee be kept in solitary confinement is always this risk (99% of all cases of solitary confinement). The legal provisions governing custody and isolation (solitary confinement) are found in Chapter 70, Section 762ff of the *Danish Administration of Justice Act*.[9]

Like custody, isolation has no specified time limits. The accused is usually not taken out of isolation until the police have ended the investigation, the case has been fully resolved and there is a confession. However, there are

---

[8] Grunewald (1967)
[9] Justitsministnet, (1979) *Justitsmimsteriets undersdgelse af isolation i Danmark og i andre europaiske lande,*

some exceptions. Reasons for keeping a person in isolation may be that there is one more accused in the same case who has not been apprehended, has not given a concordant statement, or simply because the prisons do not have the facilities for keeping the accused with others.[10] However, the last is in contravention of the provisions of the *Administration of Justice Act*.

According to a survey conducted by the Ministry of Justice,[11] Denmark is the country in Western Europe which holds the largest number of persons in custody per 100,000 citizens, and no other countries in Europe use isolation in connection with pre-trial detention to the extent used in Denmark.[12] Recent statistics[13] show that 53% of all pre-trial detainees in the prisons of Copenhagen (including the Vestre Fængsel prison) where half of all Danish pre-trial detainees are held, are kept in solitary confinement. In prisons outside Copenhagen this figure is considerably smaller.[14]

From an earlier study from 1979,[15] it appears that 50% of the detainees who were kept in isolation spent up to two weeks there, 25% up to four weeks and the rest, 25%, more than four weeks. Unfortunately, there are no particulars as to how long the last 25% spent in isolation, but from a report on isolation in Vestre Fængsel, it appears that many months in isolation are not uncommon, and there are cases where pre-trial detainees have spent between one and two years in isolation.[16]

Following an amendment of the Act in 1978, the purpose of which was to limit the number of cases where detainees were put in isolation, there has been a slight fall in the number of cases where a very short time is spent in isolation (up to two weeks), but the number of longer detentions in isolation has risen. According to a statement made by the Minister of Justice at the end of 1981, the number of cases where young people of 15-17 years are held in isolation has risen at a rate which must give rise to concern. After years of criticism of the widespread use of isolation of pre-trial detainees, the law was changed again in 1984. The law now states that - as a general rule - pre-trial detainees should not be kept in isolation longer than two months. However, this time limit is only to be used for detainees who, if convicted, could receive a maximum of six years in prison. This means in practice that all those

---

[10] Justitsministnet, (1980) Brev fra Justitsminister H Rasmussen til advokaterne S Hennksen og S Bech, 29/9/80 i lovforslag nr L22, blad nr 23, bilag 7

[11] Justitsministnet, (1981) Justitsmimsteriets undersegelse af isolationspraksis i 1981, Lovforslag nr L22, blad nr 23, bilag 6

[12] Justitsministnet, 1979

[13] Editors' note: Recent in the early 1980s

[14] Justitsministnet, 1981

[15] Justitsministnet, 1979

[16] Pauli Jensen, J, Jorgensen, F and Worsaae Rasmussen, J (1980) *Isolation/ Varetagt, Vidnesbyrd om de psykiske og sociale folger af darisk isolationsfcengsling*, Forlaget 1 Haarby,

accused of, for example, drug crime - no matter how small a crime of this kind it is - can be held in isolation with no time limit because the maximum sentence for drug crime is ten years. The change of the law has thus not changed the conditions at all for those accused who before 1984 would have spent more than two months in isolation.

It should be mentioned that isolation is also used in other stages of the legal process, during the period when the sentence is served, that is, after the person in question has received an unsuspended sentence. In such cases, isolation is used as punishment for a disciplinary offence, or if the prisoner is regarded as a danger to himself or to others. In principle, isolation here is of the same character as the isolation of pre-trial detainees, but the prisoner is kept in isolation for a specified period of time and usually for a much shorter period. Pre-trial detention in isolation must be considered a particular strain for several reasons, some of them being that the detainee is very suddenly removed from his/her everyday life when arrested; there is usually much uncertainty relating to the course of the case; the character of the charges; the period of custody and isolation and the outcome of the trial. Furthermore, the accused is frequently interrogated by the police and this is, naturally, a strain. Finally, a person who is kept in isolation for the first time is quite unprepared for the effects of isolation.

Everyday life of pre-trial detainees in isolation

Pre-trial detainees in isolation spend 23 hours out of 24 in a cell, the only interruptions being when they go to the toilet, receive their food, *etc.* On such occasions, contact with the prison staff lasts only a few minutes. Detainees in isolation are entitled to spend one hour daily out of doors. This is usually divided into two spells of half an hour each, spent (alone) in a triangular radial yard approximately six metres long. The yard is surrounded by a tall concrete wall and covered by wire netting.

The cells usually measure between six and eight square metres. The cell contains a bed, a table, a chair, a cupboard, a bookcase and a washbasin with cold water. On the wall is a radio connected to programmes one and three. Unless prohibited by the police, the detainee may borrow books, newspapers and magazines. S/he may further have a television set in the cell if s/he owns one. Usually, censured letters may be received. In some cases visits may be allowed, usually two weekly visits of half an hour each. In the case of such visits, a prison guard will always be present. At the end of the cell is a window measuring approximately 1.5 by 1.5 metres. It is set very high in the wall and can only be opened and closed by a long iron handle. Hinges are placed on the lower part of the window and the detainee cannot see the sky. This is further reinforced by the fact that the pane is made of white frosted glass and the light it allows into the cell is soft, 'greyish white' and uniform almost irrespective of the intensity of the light outside. The cell is not sound-proof, but the character of sound stimuli is extremely monotonous, *e.g.* slamming doors, shouted orders, keys in doors, *etc.* Motor mobility is naturally severely restricted. An adult may cover the cell lengthwise in three or four steps.

The work offered to the prisoners in their cells consists of fitting or assembling, such as extremely monotonous and unchallenging work like assembling clothes pegs, gluing little Danish flags onto matchboxes, mounting raw plugs in frames, *etc.* Working environment studies have shown that such work may in itself provoke mental and psychosomatic 'stress' reactions.[17]

In some prisons the detainee in isolation may ask to see a social worker, clergyman, doctor, psychiatrist or school teacher. However, the number of such staff is so low in relation to the number of detainees that it may be weeks before such a need can be met and, when it is, the contact is often of a duration of a few minutes. As an example, it may be mentioned that the Vestre Fængsel has approximately 650 pre-trial detainees and others and only six doctors, one psychiatric consultant and two and a half clergymen to cater for their needs. A prison guard at the Vestre Fængsel has stated that each prison guard on duty has three minutes for each prisoner, provided none of the guards is off work because of illness or for another reason.

In summary, pre-trial detainees in isolation are in a situation with considerably reduced sensory and perceptual stimulation and extremely limited mobility. Furthermore, there is considerable social deprivation, as the possibilities of contact with the staff do not in terms of quality nor quantity get anywhere near the necessary social stimulation.

The sequelae to pre-trial isolation

A systematically controlled study of the acute and chronic sequelae to Danish pre-trial isolation has not yet been made. However, rather extensive documentation is now available in the form of case studies, interviews and descriptions. The material is collected by lawyers who describe the process their clients go through during and after isolation; by prison clergymen who, as they come to the prison daily, can observe what happens to the prisoners they have time to see; by prison doctors and the statements and records of prison psychiatrists; and finally by the writer, who, in connection with a major study of women prisoners, interviewed 47 women, a large number of whom

---

[17] Koch, I and Jensen, K (1979) *Kvindelige spritbihlster of hceftestrajfen,* Knminalistisk Institut, Stensil, Kabenhavns Universitet

had been in pre-trial isolation. The study also comprised interviews with the prison staff.[18] The large number of letters and applications from detainees in isolation and their families is a further important contribution towards our understanding of the reactions and experience of pre-trial detainees in isolation. Pre-trial isolation has thus been described from many angles, each contributing information to a total mosaic of the harmful effects of isolation. As space is limited, no quotations from the above-mentioned material will be included in this article.[19]

Finn Jorgensen, chief physician and former physician at the Vestre Fængsel, has studied the above-mentioned material and compared it with his own observations. In the following, the main lines of his symptomatology will be used. Isolation affects the following:

1   Personal integration and sense of identity;
2   Physical/physiological and neurological state;
3   Language, perceptual and intellectual skills; and
4   Social skills.

This classification is, of course, artificial, as each individual person makes up a whole. If one area is disturbed, the others will usually be affected. It is common for the individual detainee in isolation to present several symptoms, but it is rare that the effect is equally strong in all areas.

The acute isolation syndrome

In many cases, the earliest symptoms occur after only a few days. Most common are problems of concentration, restlessness, failure of memory, sleeping problems and impaired sense of time and ability to follow the rhythm of day and night.

Intellectual life is increasingly characterised by subjective thought processes and fantasies. Many detainees in isolation describe systems and rituals they arrange for themselves in order to structure and divide their day. It is of real benefit to only a few, whereas in other cases the systems tend to dominate the life of the detainee in a compulsory way, with the effect that any interruption or alteration - for example, because of interrogation by the police or a visit from a lawyer - will provoke fear and make the detainee ill at ease. Nightmares and anxiety are very common. Suicide attempts are often

---

[18] Ibid

[19] Fuller information may be found in a book which contains more than 50 cases and interviews – see Pauli Jensen, J, Jorgensen, F and Worsaae Rasmussen, J (1980) *Isolation/ Varetagt, Vidnesbyrd om de psykiske og sociale folger af dansk isolationsfcengsling,* Forlaget 1 Haarby,

made in this period (in some cases, successfully, seven out of ten successful suicides in prisons in 1980 were by pre-trial detainees), and some detainees damage themselves severely.[20] Attempted suicides and self-damage usually mean that the detainee will be transferred to the hospital ward of the Vestre Fængsel and that s/he gets away from his/her cell and has the possibility of a little more social contact.

It is typical for detainees in isolation that in the first period they try to 'dilute' the social isolation by appealing for contact. They 'invent' all sorts of reasons for calling the staff. It is characteristic that these attempts at social contact are less numerous after some weeks and, if isolation continues, the detainee will most often reject contact This is quite often interpreted by the staff as the detainee getting used to being in isolation. However, in psychological/psychiatric terms, such behaviour must be considered rather alarming.[21]

The chronic isolation syndrome

The early pathological picture described above gradually becomes a state with symptoms which tend to become chronic, that is, they do not disappear when the detainee is taken out of isolation and may result in very protracted effects. At the same time, difficulties of memory and concentration, *etc.* intensify. This results in complaints from many detainees in isolation that they are unable to read or follow television programmes. They are unable to remember what they have just read, and unable to grasp a sequence of events. This will, of course, have serious consequences for the detainee when s/he is taken to recurring interrogations by the police who expect the prisoner to make a coherent statement which does not vary from interrogation to interrogation, to remember previous statements and to understand the questions being asked. Observations to this effect are available from defence lawyers and psychiatrists.[22] It involves a danger to the legal position and security of the accused.

Where isolation lasts for longer periods, that is, a few weeks, many detainees complain of an inexplicable fatigue. Inexplicable, because they neither move physically nor do anything. Some develop an actual lethargy, lie on their bed night and day and cannot eat or wash. A distinct emotional lability is common, where, for example, violent fits of weeping alternate with lethargy and fits of rage. The prisoners feel they have lost control of their emotions and this creates anxiety. It is extremely common for prisoners in

---

[20] Knminalforsorgens arsberetning, 1980
[21] Bowlby, J. (1966) *Deprivation of maternal care,* Schosken Paperback,
[22] Jensen et al (1980)

isolation to believe they have gone or are going mad.[23]

At this stage, physical/physiological and neurological changes may occur. These are in part due to the lack of physical exercise, the muscles become weak because they are not used, just as in the case of people who are confined to bed for a long time. Some lose weight even though they consume sufficient food. It has been described how isolation may have the effect that the body does not absorb nourishment.[24] Many also complain of diarrhoea, stomach aches, nausea, vomiting and headaches. Objectively, tics may be seen in some cases.

Many detainees who have been isolated for even a few months complain of speech impediments and problems with respect to linguistic understanding and this is especially evident in talks with lawyers and the police. The chronic syndrome can involve physical, perceptual and sensory hallucinations and delusions; the body 'melts', it goes numb, or parts of it feel cold. The detainee hears voices, sees things or animals on the wall, *etc.* These symptoms are described as psychotic or para-psychotic states, often with paranoiac features, where the detainees feel bugged or watched all the time.

Usually, it becomes increasingly difficult to make contact with the isolated detainee during this process. This appears particularly from the statements of relatives, lawyers and prison clergymen. Persons who have business in the detainee's cell are rejected or paid very little attention. Some prison psychiatrists describe this in their records as an actual state of autism.[25] In this state, some detainees are transferred to a prison institution with staff trained in psychiatric and psychological treatment (the state prison at Herstedvester), or to other closed institutions for treatment.

Most detainees in isolation are treated with psychopharmacological drugs and/or sleeping pills. It has not been possible to collect exact information in this respect, but a study from the Vestre Fængsel reveals from interviews with the staff that most pre-trial detainees, and not least those in isolation, are given medicine, often in rather large quantities.[26]

Social sequelae

In some cases the harmful effects to the detainee's social behaviour will only become evident when s/he is taken out of isolation and has the

---

[23] Cohen, S and Taylor, L (1972) *Psychological Survival the experience of long-term imprisonment,* Penguin; Jensen et al (1980)

[24] Jensen, P. (1978) J *De forfulgtes psvkologi* Bo Cavefores,

[25] Koch, I, (1981) Imod isolation Kronik I Information, d 21 12

[26] Koch, I and Jensen, K (1979) *Kvindelige spritbihlster of hceftestrajfen,* Knminalistisk Institut, Stensil, Kabenhavns Universitet; Koch, I and Jensen, K (1981) *Kvindehge fangers social baggrunk,* Knminalistisk Institut, Stensil, Kobenhavns Universitet.

possibility of relating to others, has to live up to the normal requirements of social life and his/her original social level of functioning. The symptoms appear either while the prisoner is still detained but has been taken out of isolation, in the prison after s/he has been sentenced, or when s/he is released and is confronted with ordinary civilian life.

It is very common for isolated prisoners to experience fear of having to function with other people again. And this fear is seldom unfounded. Many detainees who have been in isolation say that the first time they have to spend with others is very painful. They are unable to concentrate on conversation, have difficulty paying attention, become restless, tired of any form of social life, or are afraid of human openness and emotional intimacy. One consequence of this 'shyness' may be that the prisoner who has been isolated during his/her sentence 'shuttles' between the cell, where s/he finds the seclusion hard to bear, and the common room where s/he cannot be for long either. I have observed this behaviour in connection with my own studies in prisons. Some detainees 'choose' voluntarily to continue their isolation, they stay in their cell even though they may theoretically leave it. This social disability may continue for years after a person has been in isolation.[27] The disability may express itself in a fear of becoming attached to another person. Persons who have been in isolation have reported that they can no longer cope with physical and emotional intimacy and contact, and they feel an urge to be alone which is unnatural to them. They feel severely handicapped.

Problems of documentation

It is a fact – described in important Danish and international prison literature – that accused and convicted persons do not show their symptoms to the prison staff if they can at all avoid it. This is even truer of men than of women.[28] Very rarely do they disclose their real condition; they hide nervousness and suppress complaints.

There may be many reasons for a pre-trial detainee to try to hide to the prison staff how bad his/her condition is. Among those most often stated are that the prisoner does not want to humiliate him/herself; does not want to demonstrate the result of the suppression; is afraid it will be used against him/her, especially by the police; is afraid of an uncontrollable opening and wants to try to maintain the feeling of his/her own worth. I have seen this as a psychologist visiting a prisoner in isolation under the surveillance of a police officer. It has been described in an earlier article.[29]

---

[27] Jensen et al, (1980)
[28] Cohen and Taylor, (1972)
[29] Koch, (1981)

The fact that the detainees try to hide how bad they feel results in many problems of documentation in relation to the groups of staff who see the isolated prisoners daily. Even for a long time after having been in isolation, these persons try to hide symptoms and 'forget' the period in isolation. In connection with the prison study quoted above, it turned out that the prisoners found reliving their painful time in isolation an extremely traumatic experience. As regards hearings and radio programmes, very few wished to come before the public and relate how they experienced isolation – not because of problems of anonymity, but because they could not face living through it all again. Only in very intimate interviews was it possible for them to describe what had happened, and they did this with much distress and emotional reaction.

Criticisms levelled against isolation have come from external specialists rather than from prison staff. The reason may be the conditions mentioned above, but it may also be that the staff have got used to the situation among the prisoners and no longer notice what goes on. Prison literature, for example, Goffman[30] and Mathiesen[31] often describes that changes occur not only in people who are detained in institutions, but also in the staff after they have been employed in the system for some time. You no longer notice what you observed at the beginning. What seemed unacceptable at the beginning no longer gives any offence. The suffering complained of by patients, prisoners or others in the beginning no longer makes the same impression. Some call it becoming 'professional', others call it becoming accustomed, others brutalisation. It is very common for staff in closed institutions to experience a shift in their concept of normality and the threshold of what the individual will tolerate as acceptable and ethically/morally correct is raised.

I find that these two aspects - the victims trying to hide and the witnesses 'not seeing' - must be two important reasons for the opinion expressed by the prisons' own psychiatrists and doctors to the effect that a description like the above of the harmful effects of isolation is dramatised and emotional.[32] However, I would like to mitigate this picture by quoting our own study where one of the institutions involved was the Vestre Fængsel. Some prison guards here described the harmful effects in accordance with what has been written above.

---

[30] Goffman, E. (1968) *Anstalt og menneske*, Paludans fiol- bibliotek

[31] Mathiesen, T. (1979) *Ideologi og modstand*, Oslo, Unipax,

[32] Mikkelsen, J and Bernsten, P M (1982) fl 'Laegers deltagelse i undersegelse af isolerede varetaegtsfaengslede personer', *Ugeskr Laeger*, 144, 1982 7

Isolation - psychological torture

I do not hesitate to characterise isolation as a form of inhuman and cruel treatment. Particularly on the part of the legal system, this practice constitutes a violation of a number of provisions the Declaration of Tokyo, Conventions of Human Rights, article 3, and the United Nations Universal Declaration of Human Rights, 1948. Here it is laid down that 'no one shall be subjected to torture or to cruel, inhuman or degrading treatment or punishment'. Furthermore, Amnesty International[33] has found that isolation as such may be sufficient to seriously impair a person's mental and physical health and that isolation is a direct obstacle to rehabilitation.

The reaction of the individual detainee to isolation and the symptomatology presented by him/her in reaction varies.[34] It also varies from one individual to the next when the harmful effects will manifest themselves objectively and subjectively. But the risk of serious consequences of more than a few weeks, perhaps even a few days, of isolation seems to be extremely real when judged in the light of the above. This risk should be eliminated by not subjecting people to extreme sensory and social deprivation, whether in the case of pre-trial detainees, convicted prisoners or people with epidemic diseases.

It *is* possible for the police to obtain sufficient peace for their investigative work in other ways than by keeping the suspect in isolation.[35] It is important that information be brought together and that case histories are published. This may be a substantial contribution towards making our politicians realise the serious consequences of isolation and in the longer term the result should be that the necessary steps are taken and money made available to ensure that isolation no longer takes place in Danish prisons and jails.

---

[33] Amnesty International (1980) *Amnesty International's work on prison conditions of persons suspected or convicted of politically motivated crimes in the Federal Republic of Germany Isolation and solitary confinement*, May 1980 Index EUR 23/01/80 Distr NS/PO

[34] Jensen, (1978)

[35] Sknvelse fra advokaterne (1980) 1 Darisk Retspolitisk Forenings isolationsgruppe til Folketingets Retsudvalg af febr 1980 Vedr totahsolation under varetagtsftengsling

Bibliography

Amnesty International (1980) *Amnesty International's work on prison conditions of persons suspected or convicted of politically motivated crimes in the Federal Republic of Germany Isolation and solitary confinement*, May 1980 Index EUR 23/01/80 Distr NS/PO

Betcerikmng nr 650, (1972) 'Betaenkmng vedrorende nogle af- og nedkriminaliseringssporgsmal',

Bowlby, J. (1966) *Deprivation of maternal care*, Schosken Paperback,

Cohen, S and Taylor, L. (1972) *Psychological Survival the experience of long-term imprisonment*, Harmondsworth: Penguin,

Forest, E (1977) *Tortur i Spanien*, Gyldenal

Goffman, E. (1968) *Anstalt og menneske*, Paludans fiol- bibliotek

Goldberger, L. and Holt, R. R. (1958), 'Experimental interference with reality contact (perceptual isolation) methods and group results', *Journal of nervous and mental disease,* 127 (2),

Grunewald, K. (1967) 'Sensorisk Hamning vid isolenng\ *Nordisk tidsskrift for kriminalvideriskab,*

Hebb, D. O. (1964) *Psykologi - pa biologisk grund*, Gleerup,

Holt, R. R. and Goldberger, L., (1960) 'Personological correlates of reactions to perceptual isolation', *WADC Technical Report*, 59- 735

Jensen, P. (1978) J *De forfulgtes psvkologi* Bo Cavefores,

Jensen, P., Jorgensen, F and Worsaae Rasmussen, J 1980) *Isolation/ Varetagt, Vidnesbyrd om de psykiske og sociale folger af darisk isolationsfcengsling,* Forlaget 1 Haarby,

Justitsministnet, (1979) *Iustitsmimsteriets undersdgelse af isolation i Danmark og i andre europaiske lande,*

Justitsministnet, (1980) Brev fra Justitsminister II Rasmussen til advokaterne S Hennksen og S Bech, 29/9/80 i lovforslag nr L22, blad nr 23, bilag 7

Justitsministnet, (1981) Justitsmimsteriets undersegelse af isolationspraksis i 1981, Lovforslag nr L22, blad nr 23, bilag 6

Koch, I. (1981) Imod isolation Kronik I Information, d 21 12

Koch, I. and Jensen, K (1979) *Kvindelige spritbihlster of hceftestrajfen,* Knminalistisk Institut, Stensil, Kabenhavns Universitet

Koch, I. and Jensen, K. (1981) *Kvindehge fangers social baggrunk*, Knminalistisk Institut, Stensil, Kobenhavns Universitet

Knminalforsorgens arsberetning, 1980

Mathiesen, T. (1979) *Ideologi og modstand*, Oslo, Unipax,

McGuffin, J. (1974) *Guineapigs,* Harmondsworth: Penguin

Mikkelsen, J and Bernsten, P M (1982) fl 'Laegers deltagelse i undersegelse af isolerede varetaegtsfaengslede personer', *Ugeskr Laeger*, 144, 1982 7

Nielsen, B. (1981) 'Aspekter i den psykiske pleje af isolationspatienter', *Sygeplejersken - tidsskrift for sygeplejersker*, 40, (Tillaeg Perspektiv)

Sknvelse fra advokaterne (1980) 1 Darisk Retspolitisk Forenings isolationsgruppe til Folketingets Retsudvalg af febr 1980 Vedr totahsolation under varetagtsftengsling

Sollomon, P. and Kubzarisky, P. E. (1961) *Sensory deprivation*, Cambridge, Massachusetts: Harvard University Press

7.

Prison Politics and Prisoners' Struggles in Italy

Raffaele Caldarone and Pier Valeriani

This paper was delivered at the European Group's 9th annual conference in Derry and first published in Working Papers in European Criminology, Volume 3 'Securing the State: Politics of Internal Security in Europe' in 1982.

In this chapter we will describe the penitentiary situation in Italy and the tensions that characterise it in the context of the positions that have arisen from the class conflicts and the struggles of the workers' movement. This means describing the relations between the social situation and the political scenery in which the presence of the workers' parties is of real significance. Although there seem to be great differences between the parties of the Left movement, it is, we feel, important not to overlook the fact that various constitutional parts of the left have conquered considerable political power, that is, the political power which its institutional parts have conquered. We do not intend to take this fact as a common denominator between the various factions, nor do we glibly wish to introduce the notion of a Left unity which does not exist. Nevertheless it is the reality of this power which has raised the question: has the conquest of political space been decisive?

For the moment, we must point out that the Left's internal conflicts have meant that, at least as far as prisons are concerned, their political power has hardly been used, if at all, and so the field has been left open for the adversary. It is worthwhile restating that this is not a new experience for the Italian workers' movement. On other occasions the Left has been brought together by harsh realities which had developed through their failure to act in time. It would, for political reasons, be useful to evaluate the strength of the various positions the Left has conquered and to see how they stand up in the regressive setting of penitentiary institutions. But this type of analysis constitutes too broad a task. The aim of this paper is to describe rather than to analyse.

The strength of the political and administrative power which the Left has won is considerable. Forty-five per cent of members of Parliament are left-wing.[1] The Socialists participate in the present coalition government and many regional and local administrations are under left-wing control. Five key regions - Rome, Turin, Naples, Bologna and Florence - have Communist mayors, while Milan, Genoa, Venice have Socialist ones. This conquest of institutional power has solid roots in the sense that the Left is deeply involved in the civil and economic life of many areas, particularly in the North. It also-has strong connections with trade unions and there are links with other sectors, such as craftsmen and light industry, through organisations like co-operatives.

The parties have the power to influence the working of the prison at two levels. First, at a political level, parliamentarians and regional councillors have the right to visit penal institutions without authorisation and without giving advance warning. Second, at an administrative level, the parties have some power of intervention. Regions and Communes are responsible for providing various services for the prisons in their area - sanitation, training of prisoners, cultural activities, recreation, sport, social services and construction work. But while the penitentiary administrators must consult the local authorities, they are ultimately subordinate to the minister. In addition, the Presidents of regional councils may receive complaints or demands from the prisoners, and doctors from the provincial health offices must inspect the institutions in their area every six months to check on the conditions of hygiene.

Prison Structures

The Ministry of Justice publishes the date of construction of all the buildings controlled by the penitentiary administration, the majority of which are used as prisons. Two hundred and forty-five centres are listed. Of these, 70 were built during this century[2] – 29 of them after the last war – 57 were built in the 19th century, 17 in the 18th century, and the rest are even older. Favignana, the oldest institution, was built in 1084. The older buildings tend to be either ex-fortresses or convents. Civitavecchia, for example, is an old corn store which belonged to the Popes.

The Ministry of Justice also provides information about the capacity and quality of the institutions, as well as information about the type of space available, noting the number of the rooms, cells and cubicles. These details allow us to examine the prison structure. Ancona, for example, a reformatory school (or school-prison), with a juvenile detainee-centre, has 60 cubicles. Other institutions with cubicles include Alessandria, Augusta, Bari, Castelfrance Emilia, Catania, Favignana, Ferrara, Firenze (Florence), Imperia,

---

[1] Editors' note: Italy 1981
[2] Editors' note: 20th Century

Messina, Napoli (Naples), Palermo, Pisa, Ragusa, Tram, Turi, Viterbo and a number of smaller institutions. Even though restructuring has taken place almost everywhere - the most recent being the setting up of maximum security jails - much of the prison building is old and in very poor condition. This creates an oppressive atmosphere which in turn affects prison life. Some places are particularly bad. A council doctor visiting Castelfrance Emilia considered that the cubicles there were more appropriate for keeping cattle than human beings.

This is the background against which the idea of opening up the prisons to social life must be considered. The notion of socialisation was one of the innovations proposed by the 1975 prison reform, along with proposals for alternatives to imprisonments. All these innovations were to be introduced by local authorities - regions and communes - who would govern the prisons in a radically alternative manner. In practice, however, it was impossible to introduce one particular provision of the 1975 law - the separation of prisoners according to certain objective categories, such as people awaiting trial and convicted prisoners, young and old, first-time offenders and people with previous offences. A similar proposal had been put forward in 1931, but this too was never implemented.

While there is a lack of inertia in Italian prisons, there is also a resistance to change which is symbolised in the day to day running of the institutions by the commanding prison officer (in each institute the prison officers are commanded by a marshal, a non-commissioned officer who has come up from the ranks and who is able to guarantee continuity of procedures). However the main barrier to change lies in the actual structures of the buildings and the effect they have on prison life. The Left has succeeded in obtaining the de-militarisation of the police force but many prison warders are still soldiers. It is in fact symptomatic of the situation that, in order to resolve the problem of chronic staff shortages, soldiers doing military service are called in.

The most recent report produced in 1980 by the 'Superior Council of Magistrates' for the Italian Parliament on the subject of the penitentiary reform begins: 'The present situation, in the penitentiaries is characterised by a deep divide between the reality and the ideals of the legislators.'[3] In 1975, after ten years and more of preliminary discussion, some prison reforms were introduced. These were seen by many academics and politicians as an example of a humane law, a progressive step forward and one of the most advanced reforms in Europe. Their overall aim was to introduce substantial changes into the Italian penitentiary system but in reality the law has been a

---

[3] Superior Council of Magistrates (1980) *Penitentiary reform* Italian Parliamentary Report

failure. It was full of theoretical pronouncements but lacked the means by which the pronouncements could be carried out. For example, the articles in the law concerning prisoners' participation and re-education were never introduced. One of the principal reasons for the failure of the law was Article 90. It stipulated that the application of the reforms may be suspended, 'when there are serious, exceptional motives concerning order and security'. This meant that in practice the application of the reforms was in fact at the discretion of the state. They required the political will to apply them constantly.

The development of the reforms followed a tortuous path. In December 1973 the Senate approved a text which was extremely progressive, but just before it went to the Chamber of Deputies for approval, tragic events occurred in the prison in Alessandria. These were enough to bring about modifications to the proposed law and substantially limit its innovativeness. After the reforms had been introduced in 1975 they were affected by the upheavals in prisons in 1976. These involved almost every prison from Palermo to Turin, from Favignana to Fossano. In Florence and Vicenza prison warders were kidnapped as a protest against beatings. These actions led to the so-called mini-reform introduced in 1977. These reforms included an end to the regulation that prevented prisoners with previous criminal records from taking advantage of the new reforms. The 1977 law (No 450, of 20777) also maintained the system of permits which allowed prisoners to leave jail for a limited period (Article 30). Overall, the reforms moved in a cautiously progressive direction.

After this mini-reform, suddenly there was talk of counter-reform. It was suggested that Article 90 of the 1975 law should be applied and there was an all-out campaign against the issue of permits to prisoners by the penitentiary magistrates. It was argued that the permits were one of the fundamental causes for the mess the country was in. This point about permits is interesting because it illustrates the contradictory nature of the instructions given to the magistrates by the state. Nonetheless, they began to apply Article 30. At first, they did so only sporadically but later on a wider scale. The Article was interpreted in a very liberal fashion by the magistrates, in a way that the law did in fact authorise. The second clause of the Article gave magistrates the right to issue permits for 'serious, proven motives'. The system of permits became the only means of treating prisoners in a progressive fashion. A study of the system was undertaken by the national body of magistrates and showed how the system worked in practice. In general, it definitely helped reduce the tension inside the prisons, encouraged a sense of responsibility, not only for the individuals directly concerned but also for the whole community as a 'value' was attached to the fact of somebody returning to prison after his time-out. For the individuals concerned permits gave them a sense of responsibility and helped resolve many of the problems of aggression and anxiety which are common to prison life. As far as relations with the outside world were concerned, the permits allowed real contact between the prisoner and his family and social environment and provided a realistic preparation for the prisoner's eventual re-integration into society.

The experience of the permit system also provided information about the dynamics of the prisons. It was found that the system had particularly positive results where there was a prison population that was stable and had close links to the social environment. In addition, it was found that the more the permit system was extended, the less the prisoners demanded re-trials. The permit system also had an impact on the politics of prisons. An area of consensus was created among the prison population. People began to feel that prison as an institution could change, that a new kind of institution could develop in which security was only of secondary importance and in which innovations could be introduced.

Two other points need to be made about the system. First, it should be noted that the permit system was developed in such a way that the magistrate had only a rudimentary knowledge of the individual concerned, there were no facilities allowing them to observe and treat the permit-holder. The second point is related to the first one. Little or nothing was written down about how or why the permit was issued or whether the time spent out of prison had helped the individual become integrated into society.   The official statement regarding the results of the time-out would usually just state whether or not the subject had returned to prison.   The permits no longer exist. Article 30 was modified in such a way that it became almost impossible for the magistrates to issue them. The modified article stated that they could only be issued 'in exceptional cases, for particularly serious reasons'. The permit system was really the only provision that brought a new dynamic into the prison crisis. It was a dynamic that might have brought an end to the crisis and allowed alternative institutions to develop. In addition, the permits system allowed a closer view of prisons and prisoners, their capacities and limitations.

There are one or two more points to be made about the-permit system. Firstly, it was extremely difficult for one body, the Centre for Social Services, to take responsibility both for watching over the prisoner (control) and looking after his social and psychological needs. Yet both aspects were implicit in the work of the department. Supervision was impossible in the vast majority of cases, where there was only one Social Services Centre in the administrative capital of the region to deal with an enormous number of cases spread all over the area. Inevitably, the numbers involved affected the quality of the services provided. The second point concerned the issue as to where exactly semi-freedom could be practised as an alternative to imprisonment. Theoretically, there ought to be a section of the prison that is cut off from the rest of the buildings but which could be interconnected. This is stipulated by law. It also should be structured like a hostel, in other words a normal, inhabited building. This kind of structure has never been provided and, in a good many prisons, semi-freedom does not exist. Some of the Social Services departments have found a way of getting round the problem by letting the individual live at home, and allowing them to benefit from the permit system during the periods in which they ought to return to prison. This system was adopted, for example, in Bologna prison. It is now, of course, no longer practical to do this.

Prisons and Conflict

No effort was made to organize collective or socialising activities which, in the eyes of the reformers, could have formed the basis for the prisoners' re-education. Rather, the schools that did exist were closed down almost everywhere. Similarly, the workshops, which were run by private industry for obvious political and financial gain were also closed. A company based in Varese called 'Ticino', for example, had workshops almost everywhere in the country, producing electrical goods for export. These prison shops were very useful when sections of the workers outside prison went on strike. They enabled the company to make and deliver the goods abroad and hence meet their contracts. But these workshops too were gradually closed down.   In addition, other opportunities for the prisoners to socialise within the prisons were abolished. Even the television rooms were closed because TVs had been introduced into all the cells - a nasty, underhand aspect of modernisation. Although these opportunities for socialisation tend to mystify the nature of prison and its real function, nevertheless they did allow the prisoners a minimum of social life.

The system of dividing prisoners into groups, which in the maximum security prisons meant isolation, gradually spread into every Italian jail. There were extremely serious repercussions from this phenomenon even though the isolation techniques used in the ordinary prisons were much less strictly applied. Tension has increased. Relations between individuals are inhuman. Increasingly, outbreaks of violence occurred and new disciplinary measures were used, usually unsuccessfully, to counter them. Witnesses have stated that drugs were commonly given to prisoners. These included sleeping pills, as well as pharmaceuticals administered without due medical supervision.

In conclusion to this section, it is clear that the proposals for alternatives to prison, considered the pearl of the penitentiary 'reform' were very rarely adopted. Alternatives, which could have given credence to the principle of integrating prisoners into society, were so rarely applied that they had no impact on the rising prison population. There are now 35,000 people in prisons in Italy.[4] The history of Italian prisons is a history of conflict, both latent and explicit. A ministerial circular of 1951 speaks of 'transferring prisoners in exceptional circumstances when they are obstinately rebellious in the face of every disciplinary measure'. Another circular during the same year stated

> Pietism and the unilateral vision on the issue of punishment for crime have brought about a climate in which prisoners arrive in prison with a suitcase full of rights that they are ready to claim. I am not unaware that the most difficult cases cause us embarrassment claiming better treatment and conditions. Prison authorities are faced with threats of collective rebellion. The prison governors should be fully aware that their actions in conserving the rigorous observation of the regulations will be well appreciated. The prison sentence must aim at the prisoner's re-education - in accordance with constitutional principles - but must not be lacking in the punitive aspect which characterises it, an aspect which the law and public opinion demand. Thus it is inevitable that the prisoner will suffer from deprivation; the loss of the right to move freely, the loss of the right to work, which in prison is considered an obligation and not a right, and all the other material and spiritual needs which a free man may satisfy but which are denied to the prisoner. The constitutional principle by which a prison sentence does not involve inhumane treatment but must lead to the prisoner's re-education. This principle cannot be used to justify illicit toleration or relaxation of discipline. The most sensitive of people can well understand and accept the unsuppressible need to conserve order in prisons. I take the occasion to point out one example of relaxation of disciplinary measures - the question of newspapers. For the moment journals, which are evidently political in character, and which declare themselves to be so, must be excluded.[5]

---

[4] Editors' Note: Data from 1982
[5] Ministerial Circular (1951)

These circulars could be issued by the Ministry today.[6] One can see in the careful wording, the references to the Constitution, and in the political preoccupations, references to the press, a reflection of the conflicts going on in the prisons. They also reflect the political and social conflicts taking place in the world outside. One can also see the efforts being made to re-structure the institutions of repression, for example in the references permits to discipline and to the need for deprivation.

The circulars cover a specific moment in the history of the workers' movement which corresponds to an attempt to isolate the working class, by trying to criminalise its political behaviour. This is also a period in which governmental power is restructured – a phenomenon which will later divide the workers' movement itself – with the Socialist Party in the government and the Communist Party in opposition. This is also a time of serious economic crisis, a period in which the conflict between needs and resources brings about a system of control over the political expression of needs and the disciplinarian reorganisation of productive capacities. In this context we find a convergence between political behaviour and criminal behaviour. One specific structure, prison, is used to deal with the problems arising from the relations between the economic crisis and crime, and the conflict between the struggle for needs and the restructuring of economic organisation. In the sixties, a new element came to prominence. Organised crime now used the prisons as recruiting centres. This type of criminality had close links with the uncontrolled economic development that was taking place in those years. It had the same methods and intentions.

The situation in the prisons can be seen as a theatre of class conflict. Outside prison the workers' parties are gaining political and institutional power. Inside prison, the conflict is related to the overall structure and organisation of the prisons, the traditional way in which they are basically governed. The notion that prison is a school for crime must be seen in the context of the social dynamics that arise from the institution's repressive function. Social problems that are introduced into prisons from outside are expressed inside in a much more intransigent fashion. When repression is used at a political level, there is a process of hardening of positions.

Another element in the present conflict situation in the prisons is the high level of consciousness with which the intransigence is used. The inter-relations between the political confrontations both inside and outside the prisons could be clearly seen during the kidnapping of Judge D'Urso and the discussion about the so-called 'special prisons', maximum security jails like Asmara. These issues provoked reactions from every element in Italian

---

[6] Editors' Note: The today the authors are referring to is 1982 but it could equally be applied to 2014.

politics and were seen with great clarity from inside the prisons. In particular, special prisons were not seen as something new but always a part of the panorama of repressive institutions. Moreover, the techniques of control used inside them weren't considered as very different from the techniques in general use in prisons, particularly in cases of emergency. Furthermore, the repressive techniques used in other prisons were not undervalued. The prisoners' awareness of the nature of the conflict can be seen in the way in which their demands at the time were basically similar to those they had been making previously. They demanded that the formal regulations should be vigorously upheld in prison. This took place despite only an embryonic level of organisation.

In psychiatry the use of nosographic categories has had the result of obscuring the individuality of the patient. While the term 'schizophrenic' exists the patients afflicted with what is called schizophrenia do not exist. In the same way the institution of 'special' prisons has 'produced' dangerous prisoners. Before maximum security jails were created, every prisoner was considered dangerous and every prison was considered a security jail. This meant that no one prisoner was any more dangerous than any other, and no one jail had to be any more secure than any other. It follows that since there is no abstract category of 'dangerousness', any judgment made on an individual's behaviour and on the kind of prison that would be suited to them, will be based on a realistic, objective evaluation of the case. This is not a play on words but a true institutional paradox, 'special prisons' do not exist because dangerous criminals exist, but dangerous prisoners exist because special prisons exist. We can verify this phenomenon when we see how the label 'dangerous' is attached automatically onto certain individuals and how difficult it is for them to lose that label once it has been attached to them.

In 1977 a number of prisons were defined as special. The main ones were at Asmara, Cuneo, Fossombrone, Tram and Favignana. What really distinguishes these from the old 'hard' prisons is the level of external security. This is maintained not by normal prison warders but by a special military corps, the Carabinieri. We have to go back to 1968, a year which was characterised by the mobilisation of large sectors of the working and student population in the Western industrialised world, to find the first signs of organised struggle and planned demands on the part of prisoners in Italy. From 1968 onwards the politically and socially conscious prisoners begin to organise themselves within Italian prisons. Similar developments take place in the rest of Europe and in the United States. They are capable of carrying forward their demands and of planning strategies. They are struggling to improve the conditions of survival within divisive structures. In addition, they are capable of overcoming the existing divisions between political prisoners and common 'criminals'.

During the next few years a number of factors accelerate the process of politicisation of many proletarian prisoners. These include such factors as the emergence of political groups working outside of the institutional parties, and the increase in the number of political detainees within Italian prisons. But many prisoners were not politicised because they came from sub-proletarian rather than proletarian backgrounds. They were not aware of the political significance of their condition as prisoners. Occasionally they did join the revolts, when the conditions seemed to be favourable to them and when the struggles were for immediate demands. It cannot be claimed, however, that they were really part of the prisoners' movement because they did not understand its political value.

Expanding social conflicts and the growing importance of the role of minority and marginal groups in the class struggle made certain prisoners become more aware politically and socially. At the same time groups of young left-wing people outside of prison were going through the same experience. This phenomenon brought out the importance of prisons as a political problem in the class struggle.

Generally speaking, there are two basic ways in which a prisoner will react to his or her situation of isolation from society. One is an individual self-destructive reaction, the other is a collective reaction of active resistance. The struggles for political demands are examples of this type of resistance. They may be expressed pacifically, or they may break out in violent revolts. In 1969 many revolts did in fact break out in Italian prisons. These were sometimes a product of overcrowding.

We do not wish to undervalue the importance of these revolts which brought significant concessions from the authorities and made public opinion more aware of the seriousness of the state prisons. However, we must point out the limitations of the initial revolts. They lacked organisation and clear political positions. After the initial revolts were over, no organisational structures existed. But as the struggles went on, the prisoners' movement did make significant progress in becoming more rational and systematic. Beginning with the vague, unresolved explosion of the will to rebel – 'take hold of everything, destroy everything' – the movement produced a number of well-thought-out analytical studies of the repressive mechanisms at work in prisons. For example, during the protests at San Vittore in Milan on April 15 1970 the prisoners' behaviour was extremely well planned and correct. This demonstrated how the movement could manage the violence within the prison. Nonetheless the authorities reacted with brutally repressive methods, suffocating the protest. They were probably hoping to finish off a protest movement once and for all that had begun in Rebibbia jail in 1969 when prisoners demonstrated against the punishment bed which had been used to strap down and immobilise 'dangerous' prisoners.

In 1973 the prisoners' movement was aware of the need to establish links with progressive forces working outside of prisons, in particular, with the movement, of the free proletariat (*i.e.* non-institutionalised groups). Their principal aim was to publicise their terrible living conditions. To this end, they organised roof protests. During the protests at the Nuove prison in Turin in January 1973 the prisoners wrote an open letter addressed to FIAT workers and to the Italian working class in general. They recognised that the proletariat and the working class were basically the only elements in society who would take notice of their struggles in defence of their rights. Moreover, they saw that these elements were the only people capable of evaluating their actions. The incidents at the Nuove prison in Turin occurred mainly because of the composition of the prison population. It included militants from left-wing extra-parliamentary groups, many of whom were arrested in Turin at that time, and many detainees who had yet to be tried – people who had been in the avant-garde in earlier prison struggles.

Arising out of this situation, a document entitled 'The general programme of struggle for prisons' was published in April 1973. This established the following forms of struggle for prisoners within the penitentiary institutions: hunger strike, refusal to meet relatives and defence lawyers, refusal to present oneself before examining magistrates or in tribunals and court. The document also contained a call for the absolute ban on the use of violence, unless the prisoner was actually provoked into using it. The document also noted various demands and these were taken up in the years that followed. It demanded that the legal reforms should be approved, specifically, the Penal Code, Penal Procedures, and the regulations governing prisons; that prisoners should have the right to study, to work, and to have free association within prisons; more frequent contacts with relatives and with the outside world; and that work done in the prisons should be equal to that done in the world outside, in the sense that prison workers should have the same rights and pay as workers outside; and prisoners should be guaranteed a job once they are free. These demands were adopted by the whole of the workers' movement. They were not therefore sectarian or corporative demands. The protests steadily gained ground in places where the repression was unable to break it. Like a sinking ship, no sooner had the state managed to plug one of the holes, another one appeared somewhere else. Moreover, the policy of transferring prisoners, a policy generally used to break up incandescent centres of revolt, worked in the movement's favour. It meant that the struggles were transferred along with the prisoners, and new protest groups were formed.

As early as spring 1971, young extra-parliamentary groups led by 'Lotta

Continua' joined forces with the clandestine prisoners' movement. They attempted to set up a united front bringing together other institutions including schools, barracks and service quarters. Their aim was revolutionary, but their project failed as far as prisons were concerned. The reason for this failure can be found in their schematic, veteran-Marxist view of class reality in Italy. They believed in a programme, which oversimplified the many diverse realities, and attempted to subjugate them to the all-important organisation.

It is at this time that the Armed Proletarian Nuclei (NAP) appeared on the scene. Like the Red Brigades (BR) they believed that armed struggle was the only practicable form of 'political activity'. They felt that it was the only way of encouraging those elements who were undecided between struggling against the institutions and going back to organised crime. However, unlike the Red Brigades, NAP did not claim to be the armed avant garde of the movement. They came from marginal social forces and most of their recruits were new to political militancy. Most of the ex-prisoners who joined NAP were robbers who had become politicised in jail. NAP began its operations on October 1, 1974. Its objective was to destroy prisons and the structures that supported them. It attempted to work from both inside and outside. The stereotype of the 'nappista' was an ex-bank robber who, once he has been indoctrinated, saw himself as a romantic revolutionary and after some practice, became an urban guerrilla. He followed the road to revolution as though it was a myth. He aimed at 'all or nothing', despite what his own ideology taught him. He moved between two opposing fronts. On the one hand, he called for armed struggle, and, on the other hand, he made various reformist demands such as the improvement of living conditions in prisons. Thus NAP has always moved on two tracks the first leading to the avant garde of the prison proletariat and calling on them to take up the hardest possible forms of armed struggle, and the other tract, of a practical nature, addressing the entire prison population and encouraging them to demand greater democracy inside the jails.

The struggles that the prisoners' movement carried forward in 1976 appeared to be unplanned and lacking in an overall strategy. It is only in about mid 1977 that the movement returned to the offensive and returned once more to the battle ground of the class struggle. In August, struggles broke out all over Italy without warning, and spread with impressive speed. The forms of struggle adopted were not violent. A number of different strategies were used. Prisoners refused to work and went on hunger and thirst strikes. Those struggles began in the prisons at Fosombrone and Padova, and were soon followed by struggles in Bologna prison. Prisoners in these jails put forward again the idea of a national mobilisation for August 24. The principal demands were the abolition of the special prisons and an amnesty. After the national mobilisation the movement decided to open up negotiations on the question of the reform. The aim of this initiative was to achieve better facilities and less control.

The main causes of these struggles were overcrowding, the drastic reduction in the number of permits issued after the 1977 law, and the harder attitudes adopted by the government after the numerous scare campaigns in society. Some of the prisoners were pushing for the application of re-socialisation projects. They adopted various forms of protest, including hunger strikes. However, the majority of them tended to use the prison structure itself as ground for their protests. They refused to work and hence managed to block all internal activity in the prisons. These two forms of struggle did not however endanger the movement's unity.

The highest level of mobilisation and consciousness was reached at the beginning of 1978 during the two days of national protest on February 27-28, when the prison population refused to work for the whole 48 hours' mobilisation. This had been called by Padova prisoners. The slogans adopted were 'No to General Dalla Chiesa' and 'No to special prisons'. The demands included the immediate repeal of a ministerial decree, which handed responsibility for prison security over to the military, and the provision of salaries for prisoners performing regular work inside the prisons. The document published by the prisoners at the time showed clearly the influence of the movement's experiences in 1977. This influence was also seen in the way in which the Padova prisoners distanced themselves from the traditional left-wing parties and trade unions. They saw these organisations principally concerned in gaining power and they considered that institutionalised political choices were anti-proletarian and formed an integral part of the restructuring of capital. Moreover, they claimed that trade unions and 'official' left-wing parties had become accomplices to what they defined as 'institutionalised repression'.

Like NAP before then, they saw the question of prisons as one of the corner-stones of the class struggle. At the same time they drew attention to the role of all the groups and parties who had looked on in silence and who, in practice, had accepted the process of institutionalised repression. In the document there is a clear attempt to form a united front, to bring together the whole movement of so-called non-guaranteed elements. It concludes with two political proposals: counter-power and reappropriation according to one's needs. The notion of 'counter power' meant establishing an organisation which could function as a centre of co-ordination of initiatives and struggles on the part of proletarian prisoners, and as a political organisation able to draw attention to the external and repressive powers. In addition, it needed to be strong enough to condition the choices of the central government within the prisons.

The movement not only addressed the working class but also called for the support and mobilisation of the entire movement of marginalised young people. Its position on the issue of the reform and its failure was to disclaim those theories which argued that the reform could not succeed because prison structures could not be adapted to accommodate the reforms. In other words, it rejected those theories which considered that prisons were too archaic to be transformed into structures of re-education. In contrast, it considered that there were two main reasons for the failure of the penitentiary reform. First, the irreversible economic crisis which meant that prison functioned as an internment camp for superfluous labour and played a deterrent role with regard to the class struggle. The second reason was the overcrowding in the prisons. This was caused by the arrests of thousands of proletarians who were opposed to the restructuring of capital. These people opposed the politics of sacrifice, social contracts, wage settlements, unemployment and marginalisation.

The presence of a significant number of political prisoners had a strong influence on the character of the protests and on the analyses produced. There was a homogeneity among all the documents produced by the 'committees of struggle', organisations which co-ordinated the protests. One of the key issues was the question of differential treatment between the detainees in special prisons and those in normal ones. Special prisons differentiated between prisoners at every level. The central aim of the strategy of differential treatment was to break the spirit of politicised prisoners. It operated through a division in the role of the prison structure – a division that had been planned and directed from one centre.   The committees of struggle created a defence mechanism for the victims of this destructive logic through the use of counter-proposals. It also represented a structure which led people to believe that there could be areas of 'red power' or liberated zones which were feasible even in the isolated environment of prisons, if the prisoners themselves took control and managed their own territory.

The Emerging Counter-Reform

Italy's socio-economic situation during this period was characterised by two features. On the one hand, there was an economic crisis in which production was being restructured. This tended to affect the weakest social groups. On the other hand, there was an intensification of the level of political struggles and social conflict. The mechanisms of repression had been restructured.   The restructuring of production affected great numbers of workers and in many cases broke down the barriers built up over the years by the trade unions.   Parties and trade unions, which traditionally expressed political protest at an institutional level, were not always able or willing to counter the restructuring of projects. They adopted strategies of mediation between opposing interest groups, trying to contain the conflict within certain limits, and at the same time, defending those interests of whom they were the spokespeople.

At the same time, new forms of political expression of needs were emerging, involving direct confrontation, for example auto-reductions and occupations of houses. Often they were 'extra-legal' and were related to a generalised young people's protest movement. Finally, there was the birth and development of autonomous movements outside parties and trade unions, which challenged the traditional left-wing organisations. Young people in particular identified themselves with these.

Bibliography

Superior Council of Magistrates (1980) *Penitentiary reform* Italian Parliamentary Report

.8.

Working for the Clampdown:
Prisons and Politics in England and Wales

Joe Sim

This paper was delivered at the European Group's 13th annual conference in Hamburg and first published in Working Papers in European Criminology, Volume 7 'The Expansion of European Prison Systems' in 1986.

> Our only hope lies in the people's endeavour to hear our protest and support our cause. Building more and better prisons is not the solution - build a thousand prisons, arrest and lock up tens of thousands of people, all will be to no avail. This will not arrest poverty, oppression and the other ills of this unjust social order. (John Cluchette, 1971)

Introduction[1]

In August 1985, the average daily prison population in England and Wales reached the record level of 48,165. This was a rise of 5,400 from September 1984 and 8,000 more than the system was designed to handle. During the first six months of the year the population had been rising by 235 a week.[2] For those on remand, the rise had been even steeper. In the year ending February 1985, the remand population rose by 16%, which was four times the rate of increase for prisoners as a whole [3] Overall, the rate of imprisonment had risen to 96 *per* 100,000 of the population as compared to 29 *per* 100,000 in 1923 and 32 *per* 100, 000 in the 1930s.[4]

---

[1] Thanks to all of those who attended my session at the European Group Conference in Hamburg. The discussion and comments were very helpful in clarifying my thoughts. Special thanks to Anette Ballinger and to Rusty for their support. Finally, thanks to the Clash for providing the first part of the title to this paper

[2] See *The Guardian,* July 29, 1985, August 9, 1985, August 10, 1985, August 20, 1985 and September 3, 1985.

[3] *The Guardian,* April 18, 1985.

[4] *The Guardian,* August 10, 1985. It is also worth noting that figures compiled by the National Association for the Care and Resettlement of Offenders (NACRO) at the same time showed that in 1982 (the last year when figures were available) the United Kingdom as a whole imprisoned, both in

The juvenile prison population was also expanding at a faster rate. The latest figures available indicated that the population was 21% higher in the first half of 1983.[5] Within that category, young women were coming in for particular attention in the courts. In the first year of the operation of the 1982 Criminal Justice Act, the number aged between 15 and 20 sent to penal establishments rose by 20%.[6]

Expenditure on the prisons had also continued its inexorable rise. In the financial year 1985/6, the budget for the penal system was £822 million, a rise of 85% since 1979, and an overall rise of 176% in the ten years between 1975 and 1985. Overtime pay for prison officers alone rose by 137% in the years between 1979 and 1985.[7] By 1985 it was costing an average £11,000 *per annum* to keep an individual incarcerated.[8] This increase in expenditure was matched by an increase in the number of prison officers. By January 1984, there were 24,137 officers and civilian staff working in the service.[9] At the same time the ratio of staff to prisoners had been consistently increasing over the years. In 1971 there were 3.58 prisoners to each uniformed prison officer. By 1984 this had been cut to 2.54 prisoners *per* officer despite the fact that 'there are nowadays also many more non-uniformed specialist staff working alongside prison officers'.[10]

These developments were themselves underpinned by a major prison building programme which the government had proudly proclaimed to be the biggest undertaken this century. The programme was indeed impressive with sixteen new prisons being planned, fourteen of which would be opened by 1991. In addition, there were major developments or refurbishing schemes taking place at 100 prisons. Altogether the programme would provide an extra 11,700 prison places by the early 1990s.[11] The cost of these plans was estimated (at 1983 prices) to be around £500 million, with 5,500 new staff being recruited to support this extension in prison places.[12]

By late 1985, therefore, the prison system in England and Wales was on a major expansionist course. The government was providing the resources necessary to further extend the number of places available to the courts for

---

absolute numbers and in proportion to the population, more people than other comparable Western Europe nations. 274 men and women were imprisoned *per* 100,000 of the population in that year. NACRO, *The Use of Imprisonment: Some Facts and Figures,* 1985.

[5] *The Guardian,* December 10, 1984.

[6] *The Guardian,* August 15, 1985.

[7] *The Guardian,* May 21, 1985, June 6, 1985.

[8] *The Guardian,* August 10, 1985.

[9] Home Office, *Criminal Justice: a Working Paper,* 1984 p.24

[10] G Coogan, cited in *The Guardian,* June 14, 1985.

[11] Speech by the Home Secretary to the Prison Officers' Association National Conference, May 21, 1985.

[12] *Prison Service News,* 1983. *The Standard,* November 21, 1983.

the sentencing of offenders. The reasons for this extension are complex and sometimes contradictory but require situating the prison system, both within developments in the wider criminal justice process and also within the political and economic system itself. It is also important, however, in order to have a fuller understanding of this often complex process, to grasp the nature, extent and depth of the crisis which was affecting the prison system in 1985, a crisis which had its roots much further back in history and which had been the subject of major debates and analyses in the 1970s and early 1980s.[13]

The crisis inside

The most obvious manifestation of the crisis in the prisons was that of overcrowding. By 1985, living and working conditions for the imprisoned, especially those in the short-term and remand prisons, were appalling. This situation, clearly, was not new, as throughout the 1970s and 1980s report after report, both official and unofficial, condemned the conditions inside as 'an affront to a civilised society'[14] and as 'spartan, gloomy and stagnant'.[15] For prisoners, such rhetoric provided little comfort, especially for those locked up 23 hours a day, two or three to a cell, in a space which measured twelve feet by eight feet with only a bucket for sanitation. By 1984 16,000 prisoners were living in such conditions.[16] The 1984 *Report of the Chief Inspector of Prisons* for the fourth year running drew attention to overcrowding in prisons and was scathing about the sanitary arrangements.

> The stench of urine and excrement pervades the prison (Norwich). So awful is this procedure that many prisoners become constipated, others prefer to use their pants, hurling them and their contents out of the window when morning comes.[17]

Conditions, the Report concluded, were likely to get worse, and overcrowding, which the Chief Inspector felt was a fundamental cause of bad

---

[13] M Fitzgerald and J. Sim, *British Prisons,* London, Basil Blackwell, 1982; M Fitzgerald and J Sim, 'Legitimating the Prison Crisis: a Critical Review of the May Report', *Howard Journal,* 19, 1980 pp.73-84.

[14] *Report of the Work of the Prison Department, England and Wales,* London, HMSO, Cmnd. 8228, 1980 p.4.

[15] *Ibid* p.18.

[16] Home Office, *op cit* p.22.

[17] *The Report of Her Majesty 's Chief Inspector of Prisons 1984,* London, HMSO, cited in *The Guardian,* October 25, 1985.

conditions and 'many other evils, seemed at least in the short term more likely to get worse than better'.[18]

While media, political and public comment concentrated on debating and highlighting these conditions, other dimensions of the crisis came in for less scrutiny but were no less important in contributing to the instability of the prison system in the 1970s and 1980s. One of these dimensions was the continuing militancy of rank and file prison officers who throughout the previous decade had been in constant conflict with the Home Office, prison governors, social workers, probation officers and teachers, with members of their own union executive – the Prison Officers' Association – and with prisoners themselves. This 'crisis of authority'[19] showed no signs of abating in 1985 as prison officers in different prisons took action over a number of issues including the perennial one concerning the excessive amount of overtime which they worked. Any attempt to curtail it was met with fierce resistance. In 1985 the officers took action at, amongst other prisons, Bedford, Parkhurst and Wormwood Scrubs in support of different demands. In May of the same year the then Home Secretary, Leon Brittan, was barracked and booed at the annual conference of the Prison Officers' Association despite the fact that he had pointed out to those present that:

> the number of prison officers has increased by one fifth since 1979. The budget for the Service has gone up 85%. Annual expenditure on prison building development and repair has gone up nearly 400%.[20]

Serious conflict was also reported to be occurring between staff and prisoners in a number of prisons. In the three months between April and June 1985, for example, 316 prison officers and 135 prisoners were injured.[21] In June there was a large demonstration by 43 women in Holloway prison protesting about brutality inflicted upon a fellow prisoner who was said to have been dragged into a cell by eight prison officers, forcibly stripped, and was later refused permission to see a doctor.[22] In April probation officers at Aldington, near Ashford, reported that young offenders were being punched for forgetting to say 'Sir', for not knowing their number even though they had not been given any and for not running quickly enough.[23] Finally, in November

---

[18] *Ibid.*

[19] M Fitzgerald and J Sim, 1982, *op cit* p. 11

[20] Speech by the Home Secretary, *op cit* pp. 6-7

[21] *The Guardian,* August 10, 1985

[22] *The Guardian,* June 21, 1985

[23] *The Guardian,* April 26, 1985

1984 serious violence was also reported to have occurred at Wandsworth prison in London, a prison with the reputation of being one of the hardest in Britain. One prisoner was said to have been dragged from his cell by twelve prison officers, punched and kicked, then carried face downwards from the landing downstairs to the ground floor.[24]

This conflict between staff and prisoners was compounded by continuing disturbances in the long-term maximum security dispersal prisons. In April 1985 there was a sit-in protest by 25 prisoners at Gartree in Leicestershire, in June there was another at Parkhurst on the Isle of Wight.[25]   Finally, in September, staff at Albany maximum security prison voted to restrict the movement of prisoners on the grounds that discipline had broken down. Prisoners were to be allowed out of their cells for 30 minutes instead of the normal twelve hours. The clampdown followed a confrontation between staff and 70 prisoners after a fight between prisoners.[26]

Such protests and disturbances only highlighted the fragile and unstable nature of long-term prisons. There had been major problems of control since the dispersal system was introduced in the late 1960s.[27]   Between October 1969 and June 1983 there had been at least ten major disturbances involving five out of the eight dispersal prisons.[28]

The stability and control of the system was also threatened by prisoners engaging in other forms of direct action in an attempt to redress the balance of power inside. In particular, prisoners were increasingly turning to the law both to challenge existing penal policies and the new policies initiated in 1983 by the Home Secretary which effectively abolished parole for whole categories of offenders.[29]   While they lost the latter case after a series of convoluted court hearings, prisoners, with the assistance of the European Commission for Human Rights, finally won the right to be legally represented at prison disciplinary hearings. Although this Judgment still only applies to serious breaches of the prison rules such as mutiny, and is at the discretion of the Prison Board of Visitors, nonetheless the latest figures suggest that one in every twenty prisoners is being represented, with some success in terms of the verdicts returned.[30]   Prisoners were being supported in their endeavours

---

[24] *New Statesman,* November 25, 1984.

[25] The Sun, April 23, 1985; *The Guardian,* June 7, 1985.

[26] *The Guardian,* September 21, 1985.

[27] M Fitzgerald and J. Sim, 1982, *op cit* chapter 4.

[28] Home Office, *Managing the Long-Term Prison System,* the Report of the Control Review Committee, 1984. In Scotland similar events were happening in Peterhead, Scotland's only maximum security prison. See J. Boyle, *A Sense of Freedom,* London, Pan Books, 1977.

[29] M. Ryan and J. Sim, 'Decoding Leon Brittan', *The Abolitionist,* 16, 1984.

[30] P.M. Quinn, 'Help for Prisoners at Adjudication: Sacred Thoughts', *British Journal of Criminology* 24(4), 1984 p.396

by a number of groups and lawyers outside the prison walls, including Radical Alternatives to Prison (RAP), the National Prisoners' Movement (PROP), Women in Prison, Inquest and the Prison Reform Trust, all of whom in their different ways were providing alternative sources of information which challenged official explanations and descriptions of events and incidents inside. In that sense, prisons were increasingly becoming much less invisible as the monopoly on information which the prison authorities controlled was severely undermined,[31] a process which had started with the formation of PROP in 1972.[32]

The continuing crisis in the prisons also meant that the very legitimacy of the system itself was increasingly being called into question. These questions came from different sources but had a common theme, namely, that the prisons were not working. From the point of view of state servants, however, this was underpinned by a belief that if the prisons were failing then somehow the social order itself was in danger. The former Home Secretary, William Whitelaw, had indicated in December 1981 that the appalling conditions inside were 'a continued threat to law and order'.[33] In May 1982 the Lord Chief Justice, Lord Lane, while pointing out that 'prison never did anyone any good', nevertheless warned that if the prison system were to break down then 'all of us – judges, your Lordships and the rest of the population – would inevitably suffer catastrophe'.[34] In 1984 the right wing think-tank, the Adam Smith Institute, in arguing for the privatisation of prisons because of their ineffectiveness, complained about the escalating cost of keeping individuals incarcerated, 'three times the most expensive public school fees'.[35] Added to these pearls of criticism were the figures supplied by various reform groups, and the government's own research department in the Home Office which pointed out that overall 60% of male offenders and 41% of females were reconvicted within two years of release. For young prisoners the rates were even higher at 69% and 54% respectively.[36]

The crisis of legitimacy in particular and the prison crisis in general have raised some profound questions about the role of the prisons in England and Wales. These questions bring into sharp focus not only the relationship between prisons and the prevention of crime but also the more fundamental issue of the inter-connection between prisons and the maintenance of the social order itself. As has been pointed out:

---

[31] M. Fitzgerald and J. Sim, 1982, op cit p.6.
[32] M. Fitzgerald, *Prisoners in Revolt,* Penguin, 1977.
[33] Cited in *Report of Her Majesty's Chief Inspector of Prisons, op cit p.*17.
[34] *Hansard,* March 24, 1982, col. 987.
[35] Adam Smith Institute, *Justice Policy,* 1984 p.61.
[36] NACRO, *op cit p.*2.

The crisis of the British prison system reflects not simply a concern about the state of the prisons but a more widespread belief that the prisons of the state are not making an effective contribution to the maintenance of social order.[37]

The next part of this paper examines the connection between these two levels, first, by looking at the response to the crisis by the state as a way of highlighting and exploring the issues behind the escalation and expansion of the system, and second, by situating these issues and developments within the broader context of the changes occurring at the complex interface of the criminal justice process, the state and the political economy. It is at this latter level that the politics of the prison system become manifest.

Responding to the crisis

The state's response to the crisis of overcrowding has been classical and predictable. More prisons are to be built and more alternatives are to be sought. As indicated above, sixteen new prisons are to be built in England and Wales and others are to be refurbished at a total cost of £500 million. The reasoning behind this move was that new prisons would relieve overcrowding, a rationalisation which is contradicted by much of the sociological and criminological literature on the subject. Put simply, more prisons equals more prisoners.[38] Even before the latest building plans were announced, between 1970 and 1982, 6,000 new prison places were provided in England and Wales, but overcrowding has remained an integral feature of prison life.[39]

In a similar way, the argument for alternatives to custody has been based on the principle that such alternatives would produce a reduction in the prison population by allowing the courts to divert offenders away from custody. In England and Wales these alternatives have included fines, suspended sentences, partly suspended sentences, suggestions for weekend imprisonment and, in 1973, the introduction of Community Service Orders. The idea behind this scheme was that offenders would pay for their crimes by working in the community for between 40 and 240 hours. From 1973 until the end of 1982, 135,000 individuals were given Community Service Orders by the courts,[40] but, as Ken Pease has indicated, the Orders have not been used as an alternative to custody as the majority of those sentenced would not have

---

[37] M. Fitzgerald and J. Sim, 1982, *op cit pp.* 23-24
[38] A. Rutherford, *Prisons and the Process of Justice,* London: Heinemann, 1983
[39] *The Guardian,* June 14, 1985
[40] *Hansard,* January 24, 1984

been sent to prison anyway but would have been dealt with by some other non-custodial punishment.[41] More generally, as Stan Cohen has pointed out, the introduction and use of such alternatives has been to increase rather than decrease the total number of offenders who are pulled into the system in the first instance:

> In other words, "alternatives" become not alternatives at all but new programmes which supplement the existing system or else expand the system by attracting new populations - the net of social control is widened.[42]

It is worth noting that the parole threshold for short-term prisoners has been reduced. The Home Office has extended the eligibility of those available for parole from sentences of eighteen months down to those serving nine months. In July 1984 when it was introduced, the prison population dropped by 2,000 and it was estimated that around 8,000 extra prisoners would receive parole each year under this procedure.[43] However, while detailed figures are as yet unavailable, the steep rise in the population in 1985 would appear to confound the hope that it would reduce the population. It has also been intimated by a serving member of a Local Review Committee of a prison which is responsible for recommending parole to these kinds of offenders that the objective is to keep the system moving, that individuals are being granted parole 'on the nod', which clearly would lead to a greater increase in the use of the prison system as more offenders pass through it for shorter periods of time.[44]

This response to the overcrowding crisis has been supplemented by other suggestions and programmes for alternatives. In Leeds, unemployed people, former schoolteachers and ex-police officers have been employed as 'trackers' to monitor the movements and activities of 'offenders'. Each is paid £250 for a 16 hour week to check three times a day on the whereabouts of the offender for whom they are responsible.[45] It has also been suggested, following their introduction in New Mexico, that electronic bracelets could be fitted to offenders which would send a signal to police if the bearer moved out of a specific area which would be determined by the court, or if the tag was removed. It has been argued that the introduction of such a scheme

---

[41] K. Pease, 'Community Service and Prison: Are they Alternatives?' in K. Pease and W. McWilliams (eds.), Community Service by Order, Scottish Academic Press, 1980.

[42] S. Cohen, Crime and Punishment: Some thoughts on Theories and Policies, London: Radical Alternatives to Prison, 1979. See also S. Cohen, Visions of Social Control, Polity Press, 1985.

[43] The Guardian, March 14, 1985.

[44] Personal communication with a Parole Board member.

[45] Daily Telegraph, October 15, 1984.

would cut the jail population by 10,000 and save £100 million a year in prison costs, it was welcomed by a former prison governor as holding 'the key to a major reform in penology and for a Christian and humanitarian must be given serious consideration and trial'.[46]

The state's response to the crisis of containment[47] has been equally important in extending and expanding both old and new methods of control inside. It is important to note that this crisis has taken place against a background of a major increase in the number of long-term prisoners in England and Wales. As Stan Cohen and Laurie Taylor have pointed out:

> It does not really matter which sets of statistics are used – the overall numbers or proportion of the long-term population, average sentences served by lifers, *etc* – all document the rise in the long-term prison population and the continuing predilection of English Judges to hand out longer and longer sentences.[48]

By 1984 the number of adult male prisoners serving sentences of over five years was about 4,000. In 1983 alone there were 820 new receptions into the prisons serving sentences of this length.[49] This tendency has been exacerbated by the introduction in October 1983 of restrictions on parole for certain categories of long-term prisoners. These restrictions included no life sentence prisoners being released from custody except by the Home Secretary; life was in certain cases to mean life; those who murdered police officers, prison officers, children, terrorists and those who carry firearm in the course of a robbery would serve a minimum of twenty years; the maximum sentence for carrying firearms in the furtherance of theft was increased from fourteen years to life; no one sentenced to more than five years imprisonment for a crime of violence or for drug trafficking was to be released on parole except for a few months before the end of their sentence.[50]

The Home Office themselves recognised that the introduction of these measures 'will increase the number of long-term prisoners and (significantly) will reduce the range of incentives which bear on their behaviour'.[51] In 1984, as figures became available, it was possible to see this increase happening. In the first six months of that year only thirteen offenders sentenced to more than five years for drug trafficking or crimes of violence received parole

---

[46] *Daily Telegraph,* May 5, 1983
[47] M. Fitzgerald and J. Sim, 1982, *op cit* p.20
[48] S. Cohen and L. Taylor, *Psychological Survival,* Penguin, second edition, 1981 p.10
[49] Home Office, *op cit* p.13
[50] M. Ryan and J. Sim, *op cit* p.93
[51] Home Office, *op cit* p. 1

before their final review compared to 113 in the same period in the previous year.[52]

In this context, and in the wake of the disturbances and demonstrations already referred to, the prison authorities have introduced and utilised a number of techniques in order to maintain stability and control. The basis on which these programmes have been implemented has been the idea that it is a few 'bad apples'[53] who manipulate an otherwise quiescent prison population into confrontation, disturbance and demonstration. At a general level, the authorities have continually reinforced and consolidated prison security measures through the extension of new technology and electronic equipment.[54] Added to this, as with the rest of the criminal justice process in England and Wales,[55] the prisons are also being affected by what is happening in the North of Ireland. The Chief Inspector of Prisons pointed out in his Annual Report for 1983, for example, that the lessons to be learnt from the escape of 38 prisoners from the Maze prison that year 'apply as much to the prison system in England and Wales as to Northern Ireland when considering the custody and control of dangerous prisoners'.[56]

More specifically, the authorities have introduced and extended various techniques aimed at controlling, neutralising and isolating those individuals who are regarded as difficult, recalcitrant or subversive. The use of psychotropic drugs to control the behaviour of prisoners has been a major area of controversy in British prisons in recent years,[57] as have been a number of cases of prisoners who have died in custody either through violence or lack of care by the prison authorities.[58] The introduction of a special squad of prison officers trained in techniques of riot control – the Minimum Use of Force Tactical Intervention Squad (MUFTI) – has further consolidated this drive towards maintaining order and control inside. It has been intimated recently that all prison officers are trained in the techniques of riot control.[59] The prison authorities have also used various forms of segregation in the form of solitary confinement, segregation units and control units[60] to isolate those

---

[52] *The Guardian,* March 14, 1985.

[53] M. Fitzgerald and J. Sim, 1982, *op cit* p.93.

[54] *Ibid* pp.98-100.

[55] P. Hillyard, 'From Belfast to Britain: Some Critical Comments on the Royal Commission on Criminal Procedure', in D. Adlam et al, *Politics and Power,* vol 4, London, Routledge and Kegan Paul, 1981; P. Hillyard, 'Lessons from Ireland', in B. Fine and R. Millar (eds.), *Policing the Miners Strike,* London, Lawrence and Wishart, 1985.

[56] Home Office, *Report of Her Majesty's Chief Inspector of Prisons,* HMSO, 1983 p.11.

[57] T. Owen and J. Sim, 'Drugs Discipline and Prison Medicine: the Case of George Wilkinson', in P. Scraton and P. Gordon (eds.), *Causes for Concern,* Penguin, 1984.

[58] G, Coogan and M. Walker, *Frightened for my Life,* London, Fontana, 1982; P. Scraton and K. Chadwick, *In the Arms of the Law,* London, Cobden Trust, 1986.

[59] Personal communication with a serving prison officer.

regarded as difficult. The Prison Reform Trust has recently pointed to a 'significant rise'[61] in the use of special cells in the prisons which require no medical authorisation for their use. In particular the Trust points out that women's prisons make a quite disproportionate use of segregation in these cells. They indicate that in 1982 'women in the remand centres were 31 times as likely to be subject to restraint as men in similar prisons'.[62]

More recently, a Home Office Working Party, recognising that there have been major problems of control in the long-term prisons, and arguing that there was a 'disruptive population of the order of 150-200',[63] have called for the introduction of five or six 'long-term prisoner units' to cater for a range of prisoners who present control problems ranging from the highly disturbed to the 'calculatedly subversive'.[64] In addition to units for the 'highly disturbed and highly dangerous',[65] the Home Office proposed a further three or four units should be established for prisoners 'who present control problems of other kinds'.[66] These units would not be places of last resort, nor according to the proposals would they be punitive in purpose. In addition, the authors of the report believe that they should be run on professional lines. As they point out:

> It is essential that the different units should complement each other and should not simply be an ad hoc collection of aims and regimes. It is also crucially important that the operation and effectiveness of the various units should be centrally monitored and evaluated. We think that only a properly structured and assessed programme of this kind can provide us with the firm data that we currently lack in planning for control.[67]

Finally, the report also recommends that 'new generation' prisons should be introduced which would provide an alternative to the existing policy of dispersal. These new generation prisons, already introduced in the USA, are made up of self-contained units which hold between 50 and 100 prisoners and where architecturally cells open on to a central area so that staff can observe all of the cells, in true Benthamite fashion, without having to move about 'in a consciously patrolling manner'.[68] The authors conclude that:

---

[60] M. Fitzgerald, op cit pp.40-1
[61] Prison Reform Trust, Beyond Restraint, 1984 p.2
[62] Ibid p.7
[63] Home Office, op cit pp.15
[64] Ibid p.17
[65] Ibid p.21
[66] Ibid
[67] Ibid p.22

the requirement for very high security accommodation is unlikely to be more than 300-400 and it would appear that if 'new generation' prison designs are indeed successful, this number could be held in two small prisons of the new kind without incurring the disadvantages that we have noted as being inherent in dispersal policy. We therefore recommend that these possibilities are urgently examined.[69]

In November 1984, at a meeting of prison governors, the Home Secretary expressed the 'greatest interest' in the proposals 'I am sure that we are now going in the right direction'.[70] Evidence from the United States suggests that these new generation prisons may not after all be the panacea for the problems of the long-term prison system in England and Wales.[71] Nonetheless, the first step to implementing the new policies was taken with the announcement in September 1985 that two special units for 'disruptive' long-term prisoners would open in a year at Parkhurst and Lincoln prisons. The new Home Secretary, Douglas Hurd, said that these units would be 'an effective means of managing prisoners who jeopardise the safety of staff and other inmates'.[72]

Thus, both in terms of short-term and long-term prisoners, the prison system is expanding in England and Wales. According to Andrew Rutherford the expanding prison system is performing a dualistic role, namely to:

incapacitate very serious offenders for long periods but also to provide brief and salutary prison sentences for minor offenders. With regards to both groups there is considerable elasticity, and under conditions of expansion the incapacitation net is stretched to include persons other than those convicted of serious offences. Habitual property offenders and institutional trouble-makers become likely candidates for inclusion. At the same time the custodial threshold is lowered to include persons who earlier would have been fined or dealt with by some other non-custodial means.[73]

---

[68] *Ibid* p.7
[69] *Ibid* p.8
[70] *The Listener,* April 18, 1985
[71] *Ibid*
[72] *The Guardian,* September 18, 1985
[73] A. Rutherford, *op cit* p.58

While Rutherford rightly points to the implications of these expansionist policies in the prisons for both petty and serious offenders, and *how* they occur, he does not question *why* they are happening at this historical moment. The answer to this question is complex but some of the issues which the question raises provide the focus for the final section of this paper

Facing the future: the politics of the prisons

When Leon Brittan announced the major prison building programme and the changes in the parole system at the Conservative Party conference in October 1983, he justified the programme, and tougher law and order policies, on the grounds that crime, particularly violent crime, was out of control. He told the Party faithful that while:

> tackling lawlessness and disorder is, or course, my top priority, it is more than just my top priority. In our first term of office the fight against the evil of inflation was the Government's most fundamental task. I believe that in our second term the fight against crime is the key task of all. There is today a great wave of anger against the wanton violence which disfigures our society. That anger is not confined to this Conference and this Party. It is real, it is genuine. I share it to the full.[74]

In the speech the Home Secretary carefully utilised the populist notion that certain crimes of violence − police murders, child murders and terrorist murders − were escalating and therefore should be responded to by tougher sentencing and penal policies. In raising the spectre of such crimes, Brittan conveniently ignored their uniqueness in proportion to the overall number of crimes recorded in England and Wales. In 1982 over 95% were 'offences against property and many of these were comparatively trivial'.[75] Ideologically and symbolically the violent crimes which he highlighted became crucial for his general argument. A society which allowed such things to happen needed to be disciplined. A sense of order, respect for authority and appreciation of stability needed to be restored. Particular images of criminality once again proved to be fundamental for the mobilisation and consolidation of law and order policies. As Paul Gilroy has pointed out, 'because of their capacity to symbolise other relations and conflicts such images of crime and law-breaking have had a special ideological importance since the dawn of capitalism'.[76]

---

[74] Conservative Party News Service, Extract from Leon Brittan's Speech to the Conservative Party Conference, October 11, 1983 p.2.
[75] *Criminal Statistics,* England and Wales, London, HMSO, Cmnd. 9048, 1982.

In the mid-1980s, as a number of radical criminological analyses indicated, it is also necessary to move beyond these important connections between discussions of crime and the increase in penal sanctions. This move involves situating the prisons in a wider social, political and economic context. The work of Thomas Mathiesen, Mike Fitzgerald and Frank Pearce in Europe[77] and Ivan Jankovic, Chuck Reasons and Russell Kaplan in North America[78] raised questions about the role that the prisons played in controlling surplus populations and maintaining order itself. More recent work in England and Wales by Stephen Box and Chris Hale[79] has developed some of the issues raised by these earlier theorists. Box and Hale argue that:

> the growth of unemployment, which is itself a reflection of deepening economic crises, is accompanied by an increase in the range of severity of state coercion, including the rate and length of imprisonment. This increased use of imprisonment is not a direct response to any rise in crime but is an ideologically motivated response to the perceived threat of crime posed by the swelling population of economically marginalised persons.[80]

The authors point out that for every 1,000 increase in youth unemployment, 23 additional young males are sent to prison. This process occurs after the effects of crime rates and court workload have been controlled for. Prisoners are getting both younger and blacker and are caught in a situation where sentencing policies and law-and-order campaigns:

> are not that concerned to control serious crime. Rather they are more concerned to instil discipline, directly and indirectly, on those people who are no longer controlled by the soft-discipline-machine of work and who might become growingly resentful that they are being made to pay the price of economic recession.[81]

---

[76] P. Gilroy, 'The Myth of Black Criminality', in M. Eve and D. Musson (eds.), *The Socialist Register*, Merlin Press 1982 p. 47; See also S. Hall et al *Policing the Crisis*, London, Macmillan, 1978.

[77] T. Mathiesen, *The Politics of Abolition*, Martin   Robertson, 1974; M Fitzgerald, op cit; F Pearce, 'Crime, Corporations and the American Social Order', in I. Taylor and L. Taylor (eds.), *Politics and Deviance*, Penguin, 1973 pp.13-41.

[78] I. Jankovic, 'Labour Market and Imprisonment', *Crime and Social Justice*, 8, 1977 pp.17-34; C. Reasons and R. Kaplan, 'Tear Down the Walls? Some Functions of Prisons', *Crime and Delinquency*, 21, 1975 pp. 260-272.

[79] S. Box and C Hale, 'Economic Crisis and the Rising Prisoner Population in England and Wales', *Crime and Social Justice*, 17, 1982 pp.20-35.

[80] *Ibid.* pp.22.

[81] S. Box, *Power, Crime and Mystification*, London, Tavistock, 1983 pp.22.

A further aspect to the relationship between prisons and the maintenance of order is contained in the *Police Manual of Home Defence* which describes the procedures to be followed in the build-up to a nuclear war, including measures to 'maintain internal security, especially the detention of 'subversive' or potentially subversive people'.[82] Around 20,000 alleged subversives are thought to be on MI5's arrest list. The Special Branch would be directed by MI5 to arrest alleged subversives.

> Exact internment sites are not known, but under emergency powers legislation almost all the normal peacetime prison population would be released – leaving only the most dangerous prisoners. Whether the children of dissenting parents would be similarly detained or whether families would be forcibly split up is not clear.[83]

In considering the role that the prisons might play with regard to the maintenance of order, it is also important to situate the changes in penal policy and expansion of the system within the more general context of the changes which have occurred in the criminal justice process itself since Margaret Thatcher came to power in the spring of 1979. Since that time an impressive array of Acts and Bills have appeared and been enacted which in a number of areas have augmented the power of the state. In addition, the government has made money available to strengthen the police and prison services where in other areas spending has declined quite dramatically in real terms since 1979. A list of these developments is worth considering in order to grasp their range and scope. In the area of finance, for example, the budget for the police rose to £2.5billion in 1983/4. By 1985 this budget had risen by 40% in real terms since 1979. Overall, as the table below indicates, there has been a shift in resources towards law, order and defence expenditure and away from other public services.

---

[82] *The Guardian,* March 19, 1985.
[83] *Ibid.*

Table 1 Public Spending in Real Terms (£millions)[84]

Programme	1979-80	1985-86	% Increase 1979/80-1985/6
Law and Order	3,746	4,767	+27%
Defence	13,405	16,499	+23%
Housing	6,569	2,921	-68%
Industry, Energy, Trade and Employment	5,822	4,338	-26%
Other Environmental Services	3,833	3,153	-18%

In the general area of legislation a number of Bills have been introduced and Acts passed which have strengthened the power of the state in a range of areas: a *Juvenile Justice Act* passed in 1982 has resulted in a major increase in the numbers of young people sent to prison; three *Employment Acts* designed to regulate and control the activities of organised labour; a *Contempt of Court Act* which restricts the ability of the media to report court proceedings; a new *Prevention of Terrorism Act* which extends the already draconian powers available to the police under the old Act; *a Juries Disqualification Act* which increased the numbers of individuals who could be debarred from Jury service; a new *Police Act* which extends police powers including stop and search, arrest and detention; and 10,400 new police officers have been employed. In addition a White Paper reforming the law governing public order has been published, which, amongst other things, will give the police new powers to control the size, location and duration of static demonstrations as well as imposing conditions on marches and processions; there has been an increase and extension in the use of technology such as riot equipment and computers; there has also been an increase in the number and activities of the security services whose budget for 1986-87 increased to £1,000 million, ten times the sum publicly acknowledged; and this increase has been backed up by a widening in the definition of subversion to include activities by those individuals:

---

[84] *The Guardian*, January 23, 1985.

whose real aim is to harm our democracy but who for tactical or other reasons choose to keep (either in the long or short-term) within the letter of the law in what they do.[85]

This has allowed the security services to engage in surveillance activities and infiltrate groups such as the Campaign for Nuclear Disarmament (CND), trade unions, anti-racist groups and the National Council for Civil Liberties (NCCL). Margaret Thatcher herself has spoken of an 'enemy within', of the 'hard left operating inside our system, conspiring to use union power and the apparatus of local government to break, defy and subvert the laws'.[86] This area of surveillance has been reinforced by the formation in May 1985 of a Central Intelligence Unit at Scotland Yard to be run by their Public Order Branch. The Unit was to rely on 24 London district intelligence officers to pass on information about industrial disputes, meetings and community tension. These reports are then used to plan the deployment of the riot-trained Police Support Units.

Such surveillance techniques and the concern with subversion can also be seen in the context of military exercises such as Wintex 85, which took place between February 26 and March 16, 1985. According to the MP Dafyd Elis Thomas, this exercise tested plans for 'crisis management' at a time of war, but had more to do with fighting the enemy within than any external threat.

> The experience of the miners' strike has shown that Wintex 85 is not a hypothetical exercise. The integration of police forces, the organisation of supply convoys, the blocking of roads, the tapping of telephones and the harassing of activists show that Wintex 85 is not so much about what the state would do in the event of war, but the sinister game the state is already playing, coordinating repression in the coalfields.[87]

Finally, following major disturbances in Birmingham, Leicester, Brixton and Tottenham and London in the autumn of 1985, the Prime Minister offered what the *Times* called a 'blank cheque' to the police for more personnel and riot equipment. She told the Conservative Party conference that if the police 'need more men, more equipment, different equipment, they shall have them'.[88] Sir Kenneth Newman had already warned Londoners that they were

---

[85] *The Guardian*, January 29, 1985.
[86] Conservative Party News Service, 'Why Democracy will last', The Second Carlton Lecture by Margaret Thatcher, November 26, 1984 p.10.
[87] *The Guardian*, February 10, 1985

being put 'on notice' that he would not shrink from using plastic bullets and tear gas to restore order 'should I believe it a practical option for restoring peace and preventing crime and Injury'.[89] The process had already started with the press reporting that work was being rushed through on a £100,000 training centre at Hounslow in London which would ensure that all 26,000 uniformed police officers in the capital would train there at least four times a year in a situation which 'includes exact replicas of streets and housing estates in London'.[90] As significantly, it was also reported that from mid-October the Special Patrol Group's armoured personnel carriers would be permanently equipped with plastic bullets and CS gas and would immediately begin 'emergency training in handling the riot deterrents this week .... Police forces in other major cities are expected to follow London's lead by the end of the year.'[91]   Finally, in a speech to the London branch of the Police Federation, Newman announced that, not only would there be a new style of training for special squads, involving the regular use of plastic bullets and CS gas, but that 'senior police officers who do not normally take part in riot training would be specially instructed'.[92] Newman told the assembled audience that many more police were to be trained to use plastic bullets, and that:

> a new centre is ready for intense training of all ranks to a standard to meet the new level of viciousness and violence with which we are now faced.[93]

This further escalation in the power of the police to mobilise in response to public order situations came at the end of the year-long coal dispute, where their role in managing and controlling picket lines and mining communities was seen by many in the communities as violent and ruthless.[94] Both during and after the dispute the police have been involved in other public order situations where their response has also been ruthless. In December 1984 Thames Valley police broke up a picket of students in Oxford, arresting 35 people and allegedly turning the demonstration into a melee. In

---

[88] The Times, October 12, 1985

[89] The Observer, October 13, 1985

[90] News of the World, October 13, 1985

[91] The Mail on Sunday, October 13, 1985

[92] Dally Express, October 17, 1985.

[93] Daily Mail, October 17, 1985.

[94] Welsh Campaign for Civil and Political Liberties and National Union of Mineworkers, Striking Back, Cardiff, 1985; J. Coulter, S. Miller and M. Walker, State of Siege, Canary Press, 1984; M. Jones, Killed on the Picket Line 1984: the story of David Gareth Jones, New Park Publications, 1985; P. Scraton, The State of the Police, London, Pluto Press, 1985.

February 1985 Metropolitan police officers used wedge formations and horses to prevent demonstrators entering Trafalgar Square for a miners' rally. One person suffered a broken leg and others were injured. In March the Greater Manchester force drove a wedge through students demonstrating against the attendance of the Home Secretary at the university. One observer claimed that hundreds of police appeared without warning and charged with full force at the students, several of whom were injured as they were pushed and thrown by their hair down a flight of stairs. In June 1985 members of a peace convoy met the full force of police tactics on the road to Stonehenge.

> I witnessed women and children being hit with truncheons, glass from broken vehicle windows showering down on those inside and a mother dragged out of a shattered window with her child and thrown weeping to the ground, windows were smashed by the police and occupants were dragged out through a storm of truncheons, broken heads, broken teeth, broken spectacles. It was a whirl of destruction. Officers started to climb through the broken windows, lashing out at all sides with their sticks. Reporters screamed at the police to calm down.[95]

Finally, in October a demonstration by more than 2,000 people outside of the South African Embassy in London was met by police, who, after severely restricting the movement of the demonstrators, arrested 320 of them. Officers were seen to be using techniques of arrest, such as wrist-bending, based on Japanese martial arts. One black Anti-Apartheid member described how:

> they grabbed my leg and I fell over. Then police piled in. I was grabbed away with my wrists bent back. They lifted me clear off the ground so that all my weight was on my bent wrists. I was screaming with pain. They called me "nigger" and "cunt".[96]

During the arrests other women complained that their clothing was deliberately pulled in such a way that it amounted to sexual harassment, while a blind black man was seen being forced to the ground.[97] This kind of police response towards demonstrators is also underpinned by a secret manual drawn up by the Association of Chief Police Officers for 'riot' situations, which has abandoned the notion of reasonable force 'in arresting

---

[95] *The Observer,* June 2, 1985.
[96] *New Statesman,* October 25, 1985 p.5.
[97] *Ibid.*

offenders and instead instructs riot squads how to set about "incapacitating" *demonstrators'*.[98]

In England and Wales there has been an important political debate about the precise nature of these changes in terms of their relationship to the politics of the Conservative Party under Margaret Thatcher and the emergence and consolidation of a new-right authoritarianism in society which itself is underpinned by the adherence to a monetarist economic policy and support for a free-market economy. In the autumn of 1983 contributors to the Journal *Critical Social Policy* outlined what they saw as the increasing authoritarianism in a whole range of state provision and services, including social security, the law, housing, the National Health Service, education, the personal social services and social policies affecting women and black people.[99] These changes have been supported by the proposed abolition of the structure of local government in the main metropolitan areas of the country, the placing of individuals supportive of the monetarist thrust in key posts in industry and the civil service, the banning of trade unions in certain areas of government work and the centralisation of government decision-making within the inner sanctum of the Thatcher cabinet. While the importance of this shift has been stressed, others have pointed to the necessity of considering these changes in a much longer historical perspective. This is to stress the fact that

> the centralisation and militarisation of policing and the growth
> of repressive legal regulation have longer histories than most
> advocates of the Thatcherism concept would like to admit. This
> is principally because they are histories in which the Labour
> Party at every level has been extensively and intimately
> involved.[100]

In a number of influential articles Stuart Hall[101] has also pointed to some of the features to be considered in the analysis of Thatcherism and the emergence of a law-and-order society. Opening his 1979 Cobden Trust lecture, Hall argued that 'we are now in the middle of a deep decisive movement towards a more disciplinary, authoritarian kind of society'.[102] In developing his ideas, Hall has built upon Poulantzas' concept of 'authoritarian

---

[98] O.Hansen, 'The Armlock of the Law', *New Statesman*, October 25, 1985 p.11.

[99] *Critical Social Policy*, 8, 1983. See also T. Mainwaring and N. Sigler, *Breaking the Nation: a Guide to Thatcher's Britain*, London: Pluto Press, 1985.

[100] P. Gilroy and J. Sim, 'Law, Order and the State of the Left', *Capital and Class*, 25, 1985, p.18.

[101] Seem particular S. Hall, 'The Great Moving Right Show', *Marxism Today*, January 1979 pp. 14-19; S. Hall, 'Authoritarian Populism a Reply', *New Left Review*, 151, 1985 pp.115-124.

[102] S. Hall, *Drifting into a Law and Order Society*, London, Cobden Trust, 1980 p.3.

statism' (intensified state control over every sphere of socio-economic life), but has shifted the characterisation of the conjuncture to 'authoritarian populism'. In doing so he hoped to

> encapsulate the contradictory features of the emerging conjuncture, a movement towards a dominative and 'authoritarian' form of democratic class politics, paradoxically apparently rooted in the 'transformism' ... of populist discontents.[103]

Paddy Hillyard, again building on the concept of 'authoritarian statism' developed by Poulantzas, has pointed to significant changes in the criminal justice process in the North of Ireland which can be seen to be influencing the changes and developments in the rest of the United Kingdom. Hillyard argues that

> while neither the army nor a paramilitary police patrol the streets, the movement towards the new form of a repressive apparatus is unmistakable. Over recent years in Britain there has been an enormous growth in the technology of control and the military capabilities of the police have been greatly expanded. Moreover, there have been moves to reform the criminal Justice system along similar lines as the changes introduced into Northern Ireland in the early seventies.[104]

He outlines a number of strands in this process, including a shift from policing offences to policing areas, the decline in the power of the legislature in the development of law and order policies with a concomitant increase in the influence of the police and army, and an increasingly bureaucratised and more formal system of administering the criminal law. Hillyard's principal conclusion is that the form of repressive strategy adopted is

> far from being exceptional and a product of the unique circumstances of the political violence in Northern Ireland, is, on the contrary, the form which many modem capitalist states are evolving.[105]

---

[103] S. Hall, 1985, op cit p.118.
[104] P. Hillyard, 'Law and Order', in J. Darby (ed.), Northern Ireland: Background to the Conflict, Belfast, Appletree Press, 1983 p.60.
[105] Ibid p.32.

Finally, the contributors to *The Empire Strikes Back*[106] have also demonstrated this right-ward shift in state practices, particularly in relation to its articulation through the issues of race and racism. The authors argue that what has happened in Britain through the 1970s is not

> a simple extension of repression but a re-composition of relations of power at all levels of society. Although the more overt forms of social control are orchestrated by the police, it is important to note that the whole of society is constituted as a field of social relations structured in dominance. What were once tendencies have taken institutional form during the last few years.[107]

Conclusion

It is within this framework of analysis that the expansion of the prison system can best be understood. It is an analysis which situates initiatives in penal policies and practices within developments in the wider criminal justice system while simultaneously acknowledging the influence of changes within the political economy itself. It is also important to acknowledge that these developments in penal policies and criminal justice practices could be seen as indicative of the government's desire to establish a much more integrated and less informal process of justice in England and Wales which would approach problems of crime and public order in a manner which is rational, professional and ultimately ruthless.[108] The problems of the late twentieth century require such a response, especially in the light of the major disturbances in England and Wales in the summer of 1981 which found the police, in particular, unprepared for the scale and fury of the demonstrations. These events provided a salutary lesson to state servants such as the then Deputy Assistant Commissioner of the Metropolitan Police, Geoffrey Dear, who has argued that the disturbances of 1981 'shook the apathy out of the system'.[109] Leon Britain's short spell at the Home Office and the appointment of Kenneth Newman, the ex- head of the Royal Ulster Constabulary, as Commissioner of Police for London were important moments in the move towards a more professional criminal Justice system. Newman has since published a 60 page booklet on police ethics and professionalism, called *The*

---

[106] Centre for Contemporary Cultural Studies, *The Empire Strikes Back,* London, Hutchinson, 1982: See also P. Gordon, *Whitelaw,* London, Pluto Press, 1983.

[107] *Ibid* p.21.

[108] Thanks to Paul Gilroy and Paddy Hillyard for discussing this point with me.

[109] Cited in P. Gilroy and J. Sim, *op cit* p.49.

Principles of Policing and Guidance for Professional Behaviour, and makes clear that where a conflict arises between maintaining order and enforcing the law, 'in the last resort the maintenance of public order will be given priority'.[110] Leon Brittan himself was also quite clear in what he wanted when he went to the Home Office:

> on taking office I decided   that we needed a strategy which would enable us to pursue our priorities and objectives in a deliberate and coherent way. Such a strategy is now in place. It covers all the main areas of the Department's work, both general policies and specific legislative or administrative objectives. We shall be reviewing it regularly. Our principal preoccupation is, and I believe ought to be, the criminal justice system, which, incidentally, I wish to see treated in all that we do as a system.[111]

With regard to the prisons, Britain and his successor Douglas Hurd, in true monetarist fashion, have demanded that they start to give value for money. Each prison, therefore, has been given its own individual budget within whose limits it has to work. Furthermore, some of the most hallowed work practices of the prison officers, especially those relating to overtime, will be scrutinised and perhaps abandoned. This, needless to say, has been greeted with antagonism and hostility by the Prison Officers' Association. In demanding these changes, Britain also maintained, however, that the prison service must not be asked

> to accommodate too many changes too quickly. It has a vital task to perform and must be left to get on with it. At the same time there is much to be done if the service is to be properly trained and equipped to face successfully the challenges of the last decades of the twentieth century.[112]

In recognising the significance, extent and impact of the changes in penal policies and the political and economic context within which they are taking place, it is clearly important not to adopt a purely instrumentalist view of the

---

[110] Cited in *Policing London,* 19, August/September 1985 p.67.

[111] Leon Britain, Evidence to the House of Commons Home Affairs Select Committee, January 23, 1984, cited in *Criminal Justice a Working Paper,* Home Office, May 1984, foreword.

[112] Leon Britain, Speech to the Prison Officers' Association, *op cit* p.13. A similar theme of rationalising crime control in terms of strategic policing, private security, volunteer patrols, etc for the USA is discussed in J. Wilson (ed.) *Crime and Public Policy,* Institute for Contemporary Studies Press, 1983.

state and state power. There is no straight 'fit' between economy, class and state. As has been pointed out

> The substantial transformations of the state during the seventies are not simply an outcome of the changes in the economy. To say this would be to confuse long-term tendencies with the immediate causes of change within the state. So it is important to see that the crisis which Britain faced during the seventies, and faces today, is a crisis of hegemony, an "organic" crisis, to use Gramsci's terminology. Its content is not reducible to a cyclic economic crisis in the traditional sense or a "crisis of the political system" in the narrow sense. It consists rather of profound changes in the balances of forces, in the class struggle and in the configuration of the class alliances.[113]

Equally it is also important to recognise that much of the process of rationalisation and professionalisation is fragmentary and incomplete, is contradictory in parts and is not wholeheartedly supported by different groups of state servants. The ongoing disputes between the Prison Officers' Association and the Home Office, the hostility between the Association of Chief Police Officers and the rank and file Police Federation, and the Federation's resistance to Kenneth Newman's plans for the Metropolitan Police provide evidence of this conflict. As importantly, the struggle of prisoners inside also provides a challenge and resistance to these changes. Allied to this, the struggle of groups outside of the walls, such as the women at Greenham Common, black and mining communities and rank and file trade unionists, highlight the difficulties that the government faces in its attempts to manage an increasingly fragile social order beset by economic decline, industrial stagnation and political conflict against a background of what Colin Leys has called 'the first instance of the threatened *absolute* decline of a fully capitalist social formation'.[114]

Nonetheless, these developments pose a major threat to the very limited notions of justice and rights which citizens have had in England and Wales. The prisons are part of that process. It is a process in which they are performing a central and increasingly unambiguous role in the maintenance of order. In considering this position, it is worth remembering a point made by Michael Ignatieff concerning the reform of the prison system in England and Wales in the 1840s. The thrust of his argument is significant for the

---

[113] Centre for Contemporary Cultural Studies *op cit* p 19
[114] Leys C. 'Thatcherism and British Manufacturing: A Question of Hegemony' *New Left Review,* 151, 1985 p.*5* (emphasis in the original)

situation today:

> The persistent support for the penitentiary is inexplicable so long as we assume that its appeal rested on its functional capacity to control crime. Instead, its support rested on a larger social need. It had appeal because the reformers succeeded in presenting it as a response, not merely to crime, but to the whole social crisis of a period, and as part of a larger strategy of political, social and legal reform designed to re-establish order on a new foundation. As a result, while criticised for its functional shortcomings, the penitentiary continued to command support because it was seen as an element of a larger vision of order that by the 1840s commanded the reflexive assent of the propertied and powerful.[115]

It is that 'larger vision of order' which has to be appreciated if the politics of the prisons in England and Wales are to be clearly understood, and responded to, in the last quarter of the twentieth century.

Bibliography

Adam Smith Institute, (1984) *Justice Policy*, London: Adam Smith Institute

Box, S. (1983) *Power, Crime and Mystification*, London: Tavistock.

Box, S. and Hale, C. (1982) 'Economic Crisis and the Rising Prisoner Population in England and Wales', *Crime and Social Justice*, 17,

Boyle, J. (1977) *A Sense of Freedom*, London: Pan Books.

Centre for Contemporary Cultural Studies, (1982) *The Empire Strikes Back*, London: Hutchinson.

Gordon, P. (1983) *Whitelaw*, London: Pluto Press.

Cohen, S. (1979) *Crime and Punishment: Some thoughts on Theories and Policies*, London: Radical Alternatives to Prison.

Cohen, S. (1985) *Visions of Social Control*, Cambridge: Polity Press.

Cohen, S. and Taylor, L. (1981) *Psychological Survival*, Harmondsworth: Penguin, second edition.

Conservative Party News Service

Coogan, G. and Walker, M. (1982) *Frightened for my Life*, London: Fontana.

Coulter, J., Miller, S. and Walker, M. (1984) *State of Siege*, London: Canary Press.

Daily Express

Daily Mail

---

[115] M Ignatieff, *A Just Measure of Pain,* London, Macmillan, 1978 p.210.

Daily Telegraph

Fitzgerald, M. (1977) *Prisoners in Revolt*, Harmondsworth: Penguin.

Fitzgerald, M. and Sim, J. (1982) *British Prisons*, London: Basil Blackwell.

Fitzgerald, M. and Sim, J. (1980) 'Legitimating the Prison Crisis: a Critical Review of the May Report', *Howard Journal,* 19, pp. 73-84.

Gilroy, P. (1982) 'The Myth of Black Criminality', in M Eve and D Musson (eds.), *The Socialist Register*, London: Merlin Press.

Gilroy, P. and Sim, J. (1985) 'Law, Order and the State of the Left', *Capital and Class*, 25.

Hall, S. (1979) 'The Great Moving Right Show', *Marxism Today*, January 1979 pp. 14-19

Hall, S. (1980) *Drifting into a Law and Order Society*, London: Cobden Trust.

Hall, S. (1985) 'Authoritarian Populism a Reply', *New Left Review*, 151, pp.115-124.

Hall, S., Critcher, C., Jefferson, T., Clarke, J. and Roberts, B. (1978) *Policing the Crisis*: Mugging, the State and Law and Order, London: Macmillan.

Hansard

Hansen, O. (1985) 'The Armlock of the Law', *New Statesman*, October 25, 1985

Hillyard, P. (1981) 'From Belfast to Britain: Some Critical Comments on the Royal Commission on Criminal Procedure', in D Adlam et al, (eds.) *Politics and Power*, vol 4, London: Routledge and Kegan Paul

Hillyard, P. (1983) 'Law and Order', in J. Darby (ed.), *Northern Ireland: Background to the Conflict*, Belfast: Appletree Press.

Hillyard, P. (1985) 'Lessons from Ireland', in B. Fine and R. Millar (eds.), *Policing the Miners Strike*, London: Lawrence and Wishart.

Home Office (1980) *Report of the Work of the Prison Department, England and Wales*, London: HMSO, Cmnd. 8228.

Home Office (1982) *Criminal Statistics, England and Wales*, London: HMSO, Cmnd. 9048.

Home Office, (1983) *Report of Her Majesty's Chief Inspector of Prisons*, London: HMSO.

Home Office, (1984) *Criminal Justice: a Working Paper*, London: HMSO

Home Office, (1984) *Managing the Long-Term Prison System, the Report of the Control Review Committee*, London: HMSO.

Ignatieff, M. (1978) *A Just Measure of Pain*, London: Macmillan.

Jankovic, I. (1977) 'Labour Market and Imprisonment', *Crime and Social Justice*, 8, pp.17-34.

Jones, M. (1985) *Killed on the Picket Line 1984: the story of David Gareth Jones*, New Park Publications.

Leys, C. (1985) 'Thatcherism and British Manufacturing: A Question of Hegemony' *New Left Review*, 151.

Mainwaring T. and Sigler, N. (1985) *Breaking the Nation a Guide to Thatcher's Britain*, London: Pluto Press

Mathiesen, T. (1974) *The Politics of Abolition*, Oxford: Martin Robertson.

NACRO, (1985) *The Use of Imprisonment: Some Facts and Figures*, London: NACRO.

New Socialist

News of the World

New Statesman

Owen, T. and Sim, J. (1984) 'Drugs Discipline and Prison Medicine: the Case of George Wilkinson', in P. Scraton and P. Gordon (eds.), *Causes for Concern*, Harmondsworth: Penguin.

Pearce, F. (1973) 'Crime, Corporations and the American Social Order', in I. Taylor and L. Taylor (eds.), *Politics and Deviance*, Harmondsworth: Penguin.

Pease, K. (1980) 'Community Service and Prison: Are they Alternatives?' in K. Pease and W. McWilliams (eds.), *Community Service by Order*, Scottish Academic Press.

Policing London

Prison Reform Trust, (1984) *Beyond Restraint*, London: Prison Reform Trust.

Prison Service News

Quinn, P.M. (1984) 'Help for Prisoners at Adjudication: Sacred Thoughts', *British Journal of Criminology* 24(4),

Reasons, C. and Kaplan, R. (1975) 'Tear Down the Walls? Some Functions of Prisons', *Crime and Delinquency*, 21.

Rutherford, A. (1983) *Prisons and the Process of Justice*, London: Heinemann.

Ryan. M. and Sim, J. (1984) 'Decoding Leon Brittan', *The Abolitionist*, 16,

Scraton, P. (1985) *The State of the Police*, London: Pluto Press.

Scraton, P. and Chadwick, K.(1986) *In the Arms of the Law*, London: Cobden Trust.

The Guardian

The Listener

The Mail on Sunday

The Observer

The Times

The Sun

Welsh Campaign for Civil and Political Liberties and National Union of Mineworkers, (1985) *Striking Back*, Cardiff.

Wilson, J. (ed), (1983) *Crime and Public Policy*, Institute for Contemporary Studies Press.

·9.

'The Experiment That Went Wrong': The Crisis of Death in Youth Custody at the Glenochil Complex

Phil Scraton and Kathryn Chadwick

This paper was delivered at the European Group's 13th annual conference in Hamburg and first published in Working Papers in European Criminology, Volume 7 'The Expansion of European Prison Systems' in 1986.

Introduction[1]

The Glenochil Complex was founded as a detention centre in 1966 and it expanded in 1976 to include a young offenders' institution. It continues to combine these functions, each with its own regime, drawing its population from throughout Scotland.[2] Developed on premises acquired from the National Coal Board, the Complex is situated near the village of Tullibody, Alloa. It is a considerable distance from the main centres of population in Scotland and visitors are faced with a near impossible journey by public transport. Visits are restricted, often to just half an hour, and for many visitors coming from Edinburgh or Glasgow, or even further afield, a whole day has to be devoted to making a single, short visit. The Scottish Association for the Care and Resettlement of Offenders provides transport from Glasgow (monthly) and from Edinburgh (fortnightly). The conditions for visiting are spartan, often overcrowded and no provision is made for babies or children. Prisoners are not always unlocked and delay leads to anxiety among visitors who have tight travel schedules. Even a brief visit to the Complex confirms well-established fears that the institution represents a hostile and punitive environment which fails to take into account even the basic needs of prisoners and their families.

---

[1] Thanks to Jimmy Boyle, Sarah Boyle, Paul Gordon, Dave Godwin, Ken Murray, Sheila Scraton and Joe Sim for their help, support and critical contributions to this paper. We are grateful to Sally Channon who typed most of the text.

[2] Editors' Note: Glenochil currently (in 2014) operates as an adult male prison.

On 16th October 1981, Edward Herron, almost half-way through a 15 month sentence for theft and fire-raising, was found dead in his cell in the young offenders' institution. The Fatal Accident Inquiry (FAI) determined that the cause of death was cardiac arrest brought about as a result of the inhalation of solvents. Evidently he had used paint thinners which he had taken from the workshed. Exactly one year later, Richard MacPhie was found dead in his cell in the young offenders' institution. He was three days into a three month sentence given for road traffic offences. The FAI determined the cause of death to be asphyxia due to the inhalation of vomit and hanging. With these two cases began a sequence of deaths at Glenochil unparalleled in the custody of young people. By 13th April 1985 a further five young men had died in the Complex. Of the seven deaths, five occurred in the young offenders' institution and two in the detention centre. In June 1985 the *Scottish Mail* claimed that there had been a further 25 attempts to commit suicide at the Complex during the four year period.[3]

The details of the last five deaths are, briefly, as follows:[4]

1st November 1982, Allen Malley, ten days into a three month sentence for road traffic offences. The FAI determined that he died from asphyxia caused by hanging.

14th August 1983, Robert King, ten months into a three year sentence for road traffic offences, culpable and reckless driving and assault. The FAI determined that he had not intended to commit suicide but had an 'unhealthy interest' to 'see what hanging felt like'. In short, it was an experiment that went wrong.

16th February 1984, William MacDonald, five days before his release following a three month sentence for stealing a tin of glue and assault. At the time he was 'on report' for fighting and expected loss of remission. The FAI determined that while he died of asphyxiation due to hanging, his death probably was not deliberate suicide. Sheriff Principal Taylor, who had conducted the FAI on Robert King, considered that William MacDonald's death was an attempt to 'draw attention to himself, get sympathy or special treatment'. He had 'misjudged the extent to which he could go, or had bad luck with the loose end of the

---

[3] *Scottish Daily Mail*, '25 Suicide Bids at Glenochil', 2nd June 1985
[4] In most cases all quotes concerning FAIs are taken from the transcripts and Sheriffs determinations

knot in the sheet getting caught'. In short, it was a pretence which accidentally went wrong.

18th February 1985, Angus Boyd was found dead in the segregated cell unit of the detention centre. He was two months into a three month sentence and his failure 'to comply with the routine of the Centre' had ensured that the whole of his sentence had been spent in the segregated cell unit. He had been on 'strict suicide observation' until ten days before his death. The FAI, again conducted by Sheriff Taylor determined that he had committed suicide while suffering mental illness.

13th April 1985, Derek Harris was found dead in his cell. He had been threatened by another inmate and was facing further charges with the probable result of a further term at Glenochil. Initially, he had been sentenced to detention centre training but had been transferred to the young offenders' institution. The FAI, again conducted by Sheriff Taylor, determined that he had committed suicide by hanging. His death was 'an outburst of despair at the situations which confronted him, with which he could not cope'.

The young men who died at Glenochil were aged between sixteen and nineteen. William MacDonald and Angus Boyd died in the detention centre, the others died in the young offenders' institution. It was after the death of William MacDonald that Sheriff Taylor recommended that a working group should be set up to review the procedures at the Complex which applied in cases of suspected suicide or parasuicide. This recommendation was made against a background of mounting public and media concern over what was increasingly being claimed as a 'crisis' at Glenochil. Also under criticism, however, was the role and conduct of the Fatal Accident Inquiry, as it seemed that successive determinations by the Sheriff had focused almost exclusively on the individual characteristics and state of mind of the deceased, and had taken little note of the growing allegations concerning the operational policies and practices of the regimes at Glenochil.[5] In November 1984, the Secretary

---

[5] At the FAI into the death of Derek Harris, Sheriff Taylor emphasised that there was no evidence to suggest that the regimes were to blame for the deaths. Alternatively see David Godwin's report for SCCL (unadopted), *How Much is too Much? A Report on Deaths at Glenochil and the Feasibility of Closure*, 1985. See also, Stephen Shaw, 'Death in the Glen', *Open Mind* No 16, August/September 1985. On the issue of the role of the FAI, see Scraton, P. and Chadwick, K. (1987) *In the Arms of the Law* London: Pluto Press, Chapter 7, 'The Scottish System an appropriate alternative?'

of State for Scotland, George Younger, accepted the Sheriff's recommendation and established a Working Group. Its remit was:

> To review the precautionary procedures adopted at Glenochil Young Offenders' Institution and Glenochil Detention Centre to identify and supervise inmates who might be regarded as suicide risks, and to make recommendations.[6]

This remit closely followed Sheriff Taylor's emphasis on the actual procedures which related to suicide or parasuicide. It is not a surprising emphasis as the initial recommendation originated with Dr N Kreitman, a consultant psychiatrist who gave 'expert' evidence to the FAI into the death of William MacDonald. Inevitably, it was an emphasis on the individual, his 'state of mind' and the immediate social factors experienced by the individual. The broader structural and political contexts of detention at the Complex were effectively placed outside the remit of the Working Group's inquiry. This was reflected further in the actual composition of the Working Group. Set up under the chairmanship of Dr Derek Chiswick, a university senior lecturer in Forensic Psychiatry, six of the eight members of the Group provided a medical orientation to the Inquiry. Uniquely for an 'independent' inquiry, three people on the Working Group actually work full-time at the Complex, including Alec Spencer, the Governor of the Detention Centre, and Alan Henderson, the Principal Nurse Officer in the Young Offenders' Institution.

The Glenochil Regimes[7]

The Detention Centre

The Glenochil Detention Centre was opened in 1966 and for the next seventeen years it received mainly first-time offenders sentenced to a fixed term of three months. This changed late in 1983 when the *Criminal Justice (Scotland) Act 1980* was implemented. Under Section 45 of the Act the Prison Department allocates male young offenders, aged between 16 and 21 and sentenced between four weeks and four months (occasionally up to five months), to a detention centre. Detention centre training is avoided only on the basis of medical or related reports. Section 207(4) of the *Criminal*

---

[6] *Report of the Review of Suicide Precautions at H M Detention Centre and H M Young Offenders' Institution, Glenochil* (The Chiswick Report) Scottish Home and Health Department HMSO Edinburgh, 1985, para 1.7.1, p 11

[7] Apart from official sources much of the material contained in these sections comes from personal interviews and from statements by former inmates to the two public meetings, 'Glenochil Dare to Care', organised by the *Gateway Exchange* in Edinburgh and Glasgow, Spring 1985

Procedure (Scotland) Act of 1975 required that in imposing a custodial sentence account should be taken of 'any information concerning the offender's character and physical and mental condition'. Section 207(6) takes this further in stating that if an offender is 'physically or mentally unfit to be detained in a detention centre', then he should be transferred to a young offenders' institution. In 1981 at the Conservative Party Conference the then Home Secretary, William Whitelaw, announced the Thatcher administration's response to the 'law n' order' problem. Amidst cheers and general euphoria he told the Conference of the arrival of the 'short, sharp, shock'. 'These will be no holiday camps', he boomed, 'life will be conducted at a swift tempo, there will be drill'. The applause was rapturous and, no doubt, it echoed loudly down the spotless, scrubbed corridors of every detention centre in Britain.

Glenochil has remained the principal detention centre in Scotland even though in 1983, to accommodate the change in the law, three other institutions were designated detention centres. The 'holiday camp' jibe made by William Whitelaw could not have been further from the truth as Glenochil had a well-established reputation as a hard regime well before the arrival of 'short, sharp, shock'. The Detention Centre comprises three wings with a total capacity of 182 prisoners, referred to ironically as 'trainees', in single occupancy cell. Clothing, bedding and equipment is kept 'military style' and each cell is basically equipped, including a plastic chamber-pot. As with many UK penal institutions, there is no access to basic toilet facilities.

In 1984 1,037 prisoners passed through the Detention Centre with an average daily number of 156 in residence. They experienced a highly punitive regime comprising physical training (rather than education), running, drill and domestic cleaning. In the early weeks prisoners are castigated and cajoled into putting effort into physical tasks and a colour-coded system of tokens, related to earnings, is employed by the staff to assess 'achievement'. Failure to achieve brings a charge of 'offending against discipline for lack of effort' with probable loss of remission. Apart from slightly increased earnings and keeping free of disciplinary charges, the 'achievers' eventually graduate from scrubbing floors to work in the laundry, the garden or the kitchen. The only programme of education available is 'remedial', but even this takes second place to physical training and drill. The token system dominates the routine of the Detention Centre. Even the length of visits are dictated by where prisoners stand on the ladder of achievement. There are two visits permitted each month and new arrivals are entitled to a mere thirty minutes which increases to forty-five minutes and then to an hour according to which 'grade' prisoners have achieved. These brief moments of 'informal' contact with relatives and friends are in stark contrast to the daily routine which begins at 5.45 in the morning with slopping-out the contents of the plastic chamber-pot. From this point, prisoners are under a rule of silence with commands shouted at them, army style, by prison officers. Movement is also in a military form with prisoners marched to breakfast, marched back to their cells, change their clothes, inspected for work, marched to work, marched to tea-break, marched to their cells, change their clothes, inspected on parade and marched back to work. The time is now only one o'clock in the afternoon and the prisoners have changed their clothes three times, been inspected twice, marched everywhere and have remained in total silence. This routine continues throughout the day. At eight o'clock in the evening, following a lengthy period spent in isolation in their cells, prisoners have thirty minutes recreation. For five days every week prisoners are allowed to talk to each other for only thirty minutes per day. At the weekends only those prisoners who have reached the highest grade are allowed any evening recreation at all. Even if prisoners receive their maximum of two visits per month, and not all do, they have two full weekends per month when they have no guaranteed recreation. The rule of silence creates an atmosphere of mental isolation. At weekends that mental isolation is consolidated by long periods of physical isolation. Universally, under the 1980 Act, this regime of detention is now imposed on all young offenders given custodial sentences of under four months.

The Young Offenders' Institution

The Glenochil Young Offenders' Institution was opened in 1976 to receive prisoners whose sentences are over nine months. It is a purpose-built, high security institution separated from the Detention Centre by high level double fencing. The emphasis on security means that the Young Offenders' Institution takes short-sentence prisoners who are considered to be security risks or who have been designated as posing 'management problems' in other institutions. In that sense Glenochil's reputation is that of being the 'end of the line' for the young 'hardmen' of custody. Consequently it has a tough punishment block, known formally as a 'segregation block'.

The Young Offenders' Institution is made up of four blocks (A to D) of 124 cells, each block divided again into three wings accommodating forty or forty-two prisoners each. The wings are on either four or five levels with thirteen or fourteen cells per level. The levels are closed off at night and all gates and cell doors are controlled electronically from a central operations' room. The total capacity of the Institution is 496 but this number has rarely been approached. The average daily population early in 1985 was 270 and during 1984, 473 young offenders were admitted. The turnover of prisoners in the Young Offenders' Institution is substantially less than that of the Detention Centre. This is explained by the much higher average length of sentence in the

Institution.

D-block is the assessment and induction block where prisoners stay for one month. Psychological screening tests are used extensively and work-related aptitude tests are administered. Prisoners are assessed also by teachers and social workers with a final 'team' assessment at the end of the month, leading to either Glenochil or an 'open' allocation. These early assessments in the Young Offenders' Institution are the beginning of a grading and progression system within which 'promotion' leads to a different shirt colour, longer visits, privileges and higher wages. Promotion is granted on the basis of discretionary staff judgements and is related to cleanliness and attitude. Prisoners work their way 'upwards' from A-block to C-block. The differences between the blocks is measured in terms of access to recreation, the 'privilege' of making hot drinks during recreation (B-block) and the wearing of T-shirts and watches (C-block).

Within the Institution, as in most penal institutions where association exists, there is a strong internal hierarchy among prisoners based primarily on violence and intimidation. This internal structure of intimidation and bullying, formally labelled the 'inmate culture', is presented by the authorities as no more than the occasional acts of a few individuals - the 'aggressive behaviour of a minority'. Glenochil Young Offenders' Institution, however, with its size and reputation for a tough regime, exemplifies the institutionalisation of male violence. On the blocks the physically or mentally handicapped, the unassertive, the weak, the sex offenders and the loners are all subjected to a relentless barrage of physical torment and mental torture. They are extorted, verbally harassed, physically beaten and constantly threatened. On exercise, or alone at night in their cells, they undergo a constant hail of abuse; including direct incitement to 'top themselves' (commit suicide). Any attempt to gain the support of prison staff leads to the worst offence against another prisoner – 'grassing' – and, inevitably, to a beating. Yet the bullying and torment is visible and audible to the staff. It is the permanence of this internal regime of male violence and its apparent acceptance which leads to the conclusion that it is institutionalised. Not only is the 'inmate culture' and its hierarchy of violence recognised, it is actively used within the prison as a structure of control and containment.

Unlike the Detention Centre, the Young Offenders' Institution provides education programmes other than remedial and the daily routine, starting at six in the morning with the electronic unlocking of the cells, is more relaxed. Prisoners are allowed to talk at meal times and they are 'moved' rather than marched around the corridors. Work is more informed with regular discussion and there is a period of recreation after lunch, before work in the afternoon. Prisoners are locked in their cells for one-and-a-half hours while the officers have a meal-break and this is followed by just over two hours recreation which includes an opportunity to go to evening classes. At 20.45 in the evening they are locked in their cells for the night. In the induction block (D) and the post-assessment block (A) there is recreation only on four nights and no recreation at all on Saturday and Sunday evenings. Visiting is allowed only on Saturday and Sunday and, depending on the grade achieved, the length of visits varies between thirty minutes and one hour. If the rule of silence and the limitations imposed on recreation create conditions of mental and physical isolation in the Detention Centre, the blind-eye turned to verbal harassment and physical violence in the Young Offenders' Institution creates a climate of fear and aggression. 'Doing time' in either regime is about being able to handle the extremes of the conditions created formally (institutional) and informally (cultural). To cope with these extremes without 'bottling out' is to demonstrate publicly, with maximum visibility, that the regimes hold no fear. This not only applies to the status between prisoners but it also applies to the way in which the institution sees prisoners. For the staff, whether they are prison officers or psychiatrists, the regimes are rational and sound. The 'failure to cope' is seen as a problem within the individual, rather than as a symptom of the harsh conditions within the structure. Those individuals, who express their rationality and sensitivity by occasionally breaking down and crying, learn to cry alone.

The Chiswick Report

The 'Problem' Defined

As stated above, the remit given to the Working Group which produced the Chiswick Report was to provide a review of the precautionary procedures which are used at Glenochil to 'identify and supervise prisoners who might be regarded as suicide risks'. This closely tied the Working Group to a specifically medical/psychiatric interpretation of suicide and led to a focus on 'individuals' rather than on 'regimes'. The Working Group's report, issued on 28th June 1985, is just under 100 pages in length, contains detailed appendices including sketch plans of the two institutions and makes 63 recommendations. The Report is broken down into eleven chapters and it begins with a short introduction to the first five deaths. Chapter Two sets the agenda for the analysis of the deaths by its intention to 'examine the phenomenon of self-inflicted deaths, suicide and parasuicide'.[8] The Report

---

[8] Scottish Home and Health Department (1985) *Report of the Review of Suicide Precautions at H M Detention Centre and H M Young Offenders' Institution, Glenochil* (The Chiswick Report) Edinburgh :HMSO. Para 2.1

explains parasuicide (non fatal acts of self-poisoning or self-injury) as a release of tension, a personal indifference towards life or as a means of 'signalling distress'. Without providing any evidence, but clearly reflecting opinions given by psychiatrists at the Fatal Accident Inquiries, the Working Group states 'In the context of Glenochil, the motivations *not* concerned with the intention to die are more apparent'.[9] In other words, most of the deaths were not intentional.

The Report considers that the question of why the deaths started in 1981 'is unsolved',[10] arguing that there was no change in institutional policy at the time and no comparable occurrences elsewhere. There is, however, an acceptance of a 'pattern' of suicidal behaviour in custody which fits the events at Glenochil. One paragraph is worth quoting in full:

> Outbreaks of suicidal behaviour within closed institutions are well recognised. They tend to follow a pattern after the first one or two incidents both staff and inmates become very sensitive to the possibility of suicidal behaviour, staff anxiety rises and leads to increased surveillance and security, which may be counter-productive, among inmates, the initial shock gives way to an acceptance of self-injury and suicide, so at times of stress it becomes the most likely reaction.[11]

The Working Group provides neither references nor evidence for these broad generalisations, yet – despite ambiguous qualifications in the text *(e.g.* 'may be counter-productive') – there is a clear acceptance that this pattern applies to Glenochil.

Following on from this broader discussion of the 'pattern' of suicidal behaviour in custody, the Working Group go in search of the 'characteristics of young people who commit suicide' and conclude that there is 'no such thing as a "suicidal type" who can be identified from a formal assessment of personality'.[12] There are, however, indicators of risk. It comes as no surprise to followers of the psychological debates around individual pathology and personality disorder as to what those indicators might be:

> early history of parental loss and separation during childhood, frequently followed by unsatisfactory upbringing alienation from society, of repeated rule-breaking and of poor personal

---

[9] Ibid: Para 2.3.1
[10] Ibid: Para 2.4.5
[11] Ibid: Para 2.4.6
[12] Ibid: Para 2.5.1

relationships, isolated individuals changes in mood away from home, friends and family.[13]

This early chapter on self-inflicted deaths concludes hopefully:

> For this reason, it is important that those in charge of young people are in close touch with their thoughts, feelings and behaviour, so that they can observe and monitor any changes.[14]

Thus the stage is set. Suicides in closed institutions follow a pattern: they have a logic of their own which rolls forward on its own inevitable, mysterious momentum. Only certain individuals are at risk and, although there is some doubt about precise details, there are certain events in certain individuals' lives which inevitably render them vulnerable to the emerging pattern. They are 'inadequates', caught up in the panic of immediate social events. In all this it seems that as far as the Chiswick Report is concerned, operational policies and regime practices are irrelevant.

The third chapter of the Report outlines the programmes and routines which operate within the Complex. In conclusion, Chiswick recognises the difficult task which faces staff and commends the majority on their 'fairness' and 'consideration'. Allegations of physical aggression made against prison staff are noted as being 'isolated reports of individual members of staff who were described as having been too ready to resort to physical sanctions when others failed'.[15] While the Working Group recognises the difficulty in investigating such allegations, there is no appreciation of the problems faced by prisoners making allegations. For, not only is there the problem of a prisoner's word against that of an officer, but also a failed accusation leads to harsher treatment by officers and to a counter charge by the institution, that of making a 'malicious allegation'. Inevitably, this leads to a loss of remission.

It is in the fourth chapter - on the 'Response of the Institution' - where the Working Group takes up the issue of the deaths and their effect on the regimes. Much of the discussion here focuses again on the 'pattern' laid down previously; that the 'increased staff sensitivity' led to prisoners exploiting the situation 'by threatening suicide'. Thus an 'unprecedented number of prisoners declared themselves to be suicidal' so that they could be transferred from the main blocks and put on suicide observation.[16] This led to further tensions among staff and, mainly because of expose journalism, to a

---

[13] Ibid: Paras 2.5.2 and 2.5.3
[14] Ibid : Para 2.5.3
[15] Ibid: Para 3.6.3
[16] Ibid: Para 4.4.1

'highly destructive impact' on the staff. The Report criticises the media response to public concern over Glenochil as follows:

> The effect was to undermine confidence, make staff feel defensive of their role and over-anxious in their management of those who might be at risk.[17]

The Report notes that some changes were made in 1984 to 'alleviate the problems of identifying those at risk'.[18] Once again, however, the remedies sought reflected the official line on where the 'real problem' was rooted. The emphasis on new forms of psychological screening and quicker processing through the blocks in the Young Offenders' Institution in order to alleviate bullying is further evidence of explanations which are based on individual pathology and prisoner culture. Chiswick accepts this without question, quoting various statements of the Sheriff at the Fatal Accident Inquiries which exonerated the staff and the regimes from any contribution to the deaths.

In the following chapter - Suicide Precautions - the Working Group discusses the routine for placing prisoners on suicide observation. Strict suicide observation (SSO) is a classification which begins with a referral to the hospital staff from the prison officers on the wing. A-block accommodates thirteen prisoners classified SSO. There is also provision in the Detention Centre (punishment block and nine modified cells) and the punishment cells in the Young Offenders' Institution. The figures for 1984 show that 75 prisoners in the Detention Centre and 89 prisoners in the Young Offenders' Institution were put on SSO for periods of between two days and one year. As a proportion of the total population this was 7% in the Detention Centre and 10% in the Young Offenders' Institution.

It is in considering the regime of SSO that fundamental contradictions in the concepts of care and treatment in custody are exposed. The cells, their operation and their contents clearly deprive the senses of any 'normal' experiences or conditions. Apart from their spartan design, windows are fixed and ventilation is via a grille which cannot be closed. In the winter months the cells are 'extremely cold'.[19] The electric light is never switched off, forcing prisoners to cover their heads in order to sleep. The 'blankets' are made of coarse canvas. Prisoners on SSO are dressed in a canvas gown – a 'short-sleeved, knee-length garment shaped in a similar style to a pinafore dress'.[20] There is no other clothing, not even underwear, and slippers are provided for

---

[17] Ibid: Para 4.5.2
[18] Ibid: Para 4.6.1
[19] Ibid: Para 5.5.1
[20] Ibid: Para 5.6.1

the feet. The prisoner is kept in solitary confinement as association is forbidden; 'the regime consists essentially of the inmate sitting in his room'.[21] Exercise is half-an-hour walking up and down a corridor, work is an occasional basic cleaning task and there are two sessions per week of physical training. The daily routine is punitive even in small ways such as the removal of an prisoner's mattress throughout the day. This paragraph sums up the official line on SSO.

> The requirement to observe each inmate every 15 minutes is performed meticulously throughout the day and night. This takes the form of the officer looking through the spy-hole and ascertaining that the inmate, to all intents and purpose, appears normal. There is no conversation.[22]

The 'appearance of normality' is all that counts. On the other side of the cell door the isolated, cold, bored individual sits on a hard chair in a rough canvas gown accompanied by one paperback book and a Bible. Seventy-two times a day, as regular as a church clock, an eye appears at the spy-hole reminding the prisoner that there is life outside. This is the 'treatment' afforded to those people considered to have such a serious 'mental condition' that they require 'strict suicide observation'. The regimes adopt a medical model in defining those at risk of suicide, yet they adopt a punitive model in their response to those at risk. It represents the classic contradiction of treatment and punishment. Given the vicious nature of SSO, a response seemingly more at home in nineteenth century prison practices, all that can be hoped for is 'appearance of normality'. It is difficult to see how anyone who suffers the deprivation of the SSO regime for any length of time escapes with their sanity intact.

Yet the Working Group concludes that three main groups pose a problem for staff at Glenochil:

a) those who are mentally disturbed, either as a result of mental illness, or a temporary emotional upset;
b) those seeking protection because they are being bullied owing to the nature of their offence, or because they cannot cope in the mainstream, *e.g.* due to learning difficulties;
c) those seeking a way out of the regime (detention centre).[23]

---

[21] Ibid: Para 5.6.2
[22] Ibid: Para 5.6.11
[23] Ibid: Para 5.10.1

The only comment made on these categories by the Working Group is that it is only the 'mentally disturbed' who constitute a 'genuine risk of suicide'.

The remaining four chapters of the Chiswick Report are devoted to its 63 recommendations and their justification. These include the identification of prisoners 'at risk', their management, nursing and medical matters, general measures, fitness for detention centre allocation, contact with relatives and broader issues. It is the Working Group's conclusion that the process of SSO has been 'contaminated' by prisoners who want to escape the mainstream regimes and that the 'highly punitive element' in the SSO regime[24] (6.3.2) has arisen because of this contamination. Consequently it recommends the abolition of SSO and its replacement with the categories of 'extra care', 'close care' and 'special care'.[25] The latter two categories should be accommodated in the prison hospital and not in isolation. Other recommendations for these categories include dress and access to education.

Missing the Point

The Working Group's review of suicide precautions at Glenochil provided a rare opportunity for regimes which have remained hidden from view to be opened to some form of scrutiny. 'Independent' reviews of the institutionalised practices of custody and detention are unusual events. The Chiswick Report is unique in considering the contentious issue of deaths in custody. It was a combination of the depth of public concern about the deaths and subsequent media investigations which moved the Secretary of State for Scotland to set up the review. Consequently, the Report was awaited with real interest, particularly in Scotland. Its release, apparently delayed, inexplicably coincided with the publication of two other official investigations, the Popplewell inquiry into football hooliganism and the report of the inquiry into the sinking of the Belgrano (during the Malvinas/Falklands war). It was suggested by some members of the Scottish press that this simultaneous release was more than an unhappy coincidence. Whatever the reason, the effect was that the Chiswick Report received minimal coverage outside Scotland and was omitted from many UK radio and TV news bulletins.

The coverage which was given to the Report picked up on two central, related themes which also dominated the press conference and the statement of the Secretary of State for Scotland. First, as stated without qualification on BBC Newsnight, the Report 'cleared staff of any responsibility' for the seven suicides and the numerous 'attempts' at the Glenochil Complex.[26] The Scotsman reported the Governor of Glenochil as stating that the

---

[24] Ibid: Para 6.3.2
[25] Ibid: Paras 6.3.4, 7.4.1, 7.5.4, and 7.5.5
[26] Newsnight, BBC 2, 24th July 1985

recommendations 'imply no criticism of my staff'.[27] Secondly, the Report was portrayed as going beyond the confines of its remit in making wide-ranging recommendations which, taken together, are 'fundamental, sweeping and radical' (*Glasgow Herald*), which critically addressed 'the failings of the penal system' (The *Scotsman)* and established that 'the methods of managing prisoners thought to be suicidal were "inhumane and unacceptable" (*The Guardian).* As these represent significant interpretations of the most important official inquiry into deaths in custody to date they have to be considered with some care.

As stated earlier, the remit given to the Working Group by the Secretary of State for Scotland was concerned solely with a review of 'precautionary procedures' applied to prisoners identified within the Complex as being suicide risks.[28] The wider context, including policy decisions and staff practices within the Complex – vital to a clear grasp of the specific operation of the procedures, was absent from this remit. In fact the Working Group made a point of placing 'on record our recognition of the difficult and unrewarding task to which the great majority of staff at Glenochil show a high level of commitment'. Furthermore, it was 'impressed by the dedicated efforts that have been made by the Governor and his staff to review practices and procedures'.[29] In terms of the broader allegations made against the regime at Glenochil, however, Chiswick remains silent. The central government policy of 'short, sharp, shock' which is in operation at the Detention Centre, for example, was not scrutinised. Given the public concern over the Glenochil regime, this would have been appropriate in terms of both its general effect on prisoners and its operational interpretation by officers. In that sense, particularly as the Scottish Prison Officers' Association declined to take part in the inquiry, the broader, crucial contexts of policy and practices were not addressed. Thus to use generally supportive comments by the Working Group, three of whom are full-time staff members at Glenochil, as an 'exoneration' of the regime's policy and staff practices is misguided. While George Younger, as Secretary of State for Scotland, criticised the Working Group for going beyond the confines of its remit, a comment readily accepted by Chiswick, the fact remains that the Working Group was tightly constrained by the remit and also by the medical emphasis evident in its eight-person membership.

This leads to the second, related issue - that of the nature and extent of the recommendations. Clearly the Working Group makes significant, and occasionally serious, criticisms of the procedures adopted for handling

---

[27] All references to newspapers in this paragraph relate to publications on 25th July 1985
[28] The Chiswick Report: Para 1.7.1
[29] Ibid: Para 6.2.1

prisoners considered to be 'at risk'. For those prisoners considered to be potentially serious suicide risks, the Working Group considered the methods adopted to be 'unsatisfactory'. The seclusion of such prisoners 'for lengthy periods in a special cell' was condemned as 'inhumane and unacceptable'.[30] Also it was clear that the Group considered the procedures for assessing prisoners' fitness for the Detention Centre to be inadequate.[31] Further, the emphasis on 'macho-aggression' was criticised in terms of prisoner culture and this implied that the almost entirely male institution required reconsideration.[32] Also criticised were the arrangements, access and facilities available to visitors.[33] On a broader level the Prison Department was criticised for not providing support in times of crisis at the Complex and criticism was levelled generally against the procedures for handling young offenders. It was this range of discussion and its associated recommendations which gave an appearance of a rigorous and critical report. Given the underlying assumptions in the Report about the 'origin' of the problem at Glenochil, however, this needs to be challenged.

As pointed out above, the Working Group's remit set definite limitations on the scope of the inquiry. Rather than considering the broader institutional contexts within which the seven deaths occurred, Chiswick addresses the issue solely in terms of the 'personal' and 'situational' definitions of 'inmates at risk'.[34] Even the concept of 'situational' factors relates to those specific to the individual rather than those general to the organisation. Personal factors include 'changes within the inmate', 'alterations in mood or energy', 'loss of interest, statements that the inmate feels miserable or casual remarks indicating a degree of anxiety or despair'.[35] Situational factors include 'a crisis at home', 'bereavement, anxiety prior to release, uncertainty about the date of release'.[36] Thus the 'problem' at Glenochil is addressed exclusively in terms of the psychiatric condition and personal inadequacy of those considered to be at risk. This emphasis was first made by Sheriff Taylor at successive FAIs and was the underlying principle of Chiswick. It suggests that the regime, particularly at the Detention Centre is in itself alright and that the problem is that certain individuals (those of limited intelligence, physical disabilities, serious social or domestic problems) cannot cope and present 'major problems for the management'.[37] Those considered 'unfit for detention

---

[30] Ibid: Para 6.3.3
[31] Ibid: Paras 9.6.3 and 9.6.4
[32] Ibid: Para 8.3.5
[33] Ibid: Paras 8.6.3 and 8.6.9
[34] Ibid: Paras 7.3.4 and 7.3.5
[35] Ibid: Para 7.3.5
[36] Ibid: Para 7.3.4
[37] Ibid: Para 9.8.2

centre training' include prisoners with a history of psychiatric treatment, attendance at a special school, compulsory care orders, and any history of residential school attendance.[38] What this reflects is the obsession in traditional criminology with the idea of individual pathology - the criminal as born or created by his/her own specific environment.

When Chiswick moves beyond the individual and his personality the Report attempts to explain multiple suicides in two ways which are, to say the least, problematic. On the one hand, the Report plays down the actual extent of the problem by reasoning that as there have been seven deaths out of a transient population of 7,000 over a four-and-a-half year period, 'such deaths are rare happenings'.[39] On the other hand, as noted earlier, the Report argues that 'outbreaks of suicidal behaviour within closed institutions are well recognised' and 'tend to follow a pattern'.[40] First a couple of incidents occur, this leads to increased sensitivity by staff and prisoners, this leads in turn to staff anxiety and an increase in surveillance and security 'which may be counter-productive'; 'among inmates the initial shock gives way to an acceptance of self-injury and suicide, so that at times of stress it becomes a more likely reaction'. Chiswick argues that the events at the Complex fit this pattern. Further to this the Report describes as 'cogent' the argument that 'suicide seemed to be in the air at Glenochil, that suicidal behaviour is now ingrained in the culture and that it will continue by virtue of its own momentum'.[41] What this 'cogent' argument proposes is that somehow the pattern of suicide is a self-fulfilling prophecy. Once established by the aberrant actions of a couple of inadequate, personality-disordered individuals it adopts the quality of a disease, it becomes contagious, continuing 'by virtue of its own momentum'. The traditional criminological model is then complete – if you are not born with the problem, you will soon catch it.

Nowhere does the Report consider the regime itself in terms of the possibility of the accuracy of allegations of general harshness and acts of brutality which are institutionalised. Thus the definition and interpretation of 'discipline', either at policy or practice levels, is not analysed. However, our research shows, and is supported by extensive research on the effects of harsh regimes of incarceration on prisoners, that people who resist such regimes or who crack-up within them are not necessarily suffering from 'broken homes' or 'personal disorders', as Chiswick would have us believe, but are responding *rationally* to inhuman policies and practices which are inherent in harsh regimes of detention. It is the overemphasis on the

---

[38] Ibid: Para 9.5.3
[39] Ibid: Para 6.2.2
[40] Ibid: Para 2.4.6
[41] Ibid: Para 6.4.1

individual, clearly programmed in the Younger remit, and the failure to either recognise or come to terms with the highly punitive forms of detention which severely flaws the analysis contained within the Chiswick Report.

Conclusion

Many of the no doubt well-intentioned recommendations made in the Chiswick Report – such as officers becoming more personally involved in the welfare of prisoners – will not happen. For they flounder on a fundamental misconception of how custodial, punitive regimes actually function. They are naive in their assumption that such places have care and treatment on their agenda and they mistake professional appearance and disciplinary order, and its apparent acceptance by prisoners, as being smooth-running regimes based on the active participation and consent of prisoners. They fail to identify the underlying fear of authority – particularly that held in the discretionary practices of prison officers – and the associated climate of violence and aggression.

The hostility between prisoners and officers, noted by Chiswick, is not a one-way process nor is it rooted in personal relationships. It is generated by staff authority and the routine use of that authority. It is derived in the regimes of discipline and punishment. Consequently the hostility is institutionalised – it is how the system works. Thus it is developed in an atmosphere which not only produces bullying (both within the 'inmate culture' and by staff against prisoners) but also uses the routine violence between prisoners as a legitimate mechanism to regulate and maintain control of the institution.

The 'macho climate' identified by Chiswick is as much a part of the staffs response as it is a part of the prisoner culture. Again there is a naiveté shown by the Working Group in coming to terms with this climate - located solely within the relationships of prisoners. Chiswick assumes that a 'greater presence of female staff in a penal establishment fosters the perception that the institution is a relatively safe place and would encourage good behaviour and reduce tension'.[42] The suffering of women in the harsh, punitive conditions such as those imposed in CI Wing at Holloway[43] is real evidence that such changes will remain cosmetic unless the underlying issues of operational policies and practices are tackled effectively.

Undoubtedly the claim that the 'short, sharp, shock' intervention by

---

[42] Ibid: Para 9.3.5

[43] See Caroline Moorhead, 'The Strange Events at Holloway', New Society 11th April 1985, 'CI for Sorrow', The Abolitionist No 18 1984, also, articles in The Guardian, 25th July 1983 and 15th October 1984

William Whitelaw has been the primary cause of deaths in youth custody is wide of the mark. Official sources have been quick to point out that at Glenochil, five of the deaths occurred under the Young Offenders' regime and not in the Detention Centre. What has been shown in this paper, however, is that the regimes at Glenochil always have been punitive commanding a well-established reputation for their toughness. Any doubts about the implicit inhumanity of the regimes are dispelled by the detailed outline of the procedures for strict suicide observation. The 'short, sharp, shock' policy has served to emphasise and legitimate the hard-line approach of institutionalised state violence which existed already in certain youth custody institutions. Glenochil was such a place. The use of drill, physical exercise, menial tasks and the rule of silence together with the already tough methods used at the discretion of the officers, has brought Whitelaw's promise of 'no-compromise' to fruition. All the evidence shows that any claims for rehabilitation or reform have been lost to embitterment and resentment of the treatment received.

The punitive regime has not remained solely the prerogative of the detention centres, but is reflected in the daily working practices of all forms of youth custody. It is within this framework - the response to the demands for a law and order society in which authority would show its muscle and satisfy the near-hysterical calls for punishment – that the deaths and the breakdown of prisoners in Glenochil and in other institutions have to be located. Over one significant issue the Working Group under Chiswick was split. Some of the Group (their identities have not been revealed) considered that the solution to Glenochil lay in its closure.[44] They were over-ruled by the majority. It is our conclusion that Glenochil - both the Detention Centre and the Young Offenders' Institution - *should* be closed. We are under no illusions that the policies and practices used at Glenochil would not be generated elsewhere. There would be other tough regimes, new hard-line reputations, violent staff and non-accountable decisions. However, the closure of the Glenochil Complex would be a more than symbolic gesture that regimes which rely on punishment, brutality and violence will not be tolerated. It is some measure of how deeply the ideology of punishment is institutionalised that the closure of Glenochil - after seven deaths, twenty-five serious attempts and over a hundred on strict suicide observation - is not on the agenda.

---

[44] The Chiswick Report: Para 6.4.1

Bibliography

Glasgow Herald

Godwin, D. (1985) *How Much is too Much? A Report on Deaths at Glenochil and the Feasibility of Closure,* SCCL (unadopted).

Moorhead, C. (1985) 'The Strange Events at Holloway', *New Society* 11th April.

Newsnight, BBC 2, 24th July 1985

Scottish Daily Mail

Scraton, P and Chadwick, K (1987) *In the Arms of the Law* London: Pluto Press,

Shaw, S. (1985) 'Death in the Glen', *Open Mind* No 16, August/September 1985

Scottish Home and Health Department (1985) *Report of the Review of Suicide Precautions at H M Detention Centre and H M Young Offenders' Institution, Glenochil* (The Chiswick Report) Edinburgh :HMSO.

The Guardian

The *Scotsman*

General *Note*

This paper is part of a long-term research project, initially funded in 1981 by the Open University, into Deaths in Custody and the related procedures for their referral, investigation and examination. Melissa Benn made a significant contribution to the early development of this work and we are members of the organisation *Inquest* which monitors deaths in all forms of custody and deaths in controversial circumstances.

(Editors' note: *Inquest* continues its important and valuable work and can be contacted via their website· http://www.inquest.org.uk/)

Section C:

Beyond criminal justice

10

The Image of Power: Abolitionism, Emancipation, Authoritarian Idolatry and the Ability of Unbelief

Rene van Swaaningen

This paper was delivered at the European Group's 14th annual conference in Madrid and first published in Working Papers in European Criminology, Volume 8 'Civil Rights, Public Opinion and the State' in 1987.

'Maybe we should not have any criminology', says Nils Christie. 'Maybe the social consequences of criminology are more dubious than we like to think', he continues.[1] Herman Bianchi adds 'Criminology has predominantly been a repressive science'.[2] 'Obedience' has always been a central theme in all so-called 'social' sciences. So, why are there still criminologists? If we want to oppose the 'creation and exploitation of "law and order" issues', as it says in the Spring 1986 newsletter of the *European Group for the Study of Deviance and Social Control*, should we not begin by abolishing criminology itself?

I do not think so, but, as is so often the case, posing the question is in itself much more interesting than any possible answer. What can be said about criminologists being uncritical law enforcers – looking for ways of conditioning or catching the greatest possible number of villains? And what about 'radical' bombastic theorists who present crime like some kind of Robin Hood adventure, thereby denying the fact that most victims of crime come from the same underprivileged groups in society as the offenders? Should they remain?

If we want to present a useful critical criminology, we must – as Michel Foucault remarked at a meeting of the *Groupe d'Information sur le Prison* – not make the same mistake as our 'opponents' of the criminal law system by thinking we can present another better 'law and order' so as to create a more

---

[1] Nils Christie, 'Conflicts as Property', *British Journal of Criminology*, 17(1), 1977 p.1.
[2] Herman Bianchi, Abolition Assensus and Sanctuary', in Herman Bianchi and Rene van Swaaningen (eds) *Abolitionism, towards a non-repressive approach to crime*, Free University Press, Amsterdam, 1986, p 126.

righteous society.[3] I think this option would be too pretentious. It is indeed the critical heritage of the *Frankfurter Schule* that security and righteousness are values that can never be guaranteed, and if one were to pursue them nonetheless, it would result in an over-regulated society without any individual freedom. The *Frankfurters* considered this both ideologically undesirable and pragmatically impossible. Crime – including the so-called 'crimes of the powerful' – will always exist. It is therefore my conviction that we should not see it as our task to concentrate on factors that could possibly 'determine' crime or criminals, but to find a way of minimising the negative consequences of crime. Since empirical research always starts after ideological choices are made, we should, as Nils Christie mentioned in one of the workshops at the Madrid conference of the European Group, 'primarily improve the moral climate, not our empirical techniques, since criminology deals firstly with morals not with technique'. In this paper I shall therefore launch such a moral appeal.

The first question that arises then is which values should guide us? In this context Stan Cohen claims:

> By their overall commitment to "order through law" the left realists have retreated too far from the theoretical gains of twenty years ago. It hardly confronts the values behind the original destructuring vision. These values – which now only the abolitionist movement continues to proclaim – are worth at least a cautious re-affirmation.[4]

And Sebastian Scheerer says 'Only the labelling approach and the abolitionist perspective stand in the way of a reunion between critical criminology and the prevailing theory on a re-foundation of punishment'.[5] This paper is written from an abolitionist perspective

What is the relationship between abolitionism and critical criminology? Firstly, one has to admit that there would be no academic abolitionism if the 'new' criminology had not pre-existed.[6] Secondly, I see abolitionism, as I have

---

[3] Foucault made this remark in answer to people who pleaded for people's tribunals instead of criminal courts, but this warning can also be given to those who advocate the contradiction in terms of a 'socialist law and order', cf I. Taylor (1981) and J. Lea/J. Young (1984).

[4] Stanley Cohen, 'Community Control, to demystify or to re-affirm?' in Bianchi and van Swaaningen *op cit*, pp 127-133.

[5] Sebastian Scheerer, 'Neue soziale Bewegungen und Strafrecht', *Kritische Justiz*, Heft 3, 1985, p 253 (translation from the German, RvS).

[6] The (prison) abolitionist movement started on the North-American continent, from a mainly religiously inspired, grassroots activist context in the 1960s, before there was a 'radical criminology'. The academic abolitionist perspective has only been talked about since 1983, and was based on a rich heritage of phenomenological, labelling and critical criminology.

indicated above, as a reactive continuation of radical criminology - reactive especially in so far as it concerns concepts of crime[7] and victimisation. The 'grounded' labelling theory, that Dario Melossi presents as an attempt to overcome the crisis in which critical criminology is said to be, fits quite well into the abolitionist perspective — though I think we are outside of what used to be called 'radical criminology' by then.[8] In addition to an appropriate critique on the original labelling theory which was said to focus too much on stigmatisation and secondary deviance, thereby forgetting power-structures and primary deviance - and those who criticise radical criminology - as I have mentioned above - abolitionism can be seen as such a grounded theory. But we cannot consider abolitionism only as a criminological theory. Since 'crime no more determines the character of penalty than human need determines the specific nature of economy'[9] we must adopt a view that extends beyond strictly criminological issues. If abolitionist alternatives to penal interference are sought in family- school- or community-structures, or on the social work, psychiatric or medical circuit, without also denouncing the authoritarian relationships there, very little change in the punitive and repressive attitude towards deviance will result. There cannot be such a thing as a 'psychiatric alternative' to punishment, because medical psychiatry is as repressive as penal law. If one overlooks this fact, the basic assumption of abolitionism, the dissolution of all repressive reactions to deviance, is easily perverted. We really should bear in mind the great absorbing power of the state's machinery when we propose 'alternatives' which are otherwise doomed to fail.

I do not intend to present here a survey of abolitionism and an empirical description of the alternative process of dispute-settlement. That has been summarised in preliminary ways before.[10] Here I will concentrate on a possible foundation for the quite anti-governmental abolitionist vision on the legitimacy of authority, and on the necessity of personal responsibility whilst one is involved in a conflict. Let us for this purpose first examine how

---

[7] The 'new realist' position is even less subtle towards the problematisation of the notion of crime than the original radical position It implies a complete acceptance of the idea of punishment, only the criminalised group should change See Louk Hulsman, 'Critical Criminology and the Concept of Crime', in Bianchi and van Swaaningen op cit, note 2 , pp 25-42, and Contemporary Crises 10(1) 1986.

[8] Dario Melossi, 'Overcoming the Crisis in Critical Criminology toward a grounded labeling theory', Criminology 23(2) 1985, see also Haan, W. de (1987) 'Fuzzy Morals and Flakey Politics, the coming out of critical criminology' In Rolston, B. & Tomlinson, M. (eds.) Civil Rights Public Opinion and the State: Working Papers in European Criminology No. 8, Belfast: EGSDSC.

[9] David Garland and Peter Young, The Power to Punish, contemporary penalty and social analyses, Heinemann, London, 1983, p 21.

[10] For a survey of the development of the abolitionist movement, see among others Rene van Swaaningen, 'What is abolitionism? - an Introduction', in Bianchi and van Swaaningen op cit, note 2 , pp 9-25 (At the abolitionist congress in Amsterdam, in June 1985, many descriptions of mediation-projects in America and Europe were given (i.e. by Shonholtz, Northey, Gronfors, Theissen, Bussmann and Farrell).

emancipatory movements look at, use and are being tricked by authoritarian structures.

Emancipation and authority

In 1920, Clara Meijer-Wichmann, a Dutch pioneer of both feminism and abolitionism, said:

> if in the penal area one just wants to repeal some abuses within the boundaries of the prevailing system, or one holds that the penal system as a whole is wrong, [it] can hardly be a question of judicial conviction only. Questions of crime and punishment do not stand alone, they are linked with other social issues and questions about the philosophy of life.[11]

What is the view of the women's movement today on 'manifestations of power',[12] and, more precisely, on the criminal law system? Various analyses show that the women's movement developed from an intentionally anti-authoritarian and generally emancipatory movement towards an interest group for feminists which has quite a traditional, bourgeois and legalistic attitude towards power.[13] Whereas Meijer-Wichmann stressed the fact that the criminal law system functions as a servo-mechanism of the male status quo, many feminists of today embrace the penal system in their struggle against sexual violence. Axiomatically serious attention for these crimes is translated in terms of 'more severe punishment' for offenders. The unhappy feeling that these women must have, because their emancipatory demands are completely 'defined in' (to use Mathiesen's terminology) to the repressive (and definitely male) system, is rationalised by an escape clause, which the American essayist bell hooks describes as follows:

---

[11] Clara Meijer-Wichmann, *Misdaad Straf en Maatschappij*, Bijlevelt, Utrecht, 1920, p 23 (translation from the Dutch, RvS).

[12] This is the English translation of the title of my doctoral thesis (Manifestaties van Macht, overtuigen van abolitionistisch denken, Criminologisch Instituut VU, Amsterdam, 1986) in which I tried to analyse the tie-up between the power-symbols of criminal law, psychiatry, army, state, money, church, medicine, social work and nuclear family, and show how abolitionism could function as a 'reciprocal change', as Mathiesen calls it, to all their inter-related power-production. In this thesis, upon which theme this paper is based, I made use of concepts such as 'figurative interweaving' and 'self-compulsion' (Elias), 'the order of discourse' and 'normalising sanction' (Foucault), 'colonisation of life-worlds' (Habermas), 'fear of freedom' (Fromm), 'authoritarian personality' (Adorno), 'the will to power' and 're-estimation of all values' (Nietzsche), 'assensus' (Bianchi), and 'vernacular values' (Illich).

[13] Scheerer *op cit*, note 5 , p 245, Tamar Pitch, 'Critical Criminology, the construction of social problems and the question of rape', *International Journal of Sociology of Law* 1985, no 13, various articles and editorials in the Dutch magazine for women and justice, *Nemesis*.

By simply calling power "masculine", women do not need to discern their own urges of power that make them strive to domination and control over others. Because the feminist rhetorics emphasise the picture of the man being the enemy and the woman being the victim, women could easily withdraw from the task of formulating a new system of values.[14]

Within the women's movement there is, however, a great opposition both to this contribution to criminalisation - whereby the idea that using counter-violence is the right way to resolve problems, is reaffirmed - and to that weakly-argued escape clause. The Dutch feminist, Bernadette de Wit, therefore accuses the 'naive' part of the women's movement of 'victimism', by which she means the fact that women show themselves to be so addicted to their underlying position that they cannot even act differently while standing up for their rights:

Feminists keep wanting not to be held liable for the consequences of their deeds, including the way they embrace the penal system. Women, claiming to be oppressed people, say they have no influence whatsoever on what happens to their demands. Like those who really are powerless, these feminists are full of rancour and retaliatory urges. Indulging these leads them up a dead-end street, and preserves female vulnerability. It is this combination of moral purism, pubescent protest and demagogy which makes me revolt against the feminist victimism.[15]

This is one example of (a part of) a progressive social movement which outgrew its original struggle, and thereby became superfluous. The link with radical criminology should be clear. There are, however, numerous examples of this 'trend'. After the anti-psychiatry movement - in many ways the psychiatric variant of abolitionism - in Italy had been tackled, one of the first things the continuing 'democratic psychiatrists' did, was to abandon the original and essential ideological and political stipulations of anti-psychiatry, thereby removing the anti-thetic value of the movement. Continuing this 'trend', Sebastian Scheerer mentions some 'moral crusaders' from the Left who make the same mistakes as the women's movement. The

---

[14] bell hooks, 'Macht in een ander licht', *Nemesis* vol 2 (1985/6) no 3, p 106 (translation from the Dutch, RvS).

[15] Bernadette de Wit, 'Het slachtoffer is koning', *Nemesis* vol 2 (1985/6) no 2, p 65 (translation from the Dutch, RvS)

ecology/environmental movement in Germany seems now to translate its wishes into the most punitive terms in order to sound 'serious' in its necessary struggle against pollution and environmental exhaustion. Other progressives demand the curtailment of freedom of speech, when it concerns extreme Right political utterings Scheerer, citing Ostendorf, says:

> The dubious contention that criminal law would be an appropriate protector of the just historical viewpoint, is no different from that same anti-social belief that a repetition of nazi-dictatorship can be prevented by using the police to control the boundaries of legitimate political discussion.[16]

It seems as if we can rightly conclude that 'the social movements no longer wish to harm the state's authority, so long as it promises to do more for them'.[17] The 'moral panics of the Left' ask, just like those of the Right, for governmental, penal answers in order to give an impression of 'seriousness'. The sum of all these very legitimate struggles leads however to a dramatic extension of the punitive power of the state, and will definitely target the same groups as usual rather than rapists or chemical industries. These social movements should consider whether that is really consistent with their final goals. However, there are exceptions to this thesis. Anti-nuclear, gay and ethnic groups do appeal to (criminal) courts, but it cannot be said they want to, nor think they can, achieve their goals by punitive means.[18]

The clearest and most radical demystification of this belief comes, however, from the peace and pacifist/anti-militarist movements. The similarities in content between their goals and abolitionism are so clear, that it is hard to believe that they do not cooperate more, for example:

1   both the military and the penal institution localise evil in a 'suitable enemy';[19]

---

[16] Scheerer *op cit* note 5, pp 246-249, citing H. Ostendorf, 'Im Streit Die strafrechthche Verfolgung der Auschwitz-Luge', *NJW* 1985, p 1062 (translation from the German, RvS).

[17] Scheerer *op cit*, note 5 , p 245 (translation from the German, RvS).

[18] There were representatives from the American 'Taskforce for People of Color', along with many 'still competitive' feminists, participating at the abolitionist congress in Amsterdam, 1985, who claimed to have no choice but to opt for an abolitionist perspective on justice, because the criminal law perspective has chosen against them. The ambivalent relationship between social minorities - who have no one but the penal system to turn to - and criminal law, is described by Tony Ward of the English RAP, in his article 'Symbols and Noble Lies, abolitionism, just deserts, and crimes of the powerful', in Bianchi and van Swaaningen *op cit*, note 2 , pp 73-83.

[19] The 'suitable enemy' is a concept of Nils Christie's ('Suitable Enemies', in Bianchi and van Swaaningen op cit note 2 , pp 42-55) by which he means the ideal black sheep to blame, which is 'hated by the population, looking strong, but really being weak'.

2   the threat of war is merely of ideological and economic importance. Indeed 'War is Peace, Freedom is Slavery and Ignorance is Strength'.[20] Foucault described clearly the ideological and economic significance of a class of delinquents in the same way;[21]

3   both institutions monopolise the use of violence, and disqualify the 'unauthorised' use of what they do themselves by calling it terrorism and self-righteousness;

4   Both cherish the myth that their use of violence is necessary to protect 'democracy, people and fatherland' against violence.

The abolitionist movement has a lot to learn from the peace-activists, who have shown themselves able to make their aims into issues of the highest political priority in a relatively short time. A closer analysis of their strategy could positively influence the discussion about the struggle against the - just as useless - internal 'arms race' of the 'law and order brigades'. So-called 'conscientious objectors' to military service in my country today are rewarded for their active demystification of authoritarian myths by a year's imprisonment; they are caught by two repressive systems at the same time. Of course abolitionists are not persecuted (yet), but imagine what would happen if, for example, police service also became compulsory? Should these real radical criminologists then perhaps be martyrs like Johan Galtung or Jean Genet, and acquire the best possible information about the 'secondary victimisation' of the penal system and the metaphor of prison? Or should they rather become the victim of a crime - primary victimisation - in order to show to what extent theoretical propositions correspond with practice?[22]

What conclusions can be drawn from this short overview of social

---

[20] This Party-slogan from George Orwell's novel *Nineteen Eighty Four*, is the clearest example of what Orwell sees as 'double-thought', the saying of the opposite of what one actually means.

[21] Michel Foucault, *Surveiller et Punir, naissance de la prison*, Gallimard, Paris, 1975, and *Mikrophysik der Macht*, Merve Verlag, Berlin, 1976. Foucault can rightly be called an abolitionist, as De Folter does in his article on Foucault's analysis of the penal system ('On the methodological foundation of the abolitionist approach to the criminal justice system. A comparison of the ideas of Hulsman, Mathiesen and Foucault', *Contemporary Crises* vol 10 (1986) no 1, p 52). An anecdote which is worth mentioning in connection with this, is that Foucault, shortly before he died, told Herman Bianchi, who visited him to persuade him to come to the abolitionist congress in Amsterdam in June 1985, that he indeed planned to come - if only 'pour ecouter'.

[22] The secondary victimisation by the penal system strikes both the offender and the victim. Galtung is a Norwegian conscientious-objector who was imprisoned, and is now a professor of peace studies at Princeton University He developed the theories of 'structural violence' and of imperialism. Now he is working on a project on the 'U S foreign policy as manifest theology'. Genet is the thief who became a famous French writer. Until now, no criminologist has written merely from the perspective of a personal experience with the primary form of victimisation.

movements and their attitude towards power? I want to stress the need for any emancipatory movement, if it wishes to avoid paralysing pitfalls, to implement a clear vision for making use of, or gaining, power, into its final goal setting.[23] Whilst presenting a real alternative to penal interference, we should try to 'sanitise' the moral climate;[24] admit that crime is a serious matter, but at the same time stress that retaliation and punitive measures are immoral and are, moreover, of no use in solving this problem.

With the introduction of abolitionist alternatives the pitfalls are obvious and it is necessary that the abolitionist movement must be what Thomas Mathiesen calls a 'competing contradiction'. So, for example, we have to be careful not to stick to unreflected and unpolitical ideas - like that of the 'caring community'[25] which, next to the fact that it is an uninteresting notion, has some quite snugly idyllic and middle-class aspects as well. These ideas are easily 'defined in', absorbed by the repressive forces of the system, and are counterproductive for a movement that aims to be a progressive one. Next to the fundamentalist moralism, which is a metaphor for prison in itself, we can distinguish a moral nihilism; I think we should avoid both. And next to the danger of 'widening the net' by presenting fully worked-out 'alternatives', Richard Abel and Erhard Blankenburg warn that nice options such as 'de-professionalisation', 'delegalisation' and 'informalisation' also often lead in practice to the opposite of what one wants to achieve, namely an expansion of the legal system and a growing formalisation.[26] The question of what we should do despite all this, still remains open at this stage.

---

[23] In his article 'Pitfalls and Strategies of Abolition' (in Bianchi and van Swaaningen *op cit,* note 2, pp 147-157) Herman Bianchi analyses the pitfalls into which abolitionist movements have fallen in the past.

[24] One of my favourite quotes from Nils Christie's is 'Moralism within our areas has for some years been an attitude or even a term associated with protagonists for law and order and severe penal sanctions, while their opponents were seen as floating in a sort of value-free vacuum. Let it therefore be completely clear that I am also a moralist. Worse I am a moral imperialist' *(Limits to Pain,* p 10). During the discussions at the Madrid conference I found out that there were more of these 'moral imperialists' among critical criminologists than there were some five years ago when Christie wrote the statement.

[25] The idea of the 'caring community' of American (Quaker) abolitionists is among other ideas, presented in American Friends Service Committee, *Struggle for Justice,* Hill and Wang, New York, 1971, and P R E A P, *Instead of Prisons, a handbook for abolitionists* , Syracuse, New York, 1976. It is striking that the American (prison) abolitionism which came first - is so under-exposed in the European discussion. In the special 'abolitionism' issue of *Contemporary Crises* (no 1, 1986) not one word is said about this activist branch of abolitionism.

[26] Richard Abel (ed.), *The Politics of Informal Justice,* Academic Press, New York, 1982, mainly vol 1 chapter 10. Also, Erhard Blankenburg, 'Recht als gradualisiertes Konzept, Begriffsdimensionen der Diskussion um Verrechthchung und Entrechtlichung', in Blankenburg *et al* (eds), *Alternative Rechtsformen und Alternative zum Recht,* Westdeutscher Verlag, Opladen, 1979.

Authority as a de-skilling factor

Perhaps the most famous scene from Dostoyevsky's *The Brothers Karamazov* is the legend of the Great Inquisitor, who cynical answers to Jesus, when pleading for his idea of redeeming man is that: 'There is no sorrow for man that is more eternal and painful than, as soon as he is free, finding someone new to whom he can submit again'. Well, the church has certainly helped man 'to relive this sorrow through the ages'. At the very time man flees for his freedom into authoritarianism, narcissism, conformism, destructiveness and rationalism,[27] his ability to deal with conflict is given *or taken* over to, *or by,* institutions like the penal system, which quickly take on a more and more elusive character, and, in a way, institutionalise man's individual conscience into a collective set of morals. The influence we have on the reified core of these, seemingly deep-rooted, authoritarian structures is almost nil now. Nearly everyone accepts them, either by virtue of an institutionalised false interpretation of the letter to the Romans chapter 13, or of a belief in the existence of a 'social contract', which is said to have been drawn up during the period of Enlightenment. So, either authorities are axiomatically God's stand-in on earth, or the majority of people should have handed over their personal responsibility to an anonymous body. Those who think they can interpret the bible by themselves are heretics, and those who doubt the existence of such a thing as a 'volonte génerate' are rapidly depicted as enemies of democracy. In Habermas' terms, we could describe this latter 'enlightened' process as the communicative life-worlds which are being colonised by a system-rationality. The belief in a categorical, all-dividing rationality, which conflicts with the overall image of life, is, as we know from Nietzsche, bound to lead to nihilism.[28]

Why do people still believe in a system which creates moral panics in order to legitimise its expansion, and at the same time fails to influence the problem of crime in a positive way? On this question Herman Bianchi says:

> how mankind came across the fortunate idea of transferring his
> fears to a god who offers to his worshippers a safeguard for fear,

---

[27] This theory is developed by Erich Fromm in his books *Escape from Freedom*, Rinehart and Co., New York, 1941, and *The Sane Society,* Routledge and Kegan Paul Ltd., London, 1956. Criminal law is 'only' one of the authorities to which man gave over his freedom of measuring his deeds to standards of his own conscience. Other 'manifestations of power' - mentioned in note 12 - fulfil the same task.

[28] Friedrich Nietzsche, *Umwertung alter Werte*, (1886), Munchen, 1969, p 475. In this new edited, complete version of *The Will to Power (Der Wille zur Macht)* Nietzsche says in annotation no 112 'Result, the belief in rational categories is the root of nihilism - we have measured the world to categories, which are based on a purely fictitious world. It is still the hyperbolic naøvety of man to picture himself as the meaning and measure of things ' (translation from the German, RvS).

or how one can buy for intolerance protection against fear, or a mythology of the authoritarian personality, for an attempt at exorcism.

The image of power is that of the *Lord of the Flies*.[29] Foucault is only too right when he states that power cannot only be described in negative terms – it excludes, it represses and so on. The most important quality of power is that it produces; it produces the 'discourse of truth' on every level of reality. It produces normality and tries to wipe out all diversity between people and their cultural backgrounds, by offering a panacea solution for the most diverse situations. It creates a reality, but one that does not correspond with the reality of daily life. By claiming to bring order into the 'complex' society, alienation and complexity are indeed created.[30] The very rationale of power thus creates 'minorities, deviance and compulsive normalisation of life-styles', as is criticised in the Spring 1986 *Newsletter* of the European Group. The belief that we are dependent on authorities to solve all problems for us easily leads to an authoritarian idolatry - the *Lord of the Flies* syndrome - that results in the so-called 'victimist' attitude I described in the second section of this paper.

It is far from coincidental that Foucault analysed our criminal law system as one that has developed from a 'torture-model', via the nineteenth century 'punishment model', to the post-Industrial Revolution 'discipline-model', in which the function of the sanction came to 'normalise' all deviance, *i.e.* adapt it, and transform it into a suitable element of the capitalist mode of production.[31] In my opinion, social movements can expect little help from a penal system that has 'de-skilled'[32] it's 'worshippers' from dealing with their problems by themselves, and provides such 'super-constructing'[33] and

---

[29] Herman Bianchi, *De vliegengod: opstellen over gezag recht en orde (The Lord of the Flies: essays on authority, law and order),* Samson, Alphen a/d Rijn, 1967, p 11 (translation from the Dutch, RvS).

[30] This was stated by Louk Hulsman in his valedictory address to the Erasmus University, Rotterdam, on 19th June 1986, entitled 'Recht doen aan verscheidenheid' ('Doing justice to diversity'). He argued that the criminal law system threatens diversity, and illustrated it with Habermas' theory on the colonisation of the life-worlds (from his 'blue monster', *Theorie des Kommunikativen Handels,* Frankfurt a/M, 1981) which I described in the preceding paragraph. According to Hulsman, the abolitionist perspective does more 'justice to diversity' and corresponds better with the reality of daily life than does any abstract law/order system. Also, Hulsman, *op cit* note 7 , and, Gerhnda Smaus, 'Gesellschaftsmodelle in der abohtionistische Bewegung', *Krimmologisches Journal* no 1, 1986.

[31] These ideal-types of social control are developed by Foucault in his book *Discipline and Punish the birth of the prison, op cit* note 22.

[32] The word 'de-skilled', which is developed by the lawyer and founder/director of the community-boards of San Francisco, Raymond Shonholtz, means that mankind is being made unable to solve any problem by itself, by the expansionist and imperialist character of all kinds of 'professionals', who all create their own 'market' The idea has close links with the theories of Ivan Illich.

[33] A super-constructing idea is an idea that re-affirms and strengthens the status-quo. This concept is

normalising ideas as punitive sanctions. Put in the friendliest possible way, one could say that penal sanctions are the evident proof of the impotence really to do something about the wishes and demands of the social movements. These groups are indeed potential allies of the abolitionist perspective, in the sense in which their particular views determine how problems will be defined - instead of translating something as breach of some untouchable legal order - and finding what would be the best (or least bad, since many problems simply cannot really be solved) solution to it.[34] I am quite aware of the fact that this 'progress optimism' has little foundation in real life, but I feel that I would no longer be sincere, if I were only 'playing' theoretical 'games' of giving easy negative criticism from a safe, luxurious university post, without at least trying to achieve a more positive goal.

About victimism and self-righteousness

'The deviation is as normal as the normal. This leads to the conclusion that tolerance towards diversity is a life-necessity for the order itself', argues Bianchi.[35] This implies that 'democracy' should be more than the dictatorship of the majority, and that 'justice' means more than just the arbitrary interpretations of majority agreements by a legislative assembly. The tolerance that Bianchi means does not lead to the conclusion that we should approach crime with some kind of 'radical non-intervention', as Schur has proposed.[36] The word 'tolerance' is too often already misused, especially in the Netherlands, as a euphemism for moral nihilism, repressive tolerance or plain recklessness. But, on the other hand, the 'solution' of stigmatising and penalising behaviour which one cannot tolerate, leads to adapting the definition of this behaviour to the standards of the hegemonic ideology. And that is counter-productive for any emancipatory goal. Each 'crime', and each victim, is worthy of an approach that accords to the particular context of the situation. That is the tolerance abolitionists think is necessary; there is no such thing as a panacea solution to all the different sub-cultural and individual implications of all that is united under the penal banner such as 'murder', 'theft' or 'insult'.

The abolitionist answer to the question of how else to approach it is quite

---

developed by Thomas Mathiesen in his book *Law Society and Political Action towards a strategy under late- capitalism*, Academic Press, London, 1980.

[34] The implementing of diversity into the definition process is developed by Herman Bianchi in his theory of 'assensus', 'dissensus' and 'consensus', *op cit*, note 2 , pp 113-127 (and Bianchi 1979,1980, 1985), and by Louk Hulsman in distinguishing between 'anascopic' and 'catascopic' views on crime, *op cit*, note 7 (and Hulsman and Bernat de Celis 1982).

[35] Bianchi *op cit* note 30, p 78.

[36] Schur, E. (1973) *Radical non-intervention,* Princeton: Prentice Hall.

simple. If we want to put a stop to an undesirable situation, and we want our personal views and wishes to play a role in the settlement of the conflict, we should not just rely on some kind of authority to do it for us. We should take up our personal responsibility as well; before, during and after a criminalisable conflict. This seems logical, but as has been said, people prefer to believe in complex rationalisations rather than in their own abilities. 'Simpleness' is therefore all too often written off as 'simplicity'. Even though classical thinkers, like Herakleitos and Nietzsche have convincingly stated that conflict is the arch-principle of man's nature, people seem to show only complete incompetence in this matter. Growing interest in the role of the victim has resulted, so far, in little more than an agreement that victims should be provided with more information on 'their case'. They are allowed to be informed, but hardly a word is spoken about giving them any real, guiding influence on the process. People seem to prefer to remain in their dependent, victimist position than to reclaim their stolen property – conflict[37] and eventually to ask an independent third party to assist them, instead of the other way around - them assisting the prosecution.

The opposite of victimism is self-righteousness. In the Netherlands a psychology advisor to the Amsterdam police-forces, Frans Denkers, has broken the taboo on this aspect of criminology.[38] Pleading for a more tolerant attitude towards self-righteousness, Denkers sets out some guidelines to determine under what conditions victims and bystanders should be allowed to take the situation into their own hands. Although in all these conditions he stressed the preventive and non-violent[39] character of legitimate interference, reactions to his ideas were quite negative. Although there is an obvious risk in approving self-righteousness 'officially', the critics were, in a way, surprising. Firstly, because these ideas fit quite well into the common-sense logic of the population, and secondly, because a government commission[40] has recently made comparable recommendations concerning the most appropriate reactions to petty crimes such as shoplifting, vandalism

---

[37] Bianchi op cit note 1, see in this context also De Folter's fourth conclusion op cit note 22, p 59.

[38] Frans Denkers, Oog om oog, tand om tand, en andere normen voor eigenrichting (An eye for an eye and other norms for self-righteousness), Koninklijke Vermande by, Lelystad, 1985.

[39] Denkers does not reject the use of physical force, but he does state that it must be minimised to a reflexive, proportionate and subsidiary use, in situations when it is inevitable for one's defence. These conditions are even stricter than the legal regulations for policemen in this matter op at note 38 pp 41-48.

[40] The government commission referred to is the 'Commissie kleine cnminahteit' (Commission on petty criminality) under the presidency of the social-democrat politician H. J. Roethof. With regard to the links with abolitionism see two articles by advisors to this Commission, Erhard Blankenburg De Commissie van de Sociale Controle, in Tijdschrift voot Criminologie, October 1985, and Jacquelien Soetenhorst-de Savornin Lohman Onophoudelijk de twijfel over dit systeem aanwakkeren, in KRI-katern De Afschaffers', June 1985.

and illegal use of public transport. Both Denkers and the state's commission stressed that the police, even if they wanted to, can by no means offer direct protection against offences being committed, and that the parties directly involved must be willing to play a more active role themselves - mainly by the more obvious presence of a soft social control which will prevent people from committing these offences. If people do not feel any responsibility themselves, they cannot expect the police or the judge to do so.

However, where it concerns offences with a more emotional impact, the risks connected with self-righteousness increase rapidly. The first argument mentioned in the paragraph above should make us especially wary. It has been shown in the past that a *gesundes Volksempfinden* - being the collective of all common-sense logic - is not such a good standard for a penal policy. Since people are deskilled by the 'anomic'[41] criminal law system, which itself sets a very bad example concerning the use of violence, people's reactions to deviance are also incompetent and punitive, especially when there is emotional involvement. We saw this danger lately in Amsterdam, in the - fortunately brief - experience we had with so-called 'neighbourhood watch' groups. They turned out to be far from preventive, but were rather an extension of penal reactions. Therefore, one of the conditions for legitimate self-righteousness is, according to Denkers, that it should not be organised in groups. Particularly in groups, the internalisation of outside coercion, which develops towards a coercion that comes from the inside,[42] accelerates in a dangerous way. A re-skilling process starts with a discernment of this form of 'operant conditioning' in education.

A summarising conclusion

What should the abolitionist position be? A victimist attitude, even in its most modest form, should be rejected, because it has proved too often to be the end of any competitive and contradictory force. It turns all emancipatory strivings into authoritarian idolatry and dependency. To exclude all misunderstanding, it must be stressed that the assistance we - as bystanders - or the police must offer to the (physical, verbal, social or financial) weaker

---

[41] Anomie is a concept of Emile Durkheim, by which he indicates an existential situation of alienation and disintegration. Bianchi uses this anomie-concept (not Merton's) to describe the criminal law system. Bianchi's ideal is an eunomic (= good working norms or guidelines) system of responsive and reparative law. See his book *Gerechtigheid als vrijplaats: de terugkeer van het slachtoffer in ons recht (Justice as sanctuary the return of the victim into our legal system)*, Ten Have, Baarn, 1985, chapter 3.

[42] As we are taught by Norbert Elias theory on self-compulsion in his book *Uber den Prozess der Zivilisation Soziogenetische und Psychogenetische Untersuchungen* Falken Basel 1939, and about the accelerating influence of the group on this process, Erich Fromm's concept of the flight into conformism *op cit*, note 28 , or Nietzsche's ideas on slave-morals and herd-mentality, *op at,* note 29.

party against the more powerful, has nothing to do with 'victimism' of this weaker party, but rather it is the social duty of the stronger! It is the police's repressive function that is to be abolished, not their protective and preventive one. The problem about these functions of the police which we can see collapsing nowadays would in this case disappear as well. This, of course, implies a completely different education and organisation for the police. It must be understood in this context that I am suggesting that positive and preventive self-righteousness must be stimulated. Even in emotional situations it cannot be excluded, but the possibility of over-stepping the boundary between reasonable and proportionate reaction should be given serious consideration, just like any other criminalised deed. Surely what is to be considered as a 'serious' reaction will not be a punitive one!

Along with this, we should develop an 'ability of unbelief' in response to the discourse of truth of the 'professionals in charge'. With such an Illichian suspiciousness, people will rid themselves of the authoritarian idolatry. Ignorance is the main motor of the Right-wing populism of the law and order politics. The 'exorcism' of the myth of the *Lord of the flies*, to which Bianchi refers, should be accompanied by a 'cautious re-affirmation' of positive, contradictory values such as 'neighbourhood', 'solidarity' and 'humanity'; if only because these values 'still sound better than dependence on bureaucracies and professions'.[43] The realisation of these pretentions will start with the conscientious provision of information and education on the issue of deviance and social control, which would include a recognition of the ways in which people are conditioned to deal with conflict. This would be helpful in influencing public opinion - which right from the beginning should be favourable: in improving the moral climate; in enabling people to regard penal sanctions as the greater evil; and perhaps even re-skilling them in those 'innate dispute-settlement capacities'[44] which have been repressed for such a long time. In my opinion, academics should be more involved in existing abolitionist movements[45] when starting out with some kind of practical

---

[43] Stanley Cohen, *Visions of Social Control crime punishment and classification* Polity Press Cambridge, 1985 p 267.

[44] Raymond Shonholtz 'New Justice Theories and Practice', in Bianchi and van Swaaningen *op cit*, note 2.

[45] In the special issue of the German *Krimmologisches Journal* in which a great many articles on abolitionism have been published through the years - on the development of twenty years critical criminology (I Betheft 1986) *ie* Quensel states (on p 22) that the time had come for the abolitionist perspective to evolve into a *practice oriented* abolitionist movement, as if there had not already been such a movement on the American continent for a long time. Moreover, it often seems forgotten that many abolitionist thoughts arc also developed within European prison movements, not only the Norwegian KROM that Mathiesen (1974) has written about, but also *ie* SON (Norway) KRUM (Sweden), RAP, PROP (England) KRAK Initiative fur eine bessere Kriminalpolitik (FRG), KRIM (Denmark and Finland) BWO, Stichting Vrij Delinkwentie en Samenleving and Coornhert-Liga (Netherlands),

translation of abolitionism, because most of these groups have been active for about twenty years. So why re-invent the wheel? If the victim-perspective is included in their analyses, these movements could function as fruitful abolitionist platforms.

Although there are many other possible strategies, the abolitionist alternative of eunomic,[46] responsive and reparative law should, in my opinion, evolve in a dialectic relationship with the anomic, autonomous and repressive system of criminal law, which, for so long as is thought necessary, can continue to set limits to the 'limits to pain'[47] in order to prevent a perverted form of self-righteousness based purely on rancour and retaliatory urges. In the two-tier- system that would follow, people should be given the opportunity to choose between the two ways of dealing with conflict. In that case abolitionists must be given a fair chance to show that their options do more for both victims and offenders, are more suited for emancipatory goals and offer better possibilities for minimising the use of violence. If so-called 'alternatives' do not just want to work out as extensions of punitive measures, and only deal with those cases that otherwise would be unlikely to be handled at all - as is often the case - there should be given a (legal?) guarantee that the prosecution loses its right to prosecute if the conflict is dealt with alternatively. This suspension of the right to prosecute is the basic idea of Bianchi's proposal of the re-introduction of sanctuaries.[48] It is important that 'alternative' conflict managers should bear in mind the notion of resisting the hidden seduction to act like an authority themselves. If not, the distance between daily life and 'justice' remains, and nothing but the name of the 'trial' will change after all. They should try to set a good example, not to condition people as 'ideal' citizens and to promise them, by once more excluding their responsibilities, a more righteous society. That too is the ability of unbelief!

(together with the first two of these organisations the Dutch League for Human Rights initiated an action group for a moratorium on prison construction. About this Comite Bajesstop I refer to my article Uitbreiden of Afschaffen Feit en Fictie? Enige argumenten tegen de capaciteitsuitbreiding bij het gevangeniswezen' in *Proces* 1/1987) GIP COSYPE (France) Liberarsi dalla necessiti del carecre (Italy) and PAG (the Australian prisoners movement which George Zdenkowski and David Brown wrote about in their The Prison Struggle changing Australia's penal system, Penguin Books Australia, Victoria, (1982))

[46] The opposite of anomic, i.e. integrating, communicative, stimulating self-activity, etc. *op cit* Bianchi, note 41, pp 57-70

[47] This is a variant in title of 11 6, 'Limits to limits', of the abolitionist classic by Nils Christie, *Limits to Pain*, Universitetsforlaget, Oslo, 1981

[48] *Op cit*, Bianchi, note 41, pp 171-211

Bibliography

Abel, R. (ed.) (1982) *The Politics of Informal Justice*, New York: Academic Press.

American Friends Service Committee, (1971) *Struggle for Justice,* New York: Hill and Wang.

Becker, H.(1963) *Outsiders: studies in the sociology of deviance*, New York: The Free Press.

Bernadette de Wit, J (1985) 'Het slachtoffer is koning', *Nemesis* vol. 2, no. 2.

Bianchi, H. (1967) *De vliegengod: opstellen over gezag recht en orde (The Lord of the Flies: essays on authority, law and order)*, Samson, Alphen a/d Rijn.

Bianchi, H (1985) *Gerechtigheid als vrijplaats: de terugkeer van het slachtoffer in ons recht (Justice as sanctuary the return of the victim into our legal system)*, Ten Have, Baarn.

Bianchi, H. (1986) 'Abolition Assensus and Sanctuary', in H. Bianchi and R. van Swaaningen (eds) *Abolitionism, towards a non-repressive approach to crime*, Amsterdam: Free University Press.

Bianchi, H. (1986) 'Pitfalls and Strategies of Abolition' H. Bianchi and R. van Swaaningen (eds) *Abolitionism, towards a non-repressive approach to crime*, Amsterdam: Free University Press.

Blankenburg, E. (1979) 'Recht als gradualisiertes Konzept, Begriffsdimensionen der Diskussion um Verrechthchung und Entrechtlichung', in Blankenburg *et al* (eds), *Alternative Rechtsformen und Alternative zum Recht,* Westdeutscher Verlag, Opladen.

Blankenburg, E. (1985) De Commissie van de Sociale Controle, in *Tijdschrift voot Criminologie*, October 1985

Christie, N. (1977) 'Conflicts as Property', *British Journal of Criminology,* 17(1)

Christie, N. (1981) *Limits to Pain*, Oslo: Universitetsforlaget.

Christie, N. (1986) 'Suitable Enemies', in H. Bianchi and R. van Swaaningen (eds.) *Abolitionism, towards a non-repressive approach to crime*, Amsterdam: Free University Press, pp 42-55

Cohen, S (1985) *Visions of Social Control crime punishment and classification* Cambridge: Polity Press.

Cohen, S.(1986) 'Community Control, to demystify or to re-affirm?', in in H. Bianchi and R. van Swaaningen (eds) *Abolitionism, towards a non-repressive approach to crime*, Amsterdam: Free University Press.

De Folter, R.S. (1986) 'On the methodological foundation of the abolitionist approach to the criminal justice system. A comparison of the ideas of Hulsman, Mathiesen and Foucault', *Contemporary Crises* vol. 10, no. 1. Pp. 39-62

Denkers, F. (1985) *Oog om oog, tand om tand, en andere normen voor eigenrichting (An eye for an eye and other norms for self-righteousness)*, Koninklijke Vermande by, Lelystad.

Elias, N. (1939) *Uber den Prozess der Zivilisation Soziogenetische und Psychogenetische Untersuchungen* Falken Basel.

Foucault, M. (1975) *Surveiller et Punir, naissance de la prison*, Gallimard, Paris.

Foucault, M. (1976) *Mikrophysik der Macht*, Merve Verlag, Berlin.

Fromm, E. (1941) *Escape from Freedom*, Rinehart and Co., New York

Fromm, E. (1956) *The Sane Society,* Routledge and Kegan Paul Ltd., London.

Garland, D. and Young, P. (1983) *The Power to Punish, contemporary penalty and social analyses*, Heinemann, London.

Haan, W. de (1987) 'Fuzzy Morals and Flakey Politics, the coming out of critical criminology' In Rolston, B. & Tomlinson, M. (eds.) *Civil Rights Public Opinion and the State: Working Papers in European Criminology No. 8,* Belfast: EGSDSC.

Habermas, J. (1981) *Theorie des Kommunikativen Handels*, Frankfurt a/M.

hooks, b. (1985) 'Macht in een ander licht', *Nemesis* vol. 2, no. 3,

Hulsman, L. and Bernat de Celis, J. (1982) *Peines perdues. Le système penal en question,* Ed. du Centurion.

Hulsman, L. (1986) 'Critical Criminology and the Concept of Crime', *Contemporary Crises* 10(1) pp 63-80

Hulsman, L. (1986) 'Recht doen aan verscheidenheid' ('Doing justice to diversity'), valedictory address to the Erasmus University, Rotterdam.

Lea, J. and Young, J. (1984) *What is to be Done about Law and Order?* London: Pluto.

Mathiesen, T. (1974) *The Politics of Abolition*, Oxford: Martin Robertson.

Mathiesen, T. (1980) *Law Society and Political Action towards a strategy under late- capitalism,* Academic Press, London.

Meijer-Wichmann, C. (1920) *Misdaad Straf en Maatschappij*, Bijlevelt, Utrecht.

Melossi, D. (1985) 'Overcoming the Crisis in Critical Criminology toward a grounded labeling theory', *Criminology* 23(2) pp. 193-208

Nietzsche, F. (1886/1969) *Umwertung alter Werte*, Munchen.

Pitch, T. (1985) 'Critical Criminology, the construction of social problems and the question of rape', *International Journal of Sociology of Law* 1985, no 13,

P R E A P, (1976) *Instead of Prisons, a handbook for abolitionists* , Syracuse, New York.

Scheerer, S. (1985) 'Neue soziale Bewegungen und Strafrecht', *Kritische Justiz*, Heft 3.

Shonholtz, R. (1986) 'New Justice Theories and Practice', in H. Bianchi and R. van Swaaningen (eds) *Abolitionism, towards a non-repressive approach to crime*, Amsterdam: Free University Press.

Smaus, G. (1986) 'Gesellschaftsmodelle in der abohtionistische Bewegung', *Krimmologisches Journal* no 1

Soetenhorst-de Savornin, J (1985) 'Lohman Onophoudelijk de twijfel over dit systeem aanwakkeren', in KRI-katern De Afschaffers', June 1985.

Swaaningen, R. van (1986) Manifestaties van Macht, overtuigen van abolitionistisch denken, Unpublished PhD Criminologisch Instituut VU, Amsterdam.

Swaaningen, R. van (1986) 'What is abolitionism? - an Introduction', in H. Bianchi and R. van Swaaningen (eds) *Abolitionism, towards a non-repressive approach to crime*, Amsterdam: Free University Press.

Swaaningen, R. van (1987) Uitbreiden of Afschaffen Feit en Fictie? Enige argumenten tegen de capaciteitsuitbreiding bij het gevangeniswezen' in *Proces* 1.

Taylor, I. (1981) *Law and Order: Arguments for Socialism,* London: Macmillian Press

Ward, T. (1986) 'Symbols and Noble Lies, abolitionism, just deserts, and crimes of the powerful', in H. Bianchi and R. van Swaaningen (eds) *Abolitionism, towards a non-repressive approach to crime*, Amsterdam: Free University Press.

Zdenkowski, G. and Brown, D. (1982) *The Prison Struggle changing Australia's penal system*, Penguin Books Australia, Victoria.

11.

Sexual Violence, Criminal Law and Abolitionism

Marijke Meima

This paper was delivered at the European Group's 16th annual conference in Synnseter fjellstue, Norway and first published in Working Papers in European Criminology, Volume 10 'Gender, Sexuality and Social Control' in 1990.

Introduction

Almost from the first days of my law study at the University of Groningen I was fascinated by the phenomenon of prison. More and more, my fascination made way for astonishment and abhorrence. What keeps astonishing me is that prison – and with it the whole criminal law system – is so easily accepted both by 'lay' people and by experts as, at best, a 'necessary evil'. All too eagerly we seem to translate our feelings-of-justice-that-has-to-be-restored into the acceptance of the present criminal law system, taking the obvious disadvantages for granted because of a supposed lack of alternatives, and not bothering ourselves with questions as to whether or not the grounds of this system are 'just' anyway.

I will start with some notions on sexual violence; then I will describe what happens in the present criminal law system. Next I will try to distil some abolitionist views and suggestions apt for approaching the situation of sexual violence, and last but not least I will compare both ways of dealing with the problem and see if each of them live up to their promises.

About Sexual Violence

I have no intention of exhaustively discussing all the ins and outs of the subject of sexual violence. I will limit myself to summing up three different types of aspects that are related to this subject. But first what is sexual violence? There is of course a lot to be said about it and many books have been written about it. For my purpose in this paper a general definition will do: sexual violence is there where a person forces another person, by whatever means, into sexual contact. To avoid unnecessary complications, I will in this paper refer to the situation of a man forcing a woman.

There are three types of aspects, as I said. First of all there are those aspects related to the personal circumstances of both the man and the woman in question. Some men rape out of anger, others out of habit, and others again because they are drunk or because they think they have the right to 'take' their own wife 'with a little force'. Some women feel raped when their bed partner fails to consider their feelings, others don't feel raped because they had a drink with the man before it happened. Some men are sorry or ashamed for what they have done, others don't even know what they did and others again will be scared of what consequences may follow. Some women are helped by their close friends or relatives, others are talked into feelings of guilt because of being out so late or smiling too seductively. Some women can cope with the harm that was done to them after some time, others will suffer from agony for the rest of their lives.

Then there are the aspects related to the relationship or non-relationship of the man and the woman in question. Thus a man may start an incestuous relationship with his daughter because the same situation existed at home in his youth. And this daughter may develop a deep fear of physical intimacy because it was her father who had intercourse with her and thus made her home insecure instead of safe. A man may attack and abuse a perfect stranger because he feels dominated by all the women he knows. And this woman may develop a fear of going outside, because she can see no logical link between her going out last time and her being raped then, which means she can take no measures to avoid a second attack. These are only two examples, there are many, many more, like that of sexual violence within marriage or at work. To the complex of problems, causes and consequences a third type of aspect can be added that of the societal causes of sexual violence. In spite of the many achievements of the feminist movement, we still live in a male-dominated society. Different criteria are used to judge male and female sexuality, and apart from the sexual field many people have problems when a woman:

- directs a group of men;
- is taller, older of better educated than her husband;
- has a job outside while her husband is at home to take care of the children;
- chooses a technical profession, *etc.*

Not only the causes, but also the consequences of sexual violence have an impact on (parts of) society. Thus for example, sometimes relatives and friends call for even harsher punishment than the woman whom it concerns.

About the Criminal Justice System

The state implies that the answer to the problem of sexual violence lies in the criminal law system. Besides that, there is the system of subvention. But whereas subsidies granted to groups such as 'Women against rape' are threatened by the axe, expenditures for police and prisons only seem to grow. The sixties, with their flower power and make-love-not-war mentality are definitely over.

The line above goes, *mutatis mutantis*, for the whole field of 'crime'. As far as sexual violence is concerned, the government's no-nonsense policies against crime find support from an unexpected direction - from large parts of the feminist movement. At first when feminists started to ask for attention for sexual violence, and especially for its societal origins, they unsuspectingly asked the criminal justice system to help them fight it. By now there are others within the feminist movement (I'm talking about the Dutch situation) who reject the help of this system because they regard it as a suppressive and male dominated weapon. But still many feminists join in the choir that calls for the criminalisation of more sexual offences and higher penalties for sexual violators.

In this and the next sections I will find my way into both systems - although abolitionism is in reality not a system - along three steps; firstly the norm and how it has been worked out, secondly the apparatus and finally the result.

1   The norm and how it has been worked out

The right of physical and sexual self determination has been laid down in several articles of the criminal code (I am still talking about the Dutch situation). 'Punishability' is confined to those deeds of sexual violence that can be placed within the boundaries of the legal definition, *i.e.* within the words of the legal text. The trespasser is threatened with one or several sanction(s). Goals of such articles in the criminal code are:

1. public declaration of the norm of sexual/physical self-determination, and
2. keeping the citizens away from violating this norm by threatening them with punishment.

2   The apparatus

Those who trespass, in spite of the prohibition in the law, risk being confronted with an extensive apparatus, employing thousands of people. First of all they have to deal with the *police*, who try to find them (if they are unknown or hidden) in order to find out what has happened. The police can, with the purpose of 'finding the truth', employ several weapons, such as incarceration, interrogation, the opening of letters, *etc.* When the police think they have found the truth, they hand the case over to the *public prosecutor*, who will investigate it again, and if he thinks there is enough evidence, he will summon the trespasser to appear in court. The *judge* then will – on the basis of all the papers in the dossier and of what happens in the court-room – decide:

- whether the man has actually done exactly what the public prosecutor accuses him of in his writ, and exactly at the time and in the place and way as described, and if so
- whether what the man has done according to the public prosecutor and judge is punishable by law, that is
- whether it fits within the text of any article in the law and whether there are no circumstances that remove this punishability, if the act is indeed punishable
- whether the man himself deserves punishment (*i.e.* if he couldn't help it because of insanity, he should not be punished - in that case it might be necessary to lock him up in a mental hospital).

If the judge decides that the man is guilty and deserves punishment, he will convict him to be locked up in prison for a fixed period of time or to pay a certain amount of money to the state, both of these sanctions can, by the way, also be imposed conditionally. Recently the possibility has been created to offer 'petty' offenders a chance to perform community service instead of a prison sentence. After the verdict the man will probably meet the fourth and fifth instances the *prison authorities* and/or the *'parole board' (reclassering)*.

To summarise after the first three instances along this road there is a moment of possible escape - either because there is not enough legal evidence to prove that the man 'has done it' (the formal escape), or because the functionary in charge is willing to give other solutions (like 'making it up' or paying financial indemnities) a chance first (the informal escape).

3   The result

If the way through the criminal justice instances has led to imprisonment or another sanction, this outcome can be described as the result from the criminal justice strategy. Among the writers there seems to be agreement on the following goals (not only in the case of sexual violence, but in relation to the punishment of crime in general):

a)   keeping others away from doing the same, by setting an example of 'what happens when you do this or that';
b)   keeping the man in question from doing it again, at best by resocializing him, at worst by deterring him;
c)   preventing people taking the law into their own hands.

Goals cannot, of course, legitimate what is done. Therefore we need a more profound explanation. The basic ground of our criminal justice system, in my view, can be nothing but retaliation, the knowing or feeling that wrongdoing must be equalized, must be paid for in equal terms. Whether or not any of these goals or grounds are realized by the criminal law system will be the subject of the last section of this paper.

About Abolitionism

Before tracing the three aspects - norm, apparatus and result - I will say a little about what I conceive of as abolitionism and its main characteristics.

I think I can safely define abolitionism as the movement, grass-roots as well as academic, which tries to reach the diminishing and finally the abolition of the criminal law system (its rationale as well as its institutions). What is, in my view and especially within the context of this paper, one of the most important characteristics, is that it does not simply suggest replacing one system with another. The moment I heard of abolitionism I was attracted by its ideas, as like the abolitionists, I had come to the conclusion that imprisonment is unproductive, inhumane and illogical. But the more I learned about it, the more I found out that abolitionism is above all a different way of looking at and thinking about reality. What makes crimes so different from other types of ill, destructive, annoying or anti-social behaviour that we should need a complete and elaborated repressive system to respond to them? It seems to me that anyone who answers this question by stating 'nothing really' is on the road to abolitionism. And if you go along that road you will find no reasons to replace the criminal law system with another system doing similar things under different names. At least that is my experience until now. So, what is involved is a different way of thinking and not just another system.

But the disadvantage of what is not yet is that it is so theoretical. We have no experience with the absence of criminal law in our modern society. And so whoever tries to think of what would be just is challenged to sketch the outlines of how the good ideas would turn out in everyday life. And these outlines of course risk taking the shape of new structures. What distinguishes the abolitionist outlines principally from the criminal law system is, in my opinion, the change of roles. In our present system, the state is first and last the judge in matters of criminality. In the abolitionist perspective, the state will play no more than a background role, the first to decide are the parties in a conflict - whatever the nature of this conflict may be - and only if and when one of them calls in the help of the state, its role will increase, and even then only as much as the parties will let it increase. The state's role will thus be facilitating rather than dominant. And the structures fitting into an abolitionist perspective are really no more than a framework. No solution is prescribed in general, like in our penal codes. What must be done in this particular case must be decided in this particular case, which leaves of course a lot to the creativity of the persons in question. Now my focus switches to the three aspects of the abolitionist way.

1 The norm and how it has been worked out

Most people, and abolitionists are no exception, agree with the statement that sexual violence is wrong. Abolitionists, however, will stress the complexity of each specific situation and the coexistence in our modern society of many sub-circles with their own norms and rules and habits, rather than convicting all those who committed any form of sexual violence to a harsh and uniform punishment. Consequently they will invite those whom it concerns to try - if possible - to find a common version of what happened, and at least to try to reach an agreement on what should be done to restore or pay for what has been damaged, instead of locking a certain way of behaviour up in a phrase in the criminal code and trying to fit what has been done into the description of this article in the law.

2 The apparatus

I discern two sides to the aspect of the apparatus. First of all the abolitionist dislike of formal instances and regulations, and on the other hand the need to provide concrete suggestions as to how a country which has abolished the criminal law system should be organized. Consequently abolitionists suggest that we should make do with as little structure as possible. When a man has raped a woman, it is first of all the two of them who have a conflict that needs solving. Of course it is far too simple to propose that this woman should just tell this man what she thinks of him and what she thinks he should do to pay. She may be scared, she will probably be very much distressed, and she may not even know his name or where to find him. And he may threaten her or simply deny her accusation. But whatever practical problems there are, it is in the abolitionist view essential to recognize that the conflict is not between the state and the offender, but first of all between the parties directly concerned. Then, to become practical, what should happen to our criminal justice apparatus?

The police should no doubt stay. Even in a country where conflict-solving between the parties concerned is a normal thing, a rapist will not turn up at the woman's door the next day to solve the conflict he has caused. Public prosecutors and criminal law judges could turn around and find work in the civil law sections of their courts. The role of the civil law system will, as will become clear, be increased.[1] As for the prison system, that could really be abolished - but we would still need some provisions to keep people in custody for a little while, *e.g.* to cool down. And the parole board employees could become ordinary social workers. These would be the outer reforms - or, to be more precise, the abolitionist part of them - in a nutshell.

There is, however, a constructive part to abolitionism as well. In general, abolitionists plead for a facilitating state role. This role could consist of, for example:

- the creation of a climate in which It Is normal that conflicts are solved as closely to where they arose as possible;
- the provision of room and experts to accompany processes of negotiating;
- the control of the power equilibrium between the negotiating parties;
- the administration of justice in case the parties cannot reach agreement.

In the case of sexual violence all this could mean that the woman who has suffered any form of sexual violence can call her attacker to account. If necessary she can ask the police to help her find him or to protect her. She

---

[1] Editors' note: For a subsequent discussion of the potential role of civil courts in relation to sexual violence see Karen Leander (2013) 'The Decade of Rape' in Joanna Gilmore, J.M. Moore and David Scott (eds.) *Critique and Dissent: An Anthology to mark 40 years of the European Group for the Study of Deviance and Social Control*, Ottawa: Red Quill Books

could also ask friends or relatives to take her place, if she is too scared or too much battered (physically or emotionally). In a process of negotiating, which should take place in a neutral and safe surrounding, both she and her adversary can give their own versions of what has happened and how they think about each other. After that she can declare what she wants to happen now. Although her wish is not a command, it is the starting point for the negotiations. Also during negotiations she can ask others to represent her if she is scared or distressed or lacking energy.

Apart from representation both parties can let themselves be assisted by relatives, friends and experts. A so-called third party should watch the balance of power, to prevent the abuse of power. If the parties cannot reach an agreement, they can try to agree at least on asking an independent person to help them, for example a common acquaintance, an expert or a committee of arbitration. If nothing works at all, or if the man refuses to turn up to account for his behaviour, there is the final possibility of the civil judge, who could, after hearing both parties extensively, impose compensation or something like a street prohibition or any other measure that seems fit.

The direct aim of this approach is conflict solving. Other goals, like prevention or resocialisation or correction, depend on what both parties intend. In the background there is the long term aim of reconciliation, which is, however, especially in cases of sexual violence, very often no more than an illusion.

3   The result

The number of possible results is endless, all depends mainly on what agreement is reached between the parties in dispute. One could think of an agreement that the man would:

- pay compensation for financial and emotional harm, and/or
- take a course on the traditional role patterns between men and women and possible alternatives, and/or
- accede to a street (or town or park) prohibition being imposed, and/or
- have a few meetings with a group of women who have had the terrible experience of being raped and are willing to talk about it, and/or
- move to another (part of) town, and/or
- find another job, *etc.*

All these results have no other aim than what the parties (and especially the woman) choose as an aim. As to the basic ground of this way of dealing with sexual violence, there are no other grounds than those in civil law. People are responsible for their own deeds, they solve their own conflicts and if they cannot reach agreement, they call in the help of the state, whereby the desire for retaliation is recognized as a strong and motivating emotion, but not as a claim of justice to be imposed - if moderately - by the state.

Evaluation

I have described two ways of responding to the phenomenon of sexual violence. In this last section I will compare the two and try to find out if they have any chance of living up to what they promise or what they strive for.

1   The norm and how it has been worked out

Both abolitionists and criminal law adherents will probably agree on the fact that the state has a responsibility in relation to the problem of sexual violence. They seem to differ however on what this responsibility consists of. The present system of criminal justice sees mainly two goals; firstly that the state should publicly declare that sexual violence is not allowed; and secondly that citizens should be kept from committing sexual violence by means of a threat of punishment.

The first of these goals seems to be self-evident. Even if it is not very effective, it won't do any harm. About the effectiveness of an article in the law in respect of the second goal there is no unanimity. There seems to be no absolute proof that a penal provision in the criminal code keeps people from committing the prohibited act. But more serious is the criticism that it is not right to 'teach' people that evil shall be responded to by 'counter-evil'. In my opinion two things are often confused here: the universal notion that we all have to stand by what we do and take the consequences of our deeds, and the idea (in my view a misunderstanding) that it is the state punishment that forms the logical consequence of what is conceived of as a crime - in our case a rape. I think a more logical consequence is that a price must be paid for what is done wrong not to the state or society - a third party - but to the person to whom the wrong was done. That is the leading motive in all other law (apart of course from war law). Therefore it seems to me more apt that the juridical instance should be a civil judge and not a criminal law court. And even civil courts should be asked for help only if nothing more informal helps.

What is described above seems to be the abolitionist view. What I haven't been able to find in Dutch abolitionist literature is a clear view on the role of civil or procedural codes. Should undesirable behaviour be publicly forbidden? What then is undesirable behaviour? In what cases may the help of the police be called in and what sanctions and measures can the police dispose of? Can all these items be laid down in a code? And if so, should they be?

2   The apparatus

Our criminal justice system is in fact nothing but a big apparatus called into existence to fight against certain ways of inflicting harm, by itself inflicting or threatening to inflict a certain measure of counter-harm. Abolitionists and others formulated a number of objections against the existence of such an apparatus.

One problem with big organisations is that they tend to develop their own internal goals (like streamlining the organisation, preserving employment, or saving costs) that have nothing to do with the organisation's clients, but from which the clients suffer from nonetheless. It is the phenomenon Goffman describes in his essay on total institutions.[2] Then there is the objection of estrangement because criminal law interventions are very drastic, the law prescribes very strict security measures to guarantee the culprit's rights during and after the trial. The idea is of course very noble, but the result is a very complicated and incomprehensible system of rules and exceptions (and exceptions to the exceptions) that has little or nothing at all to do with the daily life of the people in question. Neither the 'culprit' nor the 'victim' will recognize himself or herself in the legal version of what has actually happened. The estrangement then is a matter of complicated rules, extremely legal and formal language, and - as a symbol - the unbridgeable distance between the officials and the ordinary people in the courtroom.

Another objection against our criminal justice system is that the 'victim' is more or less excluded from the procedure. All she can do is tell the police what has happened to her and then maybe the police will ask her to come and identify her attacker and that is all - except that there is the possibility of asking for a financial compensation in a civil procedure (or - for a little sum of money - in the criminal procedure). Nowadays,[3] there is a growing attention to 'victims' of 'crimes'. In police circles attention is being paid to the way a woman who has been raped should be received to tell her story, and within the court rules are being made to inform the victim about the ins and outs of the legal procedure. However there is no thinking about giving her a say in what should be done to the man. This is based on the fear that the victim

---

[2] Goffman,E. (1961) *Asylum*, Harmondsworth: Penguin.
[3] Editors' Note: In 1988

would demand too harsh a punishment and it is a logical consequence of the principle that it is not the victim but society which should judge the criminal. And finally the possibilities for help to victims of crimes are being explored, although mainly by individual organisations.

Abolitionists do not promote a counter-apparatus, they suggest that people become free to solve their own conflicts as well as they can, stimulated by the state. Abolitionists claim that we don't need a specific category of behaviour to be labelled 'crime'. Problems that arise from 'a criminal deed' can in their eyes be solved in the same way as problems that have arisen from another source. A man has raped a woman, and that causes a number of problems, depending on the specific situation. So what measures will be taken depends on the nature of the situation, the nature of the problems and the reaction of both the woman and the man.

In my opinion the abolitionist starting point is correct, not the state but the victim is the party to take measures against the committer of some form of sexual violence. Why should the state interfere with such overwhelming power without even giving space for more informal solutions, created in the immediate surroundings of where the actual conflict arose? The legal protection of the culprit could be replaced by a more effective and more logical protection - that of voluntariness. Of course the man should be answerable for what he has done in one way or another, but his rights seem to be best guaranteed if he is involved in the process of finding out in what way. Only if he refuses to cooperate reasonably ought he to be drawn into a court session - and even then not to be 'punished', but just to be forced to make up for what he has done wrong. Of course there is, in the background, a public side to sexual violence. Society as a whole suffers - theoretically speaking - when one of its members is harmed. But this public cause is, I think, better served by a common solution by the parties involved than by an imposed process that will not do anybody any good.

Although I agree with the abolitionist view on the process of conflict-solving, I do have a few questions to ask abolitionists:

- How can what has happened become clear without using humiliating practices?
- How can we manage to escape the danger of a new bureaucracy, this time of an 'abolitionist' nature? We will always need a minimum of rules in a process of negotiating or conflict-solving in general.
- How can we stimulate women to take action when they have become victims of sexual violence? How can we diminish their fear of being threatened by their attackers?

- The solving of conflicts takes much time. The same goes for the criminal justice system, by the way, but the solving of the problems caused by sexual violence by means of, for example, negotiation demands the time of the disputing parties rather than that of authorities or professionals. What if the woman concerned doesn't want to spend time on it and doesn't want to ask others to take her place? And what if the man claims to be unable to spend time on it?
- Leaving the problems to the people requires a great deal of creativity and also reasonableness. Although the idea seems logical and just, it is a practical fact that not every person can be persuaded to be reasonable - even though the stimulant to be reasonable is greater in an open process as suggested than in the closed criminal justice process? What can be done to assure a balance of power between the disputing parties? And what can be done if the man in question doesn't want to cooperate in the process? Do we need sanctions for these cases? What kind of sanctions?
- How can we prevent the conflict being taken from the parties not by the state but by the assurance companies?
- What is to be done to men who have raped out of madness? Should we simply lock them up in a mental hospital instead of in a prison? That seems to be putting off the problem instead of solving it.

3   The result

To most of us it will be evident that our criminal law system does not reach its own goals. Researchers come to different conclusions as to whether or not the example set by punishing 'criminals' keeps others from doing the same. No research at all has been done - as far as I know - into the effects of the criminal law system on the inclination of victims and their relatives to take the law into their own hands. And most researchers agree on the statement that offenders are - generally speaking - not withheld from trespassing again by a prison sentence, on the contrary, prisons are nothing short of breeding places for sexual violence. It seems clear to me that there must be a sound reason for maintaining a criminal law system even if it does not reach its own goals and that *this reason is the maintenance of the idea of retaliation*. Most of us don't like the idea, since it sounds rather barbarian – but it seems to me the only explanation of the fact that we hold on to a system that sets noble goals and has no chance whatsoever of achieving them. If we allow ourselves to give up the idea that justice is done by responding to the man who has raped a woman by locking him up for a fixed period of time or making him pay a certain sum of money to the state, we could use our energy to think of the best way to stimulate conflict-solving between parties and of more constructive ways of reaching the goals mentioned above.

Now to conclude this paper let us try and re-formulate what exactly these goals are and see what possibilities the abolitionist perspective offers in this respect. First of all we want the man who has raped to learn once and for all that what he has done-was wrong, and why it was wrong. In this goal there is an amount of revengefulness which is, in my eyes, only human and even healthy. Fantasies of castration or the death penalty occur in many a head after a gruesome rape or murder. And I think no one will blame a woman who kicks her attacker in the balls to keep him from raping her or even – out of anger – after he has raped her. This 'punishment' is prompt, it is given by the victim herself, and it has a kind of 'mirror-effect' ('feel how it feels'). But if a state called into existence an apparatus to kick rapists in the balls, this state would be said to show signs of similarity with Khomeiny's Iran with its corporal punishments. Why? Because the element of time is supposed to give us the opportunity of reconsidering things and thinking of a better solution.

Time moderating revengefulness - therein is of course the main element of this goal we want this man to never do it again, and if possible because he sees why he shouldn't do it again. There may even be a direct relation between the desire for revenge and the hope that he will learn not to do it again. The more we feel that a person is sorry for what he has done and is sincerely determined not to give problems again, the less will be the call for revenge. In a system where it is the attacked person who calls to account the attacker, both needs can be met. In the first place it creates a lot of trouble to be arrested or summoned to appear in a certain place at a certain time to account for your wrong-doings and to be made to pay or make up for them in one way or another. But in the second place the chance that a rapist will learn from this procedure, being confronted with all the suffering and problems he has caused, is much bigger than the chance that he will learn from the distant, authoritarian and uniform procedure we know now. And thirdly during negotiations or in court, agreement may be reached on the man taking a course on some subject related to sexual violence - and the more voluntarily this occurs, the more results we may expect.

Secondly we want others – the whole society – to learn that sexual violence is wrong. We want to live in a society in which sexual violence, even if it occurs, is clearly and publicly not tolerated. Well, I think if the police help to trace down culprits of sexual violence; if the state helps the process of conflict-solving by supplying room and, if necessary, expertise; and if the judge, consulted as a last resort, finds suitable measures; the message will be clear enough. As in the case of the man in question in the paragraph above, the public will at least see what happens when you are caught after committing a form of sexual violence, and at best learn that sexual violence is wrong and why. Besides this, the government will of course have to take other measures to create a climate in which sexual violence is clearly out of place.

Finally we want to keep people (especially those who have been mistreated, and their friends and relatives) from taking the law into their own hands. And also in this respect, I think the abolitionist perspective opens many possibilities. An open procedure during which all involved - including relatives and friends on both sides - can speak their minds, will leave less room for secret revenge afterwards than the procedure we know now, which excludes the victim completely and does not ask for the culprit's opinion as to what should happen next. And the result of this open procedure is an agreement, that only if one of the parties is completely unwilling will a judge dictate the result.

To end this paper, I will once again plead for the abolitionist perspective, not as a Utopia, but as a real possibility, even in the complex and painful field of sexual violence. I think in the first place it offers a more logical, pure and just look at reality than the view of our present criminal justice system, and in the second place it offers more effective ways of reaching the goals that are formulated to defend the present criminal justice system and that are fairly generally agreed to. As to the more practical problems occurring in a country with no criminal law system I think a lot of brain storming needs to be done, not only by criminologists and jurists, but also by sociologists, social workers, psychologists, psychiatrists, and so on and so forth.

Bibliography

Goffman,E. (1961) *Asylum*, Harmondsworth: Penguin.
Leander, K. (2013) 'The Decade of Rape' in Gilmore, J., Moore, J.M. and Scott, D. (eds.) *Critique and Dissent: An Anthology to mark 40 years of the European Group for the Study of Deviance and Social Control,* Ottawa: Red Quill Books

Acknowledgements

Instead of listing all the publications I've read on which this paper is based, I confine myself to heartily thanking Mr Bianchi and Mr Hulsman for writing their books *Gerechtigheid als vrijplaats (Justice as Sanctuary)* and *Afscheid van het strafrecht (Goodbye to Criminal Law)* respectively.

12

The Traitorous Temptation of Criminal Justice: Deceptive Appearances? The Dutch Women's Movement, Violence against Women and the Criminal Justice System.

Jolande uit Beijerse and Renée Kool

This paper was delivered at the European Group's 16th annual conference in Synnseter fjellstue, Norway and first published in Working Papers in European Criminology, Volume 10 'Gender, Sexuality and Social Control' in 1990.

Introduction: the Dutch women's movement and the criminal justice system until the seventies.

In its first flourishing period, from about 1870 until 1920, the Dutch women's movement didn't pay much attention to the position of women in the criminal justice system. It's focus was the legal equality of men and women and the fight against dual morals. These morals, which were very clear in issues of public morality — like prostitution and unmarried maternity — were, according to the women's movement, a sign that slavery still existed.[1]

It was from around 1870 that the present penal law of 1886 was discussed in parliament. The debates around the chapter on moral laws were not very stirring; only a small group of — exclusively male — people with the same material welfare and social status could vote. In 1873 one suggested restricting the punishability of rape to cases outside marriage. Only one member protested vainly against the proposal with the argument that it could humiliate the woman, reducing her to the status of a machine.[2]

---

[1] Wichmann.C. (1913) "Het vrouwen leven thans" In J van den Bergh van Eijsinga Elias & C. Wichmann (red) *De vrouw in Nederland voor honderd jaar en thans.* Maatschappij voor goede en goedkope lectuur, Amsterdam

[2] Doomen, J. (1979) "Verkrachting in het huwelijk" *Nederlands Juristenblad* 54 (33) 749-756

Shortly after the completion of the penal law, by a change of the constitution, the Roman Catholic and Calvinist middle classes became a significant component of the Dutch electorate. Their wish to criminalize "sinful" activities led to a revision of the moral laws twenty years later, in 1911.[3] Women were also influencial in this process. The 'Vrouwenbond ter verhoging van het zedelijk bewustzijn' ('Women's union for raising moral consciousness') for instance protested in 1885 in parliament against the trade in white slaves.

At the beginning of the second period of the women's movement, from 1968, similar topics - like contraception and unmarried maternity - were again central. Pro-choice campaigns around abortion placed the women's movement in conflict with the criminal justice system that was conceptualised as supporting the existing class society.[4] The sexual revolution promoted is a tendency towards the liberalization of moral laws. There was considerable opposition to the state interfering in the individual life of the citizen. Having introduced the free sale of contraceptives in 1970, the government placed the complete revision of the moral laws onto the political agenda and appointed an advisory committee (the Melai Committee). This committee published reports on film censorship in 1970; pornography in 1973 and prostitution in 1977.[5]

Whilst the legal liberalization of sexuality progressed the focus of the women's movement changed in response to a growing awareness that rape and the maltreatment of women occurred much more frequently than was previously thought. In 1974 the first Dutch desertion home for maltreated women was opened.[6] This initiative was followed a year later by the opening of a rape centre.[7] One of the founders of the first rape centre, Jeanne Doomen,[8] played an important role in this process by describing the experiences of sexually abused women.

Gradually it became clear that rape occurs frequently, that every man can be the rapist and every woman can be the victim and that victim and offender often know each other. It also became apparent that aggression is a more important motive for the rapist than satisfying sexual pleasure and that sex, like violence, is only a means to intimidate women. Women started to realize

---

[3] Kempe, G. Th (1976) "Uitvoerder of kruisvaarder" In: Moens, N Jorg, & P Moedikdo *Recht macht en manipulatie* Utrecht/Antwerpen, 1976

[4] DolleMina (1970) "Een rebelse meid is een parel in de klassenstrijd *"Serie: Wat te doen?* nr 2, Socialistische Uitgeverij Amsterdam, Amsterdam

[5] Prins, M. & Van der Wees, J. (1985) "Met lege handen aanpakken: Seksualiteit, geweld en strafrecht" Lover A 196-200

[6] Harmsen, P. (1984) "'Je kunt weg als je wilt'", 10 jaar Blijf van mijn Lijf" Vrouwenkrant

[7] Soest, M. van (1975) "De aanrander gaat meestal vrijuit" De Nieuwe Linie

[8] Doomen, J. (1976) *Verkrachting Ervaringen, vooroordelen, achtergronden* Anthos, Baarn

that rape, women battering, incest, prostitution, sexual harassment at work and so on are all phenomena of one power structure between men and women. In this article we shall use the general term 'violence against women'.

Through the unmasking of existing myths and contact with feminist professional helpers, women who were confronted with violence started to recognize that this violence exceeded the bounds of admissibility. Thus, in the case of violence or the threat of violence, women increasingly appealed to the police for protection and in the case of violence which took place in the past, to criminal justice for the punishment of the violator. It was these contacts with the police and the criminal justice system that led to a storm of indignation, mainly from the feminist professional helpers. The criticism focused on penal provisions, the personnel of the criminal justice system and criminal procedure.

This paper assesses the results of the encounter of women with the criminal justice system. Firstly we explore the women's movement's critique of the criminal justice system. We then show how the criminal policy makers reacted to the women's movement's critique. Then this policy is compared with practice. Finally we look at whether the criminal justice system, which in the case of abortion deprives women of their right of self-determination, can protect them from oppression by violence in other circumstances?

Criticizing the criminal justice system in dealing with violence against women

Criticizing penal provisions

Although violence against women is related to the power structure between men and women, it's various forms are allocated different values by criminal justice. Criticism was particular targeted at the categorisation of different forms of violence against women within moral laws and the distinction that is made between forced sexual intercourse by violence or threat of violence (rape) and duress to commit lewd acts or to endure these acts (sexual assault). The maximum penalty for rape is higher than for sexual assault, although woman can experience both equally seriously, because, except for 'real' sexual intercourse, which can cause pregnancy, all other acts like oral and anal sex are defined as sexual assault. In addition rape is restricted to cases in which rapist and victim are not married to each other. This restriction, the women's movement argued, expresses the patriarchal view that a married woman is sexually the property of her husband. Woman battering isn't criminalized in the moral laws. If the violator doesn't resort to the use of sex, it falls under the heading of general battering. Contrary to the case of rape, the punishment in cases of battering can be increased when the victim is married to the violator.

Criticizing criminal justice system personnel

Jeanne Doomen has highlighted the prejudices of the police and justice personnel. In discussions with police officers she observed that they made a distinction between 'good' and 'bad' rapes. They claimed not to understand why anyone would rape a victim they considered 'ugly'. She reports that a judge told her that a woman who says 'no' means 'maybe', a woman who says 'maybe' means 'yes' and a woman who says 'yes' is 'no woman at all'.[9] In response she wrote a manual for the victims of rape in which, among other things, she explained what women can do when police and justice reveal their prejudices.[10]

Complaints about treatment by the criminal justice organizations are confirmed not only by the accounts of victims and helping professionals but also by research. For example research carried out in Groningen into rape cases that were reported to the police between 1971 and 1976 shows that the decision of the police to make a report or not, of the public prosecutor to prosecute or not and of the judge to convict or not conform to the stereotypical view of rape: an unknown rapist from the lower social classes, who doesn't know the victim, has used lots of violence and has raped his victim more than once, while she offered resistance.[11]

The detective force too has to deal with violence against women in cases of woman battering. In 1985 some feminist providers of aid from shelter homes for battered women interviewed 139 women about their experiences with the detective force. Less than half of the interviewed women went to the police. Of these less than half (23) of the 53 reports were judged to be valid. In only four cases did a prosecution occur. The victim being married to the suspect proved to be the biggest obstacle to prosecution.[12]

Criticizing the criminal procedure

Women who report violence to the police do nothing more or less than inform the criminal justice system about a penal offence. The only extra opportunity the victim has, if she wants it, is to 'join' the procedure as the injured party. By participating the victim can claim damages up to 1500 Dutch guilders[13] although another consequence is that it deprives her of the right to

---

[9] Doomen, J. (1977) "Verkrachting Justitie versus slachtoffer" *Delikt en delinkwent* 7(9) 636-647
[10] Doomen, J. (1978) *Heb je soms aanleiding gegeven?* Feministische Uitgeverij Sara, Amsterdam
[11] Metz, G. & Rijpkema, H. *(1979) Mythen en feiten over verkrachting* Groningen
[12] Aktiegroep Stop geweld tegen vrouwen (1985) *Geef je 't aan of geef je 't op?* Rotterdam.
[13] Editors' note: Approx 680 Euros

claim damages in a civil procedure. Other than this small amount of compensation the criminal procedure offers the victim nothing except the possibility that the violator will be punished.

The first problem for the criminal procedure is that it is often very difficult to get sufficient evidence in cases of violence against women. Because the woman is often the only witness, a lot of co-operation is required from her. She is interrogated intensively by the police and, when necessary, medically examined by a police physician. When the suspect is not yet known, she must look at pictures and try to recognize the suspect through a mirror. When the police have sent the case to the public prosecutor, the woman will be interrogated again by the judge of instruction, at which hearing the lawyer of her violator will be present. At the end, if the lawyer of the offender requests it and the judge consents, the woman can be forced to come to the court session. The woman can't refuse any of these things. Even if she is subjected to threats by the offender, his friends or relatives, she cannot withdraw the case when the public prosecutor has decided to prosecute.

A second problem is the dependence of the victims on criminal justice organizations like the police and public prosecutor. Individual police officers can decide not to send the report to the public prosecutor because they consider that the evidence is not sufficient. The public prosecutor in turn can decide not to prosecute and the judge, at the end, can decide not to convict. The only legal opportunity of the victim to contest these decisions is a right to challenge the decision of the public prosecutor to not prosecute her case. The women's movement has highlighted that a woman can be involved with the case for months, but can in no way influence the course of things. For every decision she is at the mercy of the criminal justice system. In addition she has to tell the story over and over again, she must sometimes answer insinuating questions and can be called up at any time for an interrogation. A woman can experience this procedure as if she herself is the suspect. She feels humiliated and misused again, but now by the criminal justice system. When the violator is released, hardly any or no protection will be offered to her.

Violence against women and criminal law policy

Policy regarding penal provisions

The Melai Committee started in 1978 with the most important part of its task; to advise on the provisions on rape, sexual assault and sexual contacts with youngsters and dependent people. For this task the committee had, at the request of the Emancipation Board, been expanded to include three experts. The Committee presented its final report in 1980.[14] The starting point of the report can, like in the other reports, be found in the protection of the free will of the citizen in starting and rejecting sexual relationships. The most important issues of the report are different forms of force, the distinction between rape and sexual assault and criminalization of rape in marriage.[15] In 1981 the Bill on so-called serious moral crimes was presented. It was based on the final report of the Melai Committee and did meet the criticism of the women's movement. The distinction between rape and assault was (partially) abolished, thereby acknowledging that violence is the main element in sexual violence. Another important change was the criminalization of rape in marriage. In addition, the element of "force" used in the penal provisions was widened. In this way not only actions involving apparent force, but also more veiled ones, were acknowledged as sexual violence. Furthermore an article was introduced making joint sexual violence a qualified crime (this implies a higher punishment rate). Also the requirement that a complaint be lodged by the victim, which in Dutch criminal law is necessary before prosecution can occur in some moral crimes, was abrogated.

Policy regarding the personnel of the criminal justice system
    In 1978, due to the criticism of the women's movement, the treatment of rape victims by the police was questioned in parliament. In 1979 the De Beaufort working party was appointed to develop new regulations regarding the treatment of reports by women who were victims of a moral crime.[16] The working party reported in December 1981. As a follow up the Vaillant working party on Juridical Policy and the Victim was appointed in 1984. This working party presented its report, which concerned the development of a national victim policy by police and public prosecutors, in 1985.[17] As a result of the activities of both working parties the first new directives came into force in March 1986. Initially these applied only to victims of moral crimes, however, in April 1987, they were extended to all victims of crimes and offences with serious consequences. The directives established that the victim of crime is entitled to proper treatment by judicial officers and has a right to be informed about the settlement of the case and about the possibilities of compensation. Regarding sexual violence the directives lay down that further victimization by criminal justice processes should be avoided. Therefore the victim was entitled to be accompanied by a 'confidential person' when attending the

---

[14] *Eindrapport van de adviescommissie zedelijkheidswetgeving* (Melai, 1980), Staatsuitgeverij, 's-Gravenhage
[15] Quispel, Y. M. (1984) "Zedelijkheidswetgeving, overheidsbeleid en seksueel geweld" In *Vrouw en Recht,* NJCM-bulletin
[16] Doomen, J. (1979) "Verkrachting in het huwelijk" *Nederlands Juristenblad* 54 (33) 749-756
[17] Vaillant (1985) *Eindrapport van de werkgroep Justitieel beleid en slachtoffers* Ministerie van Justitie, s' Gravenhage

police hearing. Furthermore, the charge should be determined by specialized police officers – the moral police.

In 1985 the Ministry of Justice also presented a general report on judicial policy *Samenleving en Criminaliteit (Society and Crime)* in which the need of a uniform judicial policy regarding victim aid was explicitly acknowledged. Although the policy as set out within this plan is based upon the Melai and Vaillant reports, the starting point is that addressing the needs of the victim of crime should not lead to a subordination of the public interest. Within this framework the government intends to develop co-operative networks between the judicial authorities and the organizations for social work. The support of the government for initiatives (developed by women) in the field of social work and research, as well as the support given to the Landelijk Bureau Slachtofferhulp (National Office for Victim Aid) and the connected Landelijk Overleg Slachtofferhulp (National Consultation Platform for Victim Aid) are all part of this national victim policy.

Policy regarding criminal procedure

The working party on sexual violence published its report in 1981.[18] At its heart is the notion that the judicial interest should be subordinate to the interest of the victim. The Dutch judiciary and the Dutch Prosecution Council strongly rejected this point of view insisting that the judicial interest should always prevail. In cases of sexual violence, they argued that the violator should in every case be prosecuted and punished to prevent a second offence. Moreover, the magistracy stated that the victim of sexual violence should not be entitled to have privileged judicial treatment – sexual violence isn't supposed to affect the victim more seriously than other forms of crime. The victim who, on a voluntary basis, brought charges against someone should know that this implies an obligation towards the judicial authorities to cooperate. In later years this resistance against the proposed directives has diminished a bit, but nevertheless the government did amend the directives finally introduced to accommodate this criticism. The decision whether or not there shall be a prosecution remains firmly with the Public Prosecutor; the plea of the Dutch Emancipation Board to award the victim an official vote in this matter having been rejected.

The ratification of the treaty of the Council of Europe regarding the compensation of victims of violent crimes led to the establishment of another new committee to look into the possibilities of compensation for the victim within criminal procedure.[19] The Committee published its final report in

---

[18] *Rapport van de werkgroep aangifte seksuele geweldsmisdrijven* (De Beaufort 1981) Ministerie van Justitie, 'S-Gravenhage

[19] Council of Europe (1983) *Convention on the compensation of victims of violent crimes* Straatsburg;

March 1988 proposing the introduction of a new punishment – the compensation order.[20] A further initiative was the Committee on Threatened Witnesses (1986) whose report proposed making it possible for witnesses/victims to testify anonymously during the court session. This arrangement is already practiced in connection with the protection of undercover agents in cases involving organized crime. Now victims can also profit from this non-legislative arrangement, but only at the discretion of judicial authorities.

Policy versus practice

The penal provisions

Although the Minister of Justice has asked the Council of State for its advice, the Bill regarding serious moral crimes has never been introduced into parliament.[21] The press coverage which accompanied this advice focused on a proposed liberalization of the law concerning sexual contacts with children between twelve and sixteen years old. Public opinion was divided and in response to political pressure the Minister of Justice didn't bring the Bill before parliament.

A rape case in the spring of 1988 brought the Bill back into the limelight. The High Court ruled that a man who was accused of raping his girlfriend could not have known that she didn't want sexual intercourse at the time, because she didn't say 'no' clearly enough. Therefore the man was acquitted. The Dutch women's movement reacted furiously, in their opinion this was a clear case of rape. They stated that as a result of this judgement women were forced into the position of having to say 'no' to a man, instead of the man having to ask himself whether or not the woman would like sexual contact. They demanded the introduction of the Bill into parliament.

In spite of this the Minister of Justice came up with another solution, he introduced a new Bill into parliament and withdrew the original one.[22] This new Bill, however, is only a marginal revision of the law; the existing provisions being adapted in a marginal manner. The proposal to equalize rape and sexual assault - by means of one paramount provision - in the old law is abandoned. This denies the women movement's view that sexual violence is

---

Council of Europe (1985) *The position of the victim in the framework of criminal law & procedure* Straatsburg.

[20] *Eindrapport van de commissie wettelijke voorzieningen slachtoffers in het strafproces* (Terwee 1988), Staatsuitgeverij, 's-Gravenhage

[21] Wetsontwerp zware zedenmisdrijven, Tweede Kamer, vergaderjaar 1979-80, nr 15836, nrs 1-2, 's-Gravenhage

[22] Herzien wetsontwerp zware zedenmisdrijven, Tweede Kamer, vergaderjaar 1988-89, nr 20930 nrs 1-3 's-Gravenhage

characterized by its violence and not the sexual form in which it takes place. This also means that in court the victim of sexual violence will continue to be confronted with painful questions, necessary to establish whether sexual intercourse or lewd acts took place. Secondly, the outdated terms which are used in the penal provisions will not be replaced by more neutral terms. This puts aside the fact that women experience sexual violence in a much broader range of ways than the ones which are covered by the terms used in the penal provisions.

Whilst this setback can be viewed as a denial of the demands of the women's movement for a comprehensive review of the moral laws, it could be argued that that there is no real loss as the Bill was never meant to create a real turning point in the history of struggle against sexual violence. The motive underlying this review was not a real concern about the position of women, but merely a response to the pressure exerted by the women's movement.[23] The significance of the review for daily life (instrumental aspect) of women was minimal; its real importance lay in the consolidation of ruling values (value-expressive aspect). This review would have been merely of symbolic significance to women.[24] An example can be cited to illustrate this point of view. In the Explanatory Statement it is stated that accusations regarding sexual violence should only be taken seriously by the judicial officials when they relate to cases of objective sexual violence. This means that women will have to provide such evidence, thus proving themselves not guilty of their own rape or assault.

The personnel of the criminal justice system

As yet the directives mentioned above concerning the personnel of the criminal justice system have been executed in an insufficient manner.[25] The executive organizations do not bear the blame for this entirely as in recent years criminal justice policy has been mainly oriented towards combating serious, organised crime. As a result the technocratic aspects of the criminal law and the development of all kinds of specializations within the system have been emphasized. The policy towards victims of crime contradicts such a general policy. This lack of infrastructure has resulted in an abdication of responsibilities and connected activities by the police and its relocation with the regular social work organisations.

---

[23] Hulsman, L. H. C. (1983), "Criminele politiek en (strafrechtelijke) zedelijkheidswetgeving " In: *Bij deze stand van zaken*. Liber Amicorum A L Melai, red E Andre de la Porte (e a) 219-247 Gouda Quint, Arnhem

[24] Soetenhorst, J. & Jansz, U. (1986) *Sexueel geweld zal de wetgever een zorg zijn* Gouda Quint, Arnhem

[25] Hogenhuis, C. & De Koning-de Jong, E. (1988) Slachtoffer en politioneel beleid Vakgroep Strafrecht en Criminologie, Erasmus Universiteit Rotterdam, Rotterdam

The failure to execute the directives in a sufficient manner is also caused by the instrument chosen for the directive. Such circulars are meant as a guideline for the executive level and therefore they do not supply more detailed instructions. This is intended to enable policy implementation to be more flexible, but with respect to victim aid it works in the opposite direction. An adequate implementation of the directives can only take place by means of an alteration in mentality, suggested and supported by the central level.

In response to the attitudes highlighted above (see section titled 'Criticizing the personnel of the criminal justice system'), the Rotterdam detective force, in co-operation with feminist providers of assistance to women, produced instructions for its personnel in dealing with victims of women battering. Nevertheless, because of some changes in personnel, they have not yet been introduced. The latest information is that the instructions are hidden in some desk drawer. In the meantime, the detective force is still going on denying the problems of battered women. A recent piece of research among police officers in handling cases of women battering shows that these officers mostly look at these cases as private issues. The women, on the contrary, call for the help of the police because they decided that they no longer want to keep it private.[26] Concerning the prejudices of the other personnel of the criminal justice system, like the public prosecutor, judge of instruction and judge, there is no policy at all, either at the local or at the national level. The victim is confronted most of the time by the judge of instruction for witness interrogations. The judges of instruction are connected to one of the nineteen courts in the Netherlands. Those cabinets of judges of instruction all have developed their own policy in the treatment of victims of sexual violence. While the victim can be accompanied by confidential persons at the police interrogation, this isn't the case at all of the cabinets. In Rotterdam it was even the case that the victim's lawyer could not attend the interrogation, while the lawyer of the suspect could. A female judge of instruction once wanted to make an exception in the case of a stereotypical rape because she thought this was a serious case. It would be different, she assured, if the victim and the violator knew each other!

The criminal procedure

In relation to the position of the victim within the framework of the criminal procedure no major changes have been suggested. The introduction of a so-called compensation order, as proposed by the Terwee Committee[27] is not a real improvement, especially not for the victims of sexual violence, *(e.g.*

---

[26] Wostmann, M. (1988) *Politieoptreden bij vrouwenmishandeling* JB van den Brink & Co, Lochem
[27] *Eindrapport van de commissie wettelijke voorzieningen slachtoffers in het strafproces* (Terwee 1988), Staatsuitgeverij, 's-Gravenhage

such a compensation order is limited to material injury). Besides, due to resistance among the public prosecutors, this Bill will probably not be approved.

At the local level one can't speak of a uniform policy regarding the criminal procedure. It depends on the discretion of individual police officers and judges of instruction, for example if they keep the name of the victim/witness secret. There is an elusive combination of factors which determine this decision. The same holds true for informing the victims about the progress of the case.

Cases from practice and alternatives for criminal justice solutions

Here we will illustrate the complexity of reality, in which victims not only have to deal with the criminal justice system but can also choose other ways of handling their problems. The volunteer organization Stichting Vrouwenrechtswinkel (Women and Law) in Rotterdam started a juridicial consulting hour for women who were violated. Their caseload since 1985 can be divided as follows:[28]

- battering or sexual abuse in marriage or in a relationship;
- violence or threat of violence by the ex-partner;
- sexual abuse by the father or other male relative during the woman's infancy;
- rape, sexual assault or maltreatment by an unknown man;
- sexual abuse by professional carers.

Battering or sexual abuse in marriage or in a relationship

Most married women only want advice about divorce. Although a number of them are battered for quite a long time, most of them still hesitate in starting divorce proceedings and don't want to take other juridicial steps. The women who are not married are in a different situation. They lack the opportunity of starting divorce proceedings and have to search for other ways to show their partner that they want to break the relationship. They can report the abuse to the police, but are unlikely to have sufficient evidence. In most of these cases the man will stick to the story that the woman likes to be treated in the way he treats her and that she still loves him.

---

[28] Stichting Vrouwenrechtswinkel Rotterdam (1988) Jaarverslag Stichting Vrouw en rechtswinkel Rotterdam

Violence or threat of violence by the ex-partner

These women want to have information about the so-called 'street prohibition'. In a civil court case men can be prohibited from the street in which the woman lives. But, when a man really has a mind to make life a burden to the woman, it is very difficult to stop him. For enforcement of a 'street prohibition' the woman is dependent on the police, who have to help her when the man infringes the prohibition, which is a judicial order. We were confronted with women who were fleeing for years from place to place. Here we shall describe one of these cases.

> A thirty four year old woman was sexually abused by her brother-in-law (fifteen years older than she) between the ages of eight and of seventeen. At that time she wanted to break the 'relationship' but he did not agree and started to molest her. This lasted for several years, he followed her everywhere, battered her, broke the windows of her car when she was inside the house, *etc.* At the age of twenty one she fled from her home and left all she had. Now she has been living in Rotterdam for thirteen years; has a secret address, no telephone and no intimate friends. The only thing she had was her job and when she lost that she started to think of going back home to her mother. But every time she visits her mother she has to drive into her former home under the protection of the police because of threats from her brother-in-law. There is no way to stop him, because each of the threats is either too difficult to prove, or too small to prosecute. This woman is now seriously working on learning how to shoot. She sees no other opportunity of escaping from her terrible situation.

Sexual abuse by the father or other male relative during the woman's infancy

This concerns two groups of victims. Firstly cases in which the incest took place a short time ago or is still going on. In most of these cases the girls only want information about the criminal procedure or civil possibilities for the future. All of them are already in therapy at a feminist self-help organization and need all their energy to cope with their experiences. Secondly there are the victims who had been through the incest more than twelve years ago. In these cases a criminal procedure can't be started anymore because too long a time has passed.

Rape, sexual assault or maltreatment by an unknown man

These are the cases that most people have in mind when they speak about sexual violence. It is striking that, contrary to the cases above, all women who came to the consulting hour because of rape, sexual assault or maltreatment by an unknown man, have already reported it to the police as a matter of course. They visit the consulting hour because they are not informed about the *progress* of the procedure or about other juridicial possibilities they have. We shall give a description of one of these cases in order to show that even in these stereotypical cases criminal justice can't offer victims of violence against women any feeling of justice.

> A twenty three year old woman walks the street late at night, when a man in a car twists her arm and orders her to get into the car. Paralyzed by fear, she obliges and the man drives to a park in the neighbourhood where he rapes her and forces her to say that she loves him. After that he drives her home. Back home the woman, who is upset, calls for a taxi to go to her mother. Instead the taxi driver drives her to the police station, where she stays until the next day for a medical test, looking at pictures and telling every detail of the event.
>
> The next day the violator is caught at about the same time in the same car. The woman identifies him positively and at the same time she becomes terribly afraid that the man will be vengeful. However, the police don't want to hear about her withdrawing the complaint. They promise to keep her name secret and to make appropriate arrangements with the judge of instruction.
>
> The accused denied it was him who drove the car and during the five months of his detention on remand the woman lived with the stress of not knowing what was going to happen. During the court session the judges couldn't be completely sure about the identity of the violator and they acquitted him. At the same day of his release the woman, who didn't know about this yet, had seen the man driving slowly in his car in front of her house. She didn't feel safe anymore, searched for another house and had to cut her hair very short in order not to be recognised.

Sexual misuse by professional carers

Several women visited the consulting hour with complaints about male professional carers who used the relationship with their clients to sexually abuse them. In these cases it is even more difficult to prove what has happened. Most of the women want advice about how they can advertise in the papers to get in contact with other victims of the same psychiatrist or other professional. There are also women who brought the case before the Medical Disciplinary Committee, but who are not satisfied with the judgement of this committee. In all of these cases women wanted to warn other women but they have to be wary of a libel suit. In these cases the criminal justice system turns out to be the defender of the good name of these men.

In many cases women can make use of provisions in the civil law, in which they only have to prove that an 'unlawful deed' has happened. The disadvantage of the civil procedure is that, in contrast with the criminal one, it costs money and can take a long time (2 years more or less), but in the end the amount of compensation can be much higher than 1500 guilders.[29] In cases of a broken relationship an important factor in the civil case can be that the victim acts independently in this procedure, while this isn't so in the criminal procedure.

Conclusion: the criminal justice system - deceptive appearances?

The Melai Committee stated that the criminal justice system could only play a minor role in combating sexual violence, an opinion subsequently shared by the Minister of Justice. Now[30], a few years later, the criminal justice system is being acknowledged as a suitable means for combating sexual violence. The gains of ten years of campaigning against sexual violence have been limited to some minor reforms. Victim Aid has been set up from a system-orientated point of view and therefore in practice works out as a means of control and not as a way in which the interests of the victim of sexual violence can be served. All this is in accordance with the starting point that the public interest prevails, the victim's interest is of subordinated importance. Yet the question to be answered is when such a 'subordination' is regarded as being present and what exactly is the content of this 'public' interest. Does the criminal justice system serve the human being or is it the other way around? Within the present system-orientated settlement of conflicts it looks as if people have been made subservient to the system. For this reason the putative consensus of opinion concerning the settlement of conflicts must be regarded as of relative value, especially in view of the still increasing discontent felt by most victims in regard to their position within the criminal procedure.

---

[29] Editors' note: 681 Euros
[30] Editors' note: In 1990

The conclusion which has to been drawn is that the stated policy is not similar to the practiced policy. Apparently the government subscribes to this need for emancipation; the present policy seems to open up possibilities of improving the position of women. However, promises which have been made have not yet been implemented. Although the Explanatory Statements from the Department of Justice over the past few years contain all kinds of good intentions, the practical elaboration again and again breaks down on the lack of finances or on barriers at executive level. Therefore women who trust an official policy, and who consequently decide to co-operate with the government and choose the criminal justice system as an ally in the fight against sexual violence will see that it will prove to be a dead-end street for them. This is short-term thinking. Women should not throw away the change in moral awareness which they have gained in recent decades - for the criminal justice system has proved to be a traitorous tempter.

The criminal justice system is not a suitable starting point for such a struggle. The reason for the existence of the criminal justice system is situated in the preservation of law and order. Nowadays the prevailing opinion is that the way in which society is organized determines the relationships between men and women. The subordinated position of women is therefore to be seen as anchored in institutions, which in their turn determine the socialization of the individual - thus creating a kind of service hatch effect. Therefore to make the fight against sexual violence a successful one, the intended changes will have to find fertile ground within these institutions. For the struggle in the criminal justice system specifically to be a successful one, the intended changes will have to find a basis at the level of the aforementioned organizations. Support for the claims of the women's movement will have to get a higher priority within the criminal justice system otherwise women will have to find other ways of dealing with this phenomenon.

In this final section the question to be answered is whether or not the criminal justice system has proved to be a suitable means in the fight against sexual violence. To this end we will compare the contents of the foregoing paragraphs by means of analyzing the process of primary and secondary criminalisation as set out by Hulsman.[31] To do so we have to define the term 'society'. As we see it, 'society' is a product of the way in which people, both as individuals and as members of a group, organise their daily life. Therefore 'society' is a paramount conception, in which one can expect contradicting views and claims regarding the various subdivisions of human life. One of the

---

[31] Hulsman, L. H. C. (1983), 'Criminele politiek en (strafrechtelijke) zedelijkheidswetgeving.' In: *Bij deze stand van zaken*. Liber Amicorum A L Melai, red E Andre de la Porte (e a) 219-247 Gouda Quint, Arnhem

fields involved is the criminal justice system, which stands in open communication with the other social systems and is influenced by them. Within the criminal justice system one can differentiate between the practice of criminal policy (the criminal justice system seen as a relatively autonomous element of the paramount social strategy) and the claims regarding the practice of the criminal justice system as formulated by the members of society, as a means to change or perpetuate the social order. As there are many pressure groups within society, these claims often conflict with each other. Therefore the rewarding of claims by means of primary criminalization (to acknowledge a problem as problematic by introducing a penal provision) and secondary criminalization (the way in which the primary criminalisation is carried out in practice) implies a choice. Moreover one has to be aware of the fact that primary criminalisation presumes that the situations which are being criminalized have a uniform (problematic) meaning to all members of society.

Analyzing the fight against sexual violence, one can state that the demand of the women's movement to criminalize sexual violence has been rewarded in an inadequate way. First of all sexual violence is still interpreted in a very limited way, thus repudiating the definition of sexual violence as used by the women's movement. In doing so the government denies the degree to which women actually experience violations of their integrity (physical and spiritual) in everyday life. Secondly the intended review of the moral law will now only be marginal, thereby ignoring the importance of the matter to women. Only the 'classical' cases will continue to be acknowledged as sexual violence and even then a distinction continues to be made between rape and sexual assault. Nevertheless one could have expected such a response to the claims of the women's movement; when women identify men as guilty of reprehensible acts and insist on a change in conduct this will inevitably cause resistance among men. The male pressure group will develop counter claims, thus tempering the demands of women. In other words, primary criminalization will always be marginal, it can never award all the claims involved.[32] What is more, one could have foretold that the original Bill would be withdrawn. There was little effort made (on account of the Department of Justice) to create the infrastructure necessary to guarantee the working through to the executive level of the change in ethics embodied in the withdrawn Bill.[33]

As regards secondary criminalization - the way in which the policy towards sexual violence is carried out in practice - one can also speak of a failure. As argued earlier, the reality of the everyday life of women in regard to sexual

[32] Ibid.
[33] Soetenhorst, J. & Jansz, U. (1986) *Sexueel geweld zal de wetgever een zorg zijn* Gouda Quint, Arnhem

violence has not changed much during the past ten years. In analyzing this phenomenon we came across the following explanations. In the first place there is the conservative character of the criminal justice system, which is still pre-eminently concerned with the maintenance of the social order. Therefore the organizations involved are not suited for introducing and supporting the progressive changes asked for by women. They too will temper and adjust those claims to their own interests.[34]

Another argument for the failure of secondary criminalization is to be found in the ultimate and limited character of the means which are available within the criminal justice system.[35] As this is meant to be a last resort for the maintenance of social order, one will have to search for alternatives in order not to overstrain the system and generate opposite results. As an illustration of this the policy of the Dutch prosecution counsel concerning pre-trial detention can be mentioned – the growing appeal of the criminal justice system has resulted in a lack of penitentiary capacity. Therefore one has developed directives in which certain categories of suspects are given priority in regard to custody. Sexual offenders have a low priority and are even released to make space for other suspects. This ultimate character is accompanied by a limitation in means. Therefore women often experience the criminal justice system as inefficient in handling sexual violence,[36] especially when there is a relationship involved.[37] Alternatives such as the civil short case are nowadays more frequently used by women.[38]

This brings us to the attitudes of criminal justice the personnel. To make the fight against sexual violence a successful one a change in mentality is needed. How can one expect such a change from mainly male personnel working within a conservative organization? Both the characteristics of the criminal justice system and the contradictory interests of men in regard to women will have their impact on the attitude of personnel.

As long as society retains its present pluriform character, the claims of the women's movement will always be only partially supported by other pressure groups; moral codification will never cover the whole range of moral ethics within society. Therefore codification can never serve as a means of moral education for society; it can only be a means of instruction and a possibility for control. Women should not throw away the change in moral ethics

---

[34] Verrijn Stuart, H. (1988) 'Vrouwen en Strafrecht. het onverzadigbare slachtoffer en de onverzadigbare justitie.' In Rene van Swaaningen e a. (red.) A tort et a trovers, Liber Amicorum Herman Bianchi 215-223 Vrije Universiteits Pers, Amsterdam
[35] Hulsman (1983)
[36] Isarin, J. (1985) 'Justitie bondgenoot of tegenstander?' Nemesis 1 275-280
[37] Steinmetz, C. (1979) 'Vrouwelijke slachtoffers van misdrijven' Tijdschrift voor criminologie 5
[38] Hes, J A & Van Ringen, K (1986) Blijf uit mijn buurt Vuga, reeks 'Recht gezin en samenleving', 's-Gravenhage

awareness which has been gained in recent decades by trusting themselves to the criminal justice system, for it has proved to be a traitorous tempter.

Bibliography

Acker, H. & Rawie, M. (1982) *Seksueel geweld tegen vrouwen en meisjes* Ministerie van Sociale Zaken en Werkgelegenheid, Directie Coördinatie Emancipatie, 's- Gravenhage.

Aktiegroep Stop geweld tegen vrouwen (1985) *Geef je 't aan of geef je 't op?* Rotterdam.

Buuren, T. van & Wostmann, M. (1985) *Sexueel geweld en anticipatiestrategieën.* Ministerie van Justitie, WODC, 69, 's-Gravenhage.

Christie, N. (1977) 'Conflicts as property' *British Journal of Criminology 10(1)*

Council of Europe (1983) *Convention on the compensation of victims of violent crimes* Straatsburg

Council of Europe (1985) *The position of the victim in the framework of criminal law & procedure* Straatsburg

DolleMina (1970) 'Een rebelse meid is een parel in de klassenstrijd' *Serie: Wat te doen?* nr 2, Socialistische Uitgeverij Amsterdam, Amsterdam

Doomen, J. (1976) *Verkrachting Ervaringen, vooroordelen, achtergronden* Anthos, Baarn

Doomen, J. (1977) 'Verkrachting Justitie versus slachtoffer' *Delikt en delinkwent* 7(9) 636-647

Doomen, J. (1978) *Heb je soms aanleiding gegeven?* Feministische Uitgeverij Sara, Amsterdam

Doomen, J .(1979) 'Verkrachting in het huwelijk' *Nederlands Juristenblad* 54 (33) 749-756

Doomen, J. (1979a) 'Verkrachting, vrouwenbeweging en justitie' *Justitiële Verkenningen,* 8, 20-29

Eindrapport van de adviescommissie zedelijkheidswetgeving (Melai, 1980), Staatsuitgeverij, 's-Gravenhage

Eindrapport van de commissie wettelijke voorzieningen slachtoffers in het strafproces (Terwee 1988), Staatsuitgeverij, 's-Gravenhage

Frenken, J. & Doomen, J. (1984) *Strafbare seksualiteit* Van Loghum Slaterus, Deventer

Harmsen, P. (1984) 'Je kunt weg als je wilt', 10 jaar Blijf van mijn Lijf" Vrouwenkrant

Hes, J. A. & Van Ringen, K. (1986) *Blijf uit mijn buurt* Vuga, reeks 'Recht gezin en samenleving', 's-Gravenhage

Hogenhuis, C. & De Koning-de Jong, E. (1988) Slachtoffer en politioneel beleid Vakgroep Strafrecht en Criminologie, Erasmus Universiteit Rotterdam,

Rotterdam

hooks, b. (1986) 'Macht in een ander licht' *Nemesis* 3 105-111

Hulsman, L. H. C. (1983), 'Criminele politiek en (strafrechtelijke) zedelijkheidswetgeving' In: *Bij deze stand van zaken.* Liber Amicorum A L Melai, red E Andre de la Porte (e a) 219-247 Gouda Quint, Arnhem

Isarin, J. (1985) 'Justitie bondgenoot of tegenstander?' *Nemesis* 1 275-280

Isarin, J. (1985a) 'Misdaad als straf, straf als misdaad, abolitionisme en sexueel geweld' *Nemesis* 8 349-357

Jongste, W. de (1988) Feminism, abolitionism and power Thesis for the Common Study Programme on Criminal Justice and Critical Criminology Erasmus University of Rotterdam, Rotterdam

Justitieel Emancipatie Steunpunt (1986) Inventarisatie van onderwerpen op het terrein van Justitie met betrekking tot de positie van de vrouw 's-Gravenhage

Kempe, G. Th. (1976) 'Uitvoerder of kruisvaarder' In: Moens, N Jorg, & P Moedikdo *Recht macht en manipulatie* Utrecht/Antwerpen, 1976

Metz, G. & Rijpkema, H. (1979) *Mythen en feiten over verkrachting* Groningen

Neut, H. van der (1981) 'Het eindrapport van de adviescommissie zedelijkheidswetgeving' *Delikt en Delinkwent 11* (7)

Penders, L. (1988) 'De rechtspositie van slachtoffers van delicten' In Congres-map VOICES

Prins, M. & Van der Wees, J. (1985) 'Met lege handen aanpakken: Seksualiteit, geweld en strafrecht' Lover A 196-200

Rapport van de werkgroep aangifte seksuele geweldsmisdrijven (De Beaufort 1981) Ministerie van Justitie, 'S-Gravenhage

Quispel, Y. M. (1984) 'Zedelijkheidswetgeving, overheidsbeleid en seksueel geweld' In *Vrouw en Recht,* NJCM-bulletin

Soest, M. van (1975) 'De aanrander gaat meestal vrijuit' De Nieuwe Linie

Soetenhorst, J. & Jansz, U. (1986) *Sexueel geweld zal de wetgever een zorg zijn* Gouda Quint, Arnhem

Steinmetz, C. (1979) 'Vrouwelijke slachtoffers van misdrijven' *Tijdschrift voor criminologie 5*

Steinmetz, C. Buuren, E. van & Andel, H. van (1987) 'De slachtoffercirculaires' *Delikt en Delinkwent* 17 (9)

Stichting Vrouwenrechtswinkel Rotterdam (1988) Jaarverslag Stichting Vrouw en rechtswinkel Rotterdam 1987 Rotterdam

Vaillant (1985) *Eindrapport van de werkgroep Justitieel beleid en slachtoffers* Ministerie van Justitie, s' Gravenhage

Verrijn Stuart, H. (1988) 'Vrouwen en Strafrecht. het onverzadigbare slachtoffer en de onverzadigbare justitie' In Rene van Swaaningen e a. (red.) *A tort et a trovers, Liber Amicorum Herman Bianchi* 215-223 Vrije Universiteits Pers, Amsterdam

Verijn Stuart,H. (1989)'Kort van memorie, redactioneel' *Nemesis* 1

Wessehus, E. T. (1986) 'Slachtofferhulp-hulp aan slachtoffers?' *Delikt en*

Delinkwent 16 (8)

Wichmann, C. (1913) 'Het vrouwen leven thans' In J. van den Bergh van Eijsinga Elias & C. Wichmann (eds.) *De vrouw in Nederland voor honderd jaar en thans.* Maatschappij voor goede en goedkope lectuur, Amsterdam

Wostmann, M. (1988) *Politieoptreden bij vrouwenmishandeling* JB van den Brink & Co, Lochem

Parliamentary Papers

Ministerie van Justitie

Wetsontwerp zware zedenmisdrijven, Tweede Kamer, vergaderjaar 1979-80, nr 15836, nrs 1-2, 's-Gravenhage

Begroting, Tweede Kamer vergaderjaar 1984-85, nr 18600 H VI 's-Gravenhage

Samenleving en criminaliteit, Tweede Kamer, vergaderjaar 1984-85, nr 18995 nrs 1-2 's-Gravenhage

Begroting, Tweede Kamer, vergaderjaar 1985-86, nr 19200 H VI 's-Gravenhage

Begroting, Tweede Kamer, vergaderjaar 1986-87,nr 19700 H VI 's-Gravenhage

Voortgangsrapportage Samenleving en Criminaliteit, Tweede Kamer, vergaderjaar 1986-87, nr 18995 nr 3 's-Gravenhage

Begroting, Tweede Kamer, vergaderjaar 1987-88, nr 20200 H VI 's-Gravenhage

Herzien wetsontwerp zware zedenmisdrijven, Tweede Kamer, vergaderjaar 1988-89, nr 20930 nrs 1-3 's-Gravenhage

Ministerie van Sociale zaken en werkgelegenheid

Voorlopige nota met betrekking tot het bestrijden van sexueel geweld tegen vrouwen en meisjes, 's-Gravenhage, Oktober 1983

Beleidsplan emancipatie, Tweede Kamer vergaderjaar 1984-85, nr 19052, nrs 1-2 's-Gravenhage

Ministerie van Welzijn, volksgezondheid en cultuur

Sexueel geweld tegen vrouwen en meisjes, voortgangsrapportage, Tweede Kamer, vergaderjaar 1987-88, nr 18542,nr 17 's-Gravenhage

Stoatscourant

Richtlijnen voor het Openbaar Ministerie en politie voor het omgaan met slachtoffers, 1986 nr 33, p 4-7 's-Gravenhage

Richtlijnen aan politie en Openbaar Ministerie ten aanzien van uitbreiding slachtofferhulp, 1987 nr 64, p 64 's-Gravenhage

13

The Protection of Women by the Criminal Justice System?
Reflections on Feminism, Abolitionism and Power

Willemien de Jongste

This paper was delivered at the European Group's 16th annual conference in Synnseter fjellstue, Norway and first published in Working Papers in European Criminology, Volume 10 'Gender, Sexuality and Social Control' in 1990.

Introduction[1]

This paper is about feminist responses to sexual violence, the abolitionism of Louk Hulsman and their respective concepts of power. Feminism, especially during the second wave when sexual violence became an important issue, and Louk Hulsman's abolitionism are closely allied to each other in several ways. Both movements are liberation movements and are based on a comparable view of the world and human beings. They attack the *status quo* in industrialized societies in order to do justice to people's personal experience and authentic existence. They both analyse the criminal justice system as a patriarchal bastion in which women hardly play a role and which reinforces existing power inequalities between people.

However, when it comes to problems of sexual violence, the possibility of women receiving protection from the criminal justice system is a point of disagreement. Whereas abolitionism considers that criminalisation provides no fruitful solution to the problems posed, feminism advocates criminalisation of sexual violence. By exploring some of the central points within both theories this paper seeks to make a contribution to the on-going discussion between these two views.

---

[1] This paper is an adaptation of my thesis "Feminism, Abolitionism and Power on Feminism with regard to Sexual Violence and the Abolitionism of Louk Hulsman". The thesis was written for the first Common Study Programme on Criminal Justice and Critical Criminology, which was held from 1984 to 1986 at the Universities of Bologna, Rotterdam and Saarbrucken.

I first summarise a recent controversial decision of the Supreme Court of the Netherlands in a case of rape, before summarising the feminist position on the role of penal legislation concerning sexual violence. It is my thesis that this position can be understood best if we take into consideration that feminism is a theory of power. I will then clarify some of the foundations of Louk Hulsman's abolitionist perspective as well as of his understanding of the concept of power. For abolitionism conflict solving is of chief importance, whereas feminism considers and reconsiders patriarchal relationships. However, this does not mean that both theories can afford not to pay attention to each other. Both the feminist movement's second wave and the abolitionism of Louk Hulsman are recent developments which can be enriched by engaging with each other's ideas.

A sensational decision

The women's liberation movement in the Netherlands has been thrown into confusion. The Supreme Court has decided[2] that rape in lasting relationships which are not marriages will go unpunished as long as the woman has not let the man know clearly she intends to finish the relationship. In the case a man who had, in addition to his marriage, a long-term relationship with a woman. The man was prosecuted because he had taken the woman by means of violent acts and by threatening her with more violence; 'if you keep on opposing me I will break your arm'. In court the man was accused of rape but the woman's word was not believed. The acquittal was confirmed by the court of appeal, but on different grounds. It was not fully convinced that after a long relationship, a process of attraction and repulsion, the woman wished to bring the relationship to a definitive end and consequently wished to have no more intercourse. With regard to the wording of the law[3] the court of appeal considered the intent to force the woman not proven because it is not clear whether the man sought to compel the woman by threatening her. At the third stage of the judicial procedure the Supreme Court agreed with the court of appeal, and thus the woman was oppressed not only by the man but also in three judicial decisions.

---

[2] *Nederlandse Jurisprudents* 1988 156 Information derived from Prof Mr Henc van Maarseveen, "Een arrest dat schoffeert" *Nederlands Junsten Blad,* 11 June 1988, 23.

[3] The present paragraph 242 of the Penal Code, dating from 1866, says 'He who by violence or threat of violence forces a woman to have intercourse with him outside of marriage shall be punished as guilty of rape with imprisonment not exceeding 12 years or a money fine from the fifth category'.

Liberation of women's sexuality

For women this decision feels like a major reversal in the progress made towards the liberation of women's sexuality which started in the late sixties and was broadened and deepened during the second wave of the feminist movement in the seventies. During that period the feminist perspective on rape gained ground. In the Netherlands, like in the USA, consciousness-raising groups were set up as well as centres for battered women and children, where women found out that their experiences were shared by many other women. Articles were published – including in the non-feminist press – criticising existing concepts of rape.[4] Rape was no longer conceived of as a personal misfortune but an experience shared by all women in one form or other.

Furthermore the women's liberation movement contended that the problem of rape was related to other forms of the subordination of women in society at large and was therefore a structural rather than an individual problem. Instead of speaking of 'rape' the term 'sexual violence' was increasingly used, expressing the rejection of both the violence and existing notions of sexuality. It is a broad term in that it covers the full range of violence from pornography to rape.

Most of the subjects in this range are dealt with within Dutch penal legislation under the heading of 'morality offences'. From 1970 this legislation was reconsidered by the Melai Committee, set up by the Minister of Justice and called after its president, the Emeritus Professor in Penal Law, A. L. Melai. When at the end of the seventies the subject of sexual violence had to be dealt with, three feminists were appointed as additional members of the Melai Committee. In June 1980 the Committee finished its work, recommending with regard to rape and assault:

- the abolition of the exceptional disposition of rape in marriage;
- an extension of the definition of rape to include acts to be considered equal to sexual intercourse;
- an extension of the description of 'force' in two paragraphs of the Penal Code into 'by violence or another facility or by threatening with violence or another facility';

---

[4] Existing dominant perspectives on rape criticized in national and international literature focus on the extent of the problem, the assertion that cases of rape are rare, the myth that the victims themselves are to blame by taking unnecessary risks or not offering enough resistance, the notion that the "real rapist" is unknown to his victim, the myth that victims are especially good looking girls, and the conclusion that the rapist is to be characterized as mentally handicapped and sexually perverse.

- a gender neutral formulation of the criminal offence.[5]

The feminist struggle against dominant notions concerning sexuality and rape will therefore lead to a different definition of sexual violence in the Penal Code, mainly by an extension of the number of grounds for prosecution. This enlargement of the scope of penal law has led Louk Hulsman to criticise both the feminists' objectives and the activities of the Melai Committee. According to Hulsman, they, on the one hand seek to free people's authentic existence and defend limited pretensions of the state towards citizens, but on the other hand increasingly seek to involve a system as repressive as the criminal justice system.

Louk Hulsman's critique

In order to understand the field covered by the criminal justice system and the inter-relations within that field, Hulsman has developed a model, known as 'the apple'.

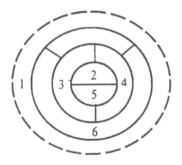

1   representations of criminal justice activities, people who report to the police, movements;
2   legislation, case law, dogmatics;
3   police, magistrates, prison system;
4   legislature, Department of Justice, government, parliament;
5   criminal justice myths;
6   mass media, novels, pictures.

By means of this model, Hulsman has visualised the criminal justice system from which his abolitionist perspective is derived. It is on basis of his conception of the totality of activities within criminal justice that Hulsman

---

[5] See also the discussion in chapter 12 of this volume.

formulates his criticism. He states:

> The criminal justice system does not deal with the original matters of the people involved but is concerned with the problems it defines itself, corresponding with its structure.[6]

This distinction between face-to-face situations and the criminal justice reality is, according to Hulsman, hardly ever made, particularly because of the way language is used with regard to criminal justice. A notion like 'punishment' clouds the difference between people directly involved and those within the system, those indirectly involved. The purpose of punishment within a criminal justice system is quite different from that within, for example, a family, a sporting club or a neighbourhood. Therefore the criminal justice system cannot give adequate answers to the difficulties experienced outside the system.

For Hulsman the abolition of the criminal justice system does not mean that all criminal justice organisations should disappear. What should be done away with is the penal reference scheme most often used within this system. The institutions of social control as they are represented in section 3 of Hulsman's 'apple', the legislature (section 4) and organisations of social control in general (sections 1 and 6) belong to the criminal justice system only in so far as their activities and legitimacy are focussed on the central criminal justice rules and myths (sections 2 and 5). The abolitionist perspective thus implies doing away with the core of the apple as the main point of orientation. The feminist activities with regard to the text of the Penal Code imply a strengthening of this core as an important point of orientation, thus effectively pushing aside many other reference points.

Feminism, a theory of power

Power inequalities between women and men

In relation to sexual violence feminism's main criticism of abolitionism is that it leaves the power aspect out of the picture. During the last decade sexual violence, has in feminist theory, been explained by means of a theory of power, namely the unequal division of power between women and men. Power inequalities can be recognised on a social-structural, an interpersonal and an intra-psychological level.[7] Women are less educated, have fewer

---

[6] L.H.C. Hulsman, "Een abolitionistisch (afschaffend) perspectief op het strafrechtelijk systeem", in *Problematiek van de strafrechtspraak* Een publikatie van het Nederlands Gesprek Centrum, Baarn 1979 p.54.

opportunities in professional life and lower income and fewer possessions in comparison with men. Their position in the labour market is therefore weaker. When entering the labour market women find that only badly paid jobs, or jobs which replicate the role of the housewife (*e.g.* nursing, social work, shop assistance) and therefore have a low status, are available.

At the interpersonal level research into the experiences of individual women and men shows that both estimate the social position of men better than that of women. Men judge themselves higher than women in terms of both their personal and their cognitive competence. Alongside this, the women interviewed also gave their husbands higher scores both in terms their personal, and (even more so) their cognitive competence. The conclusions with regard to the intra-psychological level were also clear. The women in the study had less self-confidence and less self-appreciation than the men and also had quite ambivalent and unclear expectations of their (professional) future life. These psychological characteristics invade the interpersonal relationships of women and men and the way they form their social position.

At the beginning of the 1970s women's neglected position and lack of power at the social-structural level was supposed to be met by the redistribution of opportunities in the fields of education, income and paid labour. Furthermore, a redistribution of roles inside and outside the home and a proportional distribution of women and men in political and official functions were aimed at. In the mid-1970s women gradually came to the conclusion that power inequalities between women and men also existed within the sphere of so-called 'body politics'. This implied that phenomena such as rape, battering of women, incest and abortion have a common structural element, namely the antagonism between the sexes, brought to the fore through sex role differentiation and inequality.

Patriarchy

In feminist theory the term 'patriarchy' indicates the rule of men. The word stands in a (juridical) historical tradition in which it refers to might, power and authority being centred on the *'pater'*, the man and father.[8] Women have used 'patriarchy' to explain the social and cultural factors and forces that maintain women's oppression and sexism. The supremacy women experience in the fields of labour and production, family and the relations

---

[7] A. E. Komter, *De macht van de vanzelfsprekendheid in relaties tussen vrouwen en mannen* (The power of self evidence in relationships between women and men) Gravenhage 1985 p.55 ff.

[8] H. Th. J.F. van Maarseveen,' "Rechtstheorie en vrouwen patiarchie als juridisch concept", ("Theory of law and women patriarchy as a judicial *concept",)* Nederlands Juristen Blad 1984 24

between the sexes is characterized as essentially masculine. The public and private spheres can in this sense not be separated: 'the personal is political'. In addition, sexual violence should be understood against the background of this patriarchal structure of our social world. Feminist theory has developed a theory of power and its unequal distribution. The starting point is sexuality, controlled by men, which thus determines the social division of gender.

Women's personal intimate experiences of rape, prostitution, abortion, *etc.* are not a random collection of details, but form the basis of the feminist explanation of women's oppression. Feminism thus is a theory which has sexuality as its central point and intends to explain the social and political order in terms of power relations between women and men. It is not limited to a theory of the state or state law. In this sense the door towards abolitionism is open – the abolitionism of Louk Hulsman with its aim of replacing the centrally regulated criminal justice system with a system of autonomous conflict regulations.

The concern of women that abolitionism takes away the protection of the criminal justice system is to a large extent based on a misunderstanding of the abolitionist view, as well as on an over-estimation of the ability of the criminal justice system. In the following paragraphs I will reflect on some more aspects of Hulsman's abolitionism as well as on his notion of power.

Further aspects of Hulsman's abolitionism

Conflict solving

Several theories have been developed to legitimate the existence and use of criminal justice. The grounds for these theories vary from violation of the so-called 'social contract' to ideas about (a combination of) retribution and prevention. All of these legitimating theories focus on the relation between the culprit and society, mostly represented by the state. It is on behalf of the whole of society that the state intervenes through the criminal justice system to take action against a suspect or offender. State intervention does not take place primarily on behalf of the victim. The position of the victim in the criminal justice system is peripheral. The victim plays a minor role activating the system through complaints and giving evidence during pre-trial and trial proceedings.[9] It is thus a misunderstanding to conclude that women's role becomes more active when they start reporting to the police.

The aim of intervention of state organs in conflict situations is not

---

[9] M. Spector and S. Batt, "Towards a more active victim", in J. R. Blad; W. van Mastrigt and N. A. Hildriks (eds). *The criminal justice system as a social problem, an abolitionist Perspective,* Mededelingen van het Juridisch Instituut van de EUR, no 36.1987.

primarily to solve the conflict of the people involved. According to Louk Hulsman, this could be the only reasonable ground for the interference of a third party. Drawing on Nils Christie[10] Hulsman conceives of conflicts as the property of those directly involved. By taking over problematical situations the state removes the possibility of those directly involved learning from their conflict and destroys its potential solution. Hulsman talks in this respect of 'revitalizing the social fabric'. By doing away with the macro level of state conflict regulation in favour of meso and micro levels of more autonomous conflict regulation, the conflict can be solved where it arose. The micro level stands for inter-individual face-to-face relationships. The meso level includes intermediary institutions like schools, churches, *etc.* At those levels the victim and more especially the offender do not exist as ontological categories, as is the case in the criminal justice system. Elements of victimization and offence are much more dispersed. The feeling of being a victim is not restricted to events over which the penal system is or could be involved. People usually associate this feeling with situations in their work or family. And it is also in such spheres that 'offenders' can be recognized who are hardly labelled as such. The firm definitions of 'criminality', 'crime' and 'culprit' in penal law procedure are not only far away from conflict regulation at the meso or micro level, but other language games and their corresponding practices are also ignored. For Hulsman, in order to make room for diversification in a tribal society, a new language is needed. Our present day notions of criminality and the culprit refer to stereotypes and are oriented towards centralized legislation. They are not related at all to our everyday life and we would be better off without them.

This does not mean that there is no function for juridical intervention, but that instead of constituting law it should follow law. This means that the solving of conflict situations should not be determined at the macro level but should be supported at the meso and micro levels of social interaction where solutions (potentially) exist.

What Hulsman says about power

Unlike Michel Foucault, Hulsman has not devoted lengthy contemplations to the notion of power. However he is very much inspired by Foucault's view on the topic. Like Foucault, Hulsman states that 'power inequalities are not absolute'. But he goes further. Power always, according to Hulsman, implies the existence of 'counter-power'. He mentions as an example the relationships between parents and (young) children. Although parents occupy

---

[10] Nils Christie, (1977) 'Conflicts as Property' *British Journal of Criminology,* Vol. 17, No. 1. pp. 1-15

a structurally more powerful position than their children, nearly all children are aware of the moments when they have a preponderance of power and exploit it. 'This also counts in other relationships within which structural power inequalities exist', Hulsman contends.[11]

Hulsman also follows Foucault when he states that power is much more than what is executed by means of law. Hulsman has characterized the attempts of women to expand the legislation concerning sexual violence as belonging to the Ten Commandments approach. By characterising them thus, he points out that the women movement approach to influencing the power relations between women and men is too simplistic. It is based on the idea of society in Moses' day. Nowadays our society, of which power relations form an integrated part, is more complex. It is definitely not enough to look primarily at legislation as the means of influencing human interaction. Hulsman invites us to take a closer look at those places where interaction actually takes place. In practice it appears to be much more complex than one could ever think of in theory.

The question of how people interact is of more relevance than why one has more power than the other. Hulsman aims to strengthen individuals and revitalize the 'social tissue'. He warns us to beware of the definition power of legislation and the powerful impact of concepts like 'crime' and 'criminality'. Hulsman stresses the power that fixes the border lines between legality and illegality, between 'non-crime' and 'crime', and consequently between activating the criminal justice system machine or not. Criminal justice, if activated, leaves no bargaining power to those directly involved.

Concluding remarks

The women's liberation movement considers the sensational decision of the Dutch Supreme Court acquittal in the case of rape as a setback in their struggle for a different conception of the problem of sexual violence. By means of various kinds of actions and activities, women have emphasized that sexual violence should be conceived of as a structural problem. One of those activities consisted in pleading for more grounds for prosecution. According to Louk Hulsman, this is the most one-sided and non-creative solution to the problems posed. We can understand this criticism if we keep in mind the apple of Louk Hulsman. Enlarging the number of grounds for prosecution implies that solutions are sought within the core of the apple, not in other parts or outside of it. On the other hand, the feminist criticism of Hulsman's

---

[11] L.H.C. Hulsman *Afscheid van het strafrecht: een pleidooi voor zelfregulering* (A farewell to criminal justice: a plea for self-regulation) Houten 1986 p. 122

analysis is that certain aspects are left out of the picture. What happens in cases of rape should, according to most feminists, be considered as the reflection on a micro scale of power inequalities that exist between women and men in society at large. As the abolitionism of Louk Hulsman doesn't explicitly go into societal structures, it will not explain the problems of sexual violence as being part and parcel of women's powerlessness.

Like Foucault, Hulsman is of the opinion that power in itself does not explain anything, rather, it itself needs explanation. Instead of posing the question 'why are women time and again the suffering party?' it tries to answer the alternative question 'how does the woman nearly always become the victim?' In this way it tries to avoid essentialist notions that feminists also try to eliminate. They state:

> The meaning of assault and battery is not settled by stating that it deals with women/girls as opposed to men/boys. That meaning depends, for example, on the specific context or the subjective experience of people involved[12]

In the abolitionist view solutions to problematical situations which arise should be sought in each specific context. 'Feminist practice' already shows how problems of sexual violence can be dealt with in non-criminal justice ways, for example by initiating social aid, organizing mental aid, founding rape crisis centres and centres for battered women. Furthermore, women claim street prohibition, park prohibition, housing prohibition, dial and contact prohibition within civil jurisdiction, as well as financial compensation for damage. Also, with regard to prevention and defence, women themselves have found how rape and injury could be avoided and what methods of defence can be used.

The above-mentioned sensational decision shows it is hardly of any use to fight for a different text of the Penal Code. With regard to cases of rape, the decisive factor is not the text of the law, nor the report of the woman, but a dominant vision of what in our society counts as rape. The administration of justice thus turns out to be an implementation of a dominant view of rape rather than a means of fighting against it. Feminist theory can benefit from the decision of the Dutch Supreme Court. It appears to be of no use to apply energy to changing the words of the Penal Code's articles. On the contrary, feminism's strong and creative characteristics are threatened.

---

[12] *Tijdschrift voor Vrouwenstudies* 2, 1986 p.140

Bibliography

Christie, N. (1977) 'Conflicts as Property' *British Journal of Criminology*, Vol. 17, No. 1. pp. 1-15

Hulsman, L.H.C. (1979) 'Een abolitionistisch (afschaffend) perspectief op het strafrechtelijk systeem', in *Problematiek van de strafrechtspraak* Een publikatie van het Nederlands Gesprek Centrum, Baarn.

Hulsman L.H.C. (1986) *Afscheid van het strafrecht: een pleidooi voor zelfregulering* (A farewell to criminal justice: a plea for self-regulation) Houten.

Komter, A. E. (1985) *De macht van de vanzelfsprekendheid in relaties tussen vrouwen en mannen* (The power of self evidence in relationships between women and men) Gravenhage.

Maarseveen, H. van (1984) 'Rechtstheorie en vrouwen patiarchie als juridisch concept', (Theory of law and women patriarchy as a judicial *concept,) Nederlands Juristen Blad*.

Maarseveen, H. van (1988) 'Een arrest dat schoffeert'" *Nederlands Junsten Blad*, 11 June 1988.

Spector M. and Batt, S. (1987) 'Towards a more active victim', in J R Blad; W van Mastrigt and N A. Hildriks (eds). *The criminal justice system as a social problem, an abolitionist perspective,* Mededelingen van het Juridisch Instituut van de EUR, no 36.

Tijdschrift voor Vrouwenstudies 2, 1986

14

Mediation: An Experiment in Finland

Marti Gronfors

This paper was delivered at the European Group's 15th annual conference in Vienna and first published in Working Papers in European Criminology, Volume 9 'Justice & Ideology: Strategies for the 1990s in 1989.

Introduction

In 1984 a locally modified version of community mediation was started in the city of Vantaa, Finland, alongside which research was carried out during 1984 and 1985. This paper is based mainly on this empirical research. The final analyses are still in progress, so in some instances the results are tentative. The empirical work consisted of interviews with participants in mediation, conducted as focused personal interviews, interviews with the mediators themselves, a review of the documentation kept during the two year observation period, including prosecution files, police files and court records. Finally, the personal experiences of the two researchers (who had been with the project right from the start) were utilised as additional material.

Conflict and its Resolution

Conflicts differ in their nature, and it is important to recognise what kind of conflict is being dealt with before its resolution can be attempted. Also, conflict is not always negative as it can contain energy for change at the level of individual human interaction, the community or the whole society. Conflict is also something different from a mere problem. To make a somewhat simple distinction between the two a conflict refers to communication and interaction, while a problem relates primarily to an individual person. While a conflict cannot be satisfactorily resolved unilaterally, the solution to a problem lies mainly within the person having the problem. In the long run the consequences of ignoring conflicts can be more destructive than attempts at handling or resolving them.[1]

---

[1] See A. D. Sarat (1984) 'The Emergence of Disputes' in *A Study of Barriers to the Use of Alternative*

Dispute-processing options[2]

The following are possible ways of processing disputes:

1   Unilateral actions on the part of a disputant:
    a)   Inaction,
    b)   active avoidance,
    c)   self-help,
        i.   re-definition of problem,
        ii. elimination of the deficit,
        iii. use of social work and other agencies.
2   Dyadic options—contacts between disputing parties:
    a)   coercion (threats and use of force),
    b)   negotiation.
3   Third party resolution techniques:
    a)   Conciliation   (bringing   parties   together   for negotiation),
    b)   Mediation (structured communication, recommendations),
        i.   General meditational projects,
        ii. Projects mediating limited disputes for the general public,
        iii. Projects mediating general disputes for a limited segment of the public.
    c)   Arbitration,
        i.   General arbitration projects,
        ii. Arbitration of small claim matters,
        iii. Consumer arbitration,
        iv. Contractually based arbitration.
    d)   Fact-finding,
        i.   Media action lines,
        ii. Trade association projects,
        iii. Government projects.
    e)   Administrative procedures,
        i.   Court-oriented processing,
        ii. Informal court-operated processing,
        iii. Routine administrative processing,

Methods of Dispute Resolution, South Royalton, Vermont: Vermont Law School pp. 29-36.
[2] See D. McGillis and H. Mullen *Neighborhood Justice Centers an Analysis of Potential Models*, US Department of Justice, October 1977, p. 5.

        iv. Measures reducing or eliminating the need
            for adjudication,
        v. Measures simplifying adjudication.
  f) Adjudication.

In attempting to resolve the conflict it is necessary to take account of the various characteristics which influence the birth of the conflict, its nature and progress. Firstly, there are the *personal characteristics* of the participants, their values, motivations, aims, their physical, psychological and social resources, their beliefs about the conflict and their thoughts about how the matter should proceed. Second is the *relationship between the participants*, their attitudes, beliefs and expectations of each other. Thirdly, there are the *types of matters* under dispute, matters relating to the conflict's birth, its extent, the degree of seriousness, the motivation for continuing or resolving the conflict, how it is seen and whether it is thought to be a unique event or a continuation of events. Fourth is the *social setting* which influences the continuation or resolution of the conflict and the prospects of resolution. Fifthly, the progress of the conflict is influenced by the existence of *other interested parties* who have their own outside reasons for continuing or resolving the conflict. Sixth are the various *strategies and tactics* used in disputing positive or negative factors such as promises, threats and punishments, openness or the lack of it, what the parties attempt to influence and by what means. And lastly, what are the *consequences* of keeping up conflict or resolving it? What is gained or lost, and how are the participants' reputations affected by it?[3]

There are two main opposing ways of handling disputes, namely, co-operative and competitive styles. The former is characterised by open and honest exchange of information, while the competitive style is marked by secrecy and wrong information. If positive solutions are attempted, at least the following are important. The attitude of both parties should be positive towards the resolution of their conflict. Information supplied for the resolution should be open and accurate. There should be an active search for common aims and advantages. Parties should develop a trust of each other and behave honestly and with friendliness towards each other. The matters under dispute should be clearly defined and a non-accusatory attitude should be employed. The substance of the conflict should be in focus, not the personalities involved.

---

[3] M. Deutsch *The Resolution of Conflict: Constructive and Destructive Processes,* New Haven, Yale University Press, 1973, pp. 5-7.

The Vantaa project: aims and framework

Either at the outset of the project or as a result of the early mediation experiences, certain broad and general aims were established for the project. Among the more important were the following:

1   an attempt to hand back some power to the community and individuals;

2   an assumption that conflicts (including criminal ones) are a part of normal communication processes;

3   solutions to conflicts should be attempted as quickly as possible and as close to the place of their occurrence as possible;

4   acceptance of differences is positive and enriching, handling conflicts develops communal life positively and can unite community members;

5   it is desirable that the horizons of all people are widened, open-minded people are a positive community resource;

6   instead of treatment or punishment, it is important to develop the communicative skills of people, and shift attention to compensation;

7   non-judgemental interaction is encouraged.

On a practical day-to-day basis certain general operating principles were considered important. The mediators should work *with* the participants, not for them. Mediators are not solving problems, they are not experts, but they are helping the participants to develop their own communicative skills. It is of paramount importance that mediators recognise what is under dispute, as often the dispute which participants bring forth is not the real dispute between them. In mediation negotiations the actual process of mediation is more important than the practical and/or concrete end results. The mediators' overall aim is to provide the participants with survival skills, and to provide a model by which the disputants can in future resolve their conflicts without the aid of a professional mediator.

Structure and Organisation of the Vantaa Project

The project was established as an 'open system', with no clear decisions made in advance as to where the cases should come from, what kinds of cases were to be handled and so on, as these were considered part of the experimentation. One purpose that the project had was to develop guidelines for other possible similar mediation schemes in future. It was emphasised from the beginning that the scheme should operate as an alternative to the official system, not a supplement to it.

Finance for the initial project came from a variety of sources: state finance for the research; municipal and church finance for the practical operations of the project. During the experimental years the control of the project was largely in the hands of the researchers and voluntary mediators although the advisory panel (of the local authorities) also exercised considerable power, as they, in part, controlled the case input. Mediators, who were voluntary and unpaid, were trained for their task in three different ways, including firstly, an initial 30-hour theoretical course organised by the local adult education college. In that course they were given some rudimentary knowledge of the workings of the justice system and some theoretical knowledge about mediation and related matters. Secondly, mediation skills were primarily learned in weekend live-in seminars, where role play was used extensively. Thirdly, on-the-job individual and group supervision was provided throughout the experimental period.

Cases

Cases for mediation came directly from the participants, either from the aggrieved party or from the party against whom certain accusations or claims were made. These could, in principle, be of any kind, either civil matters or matters which would be defined as criminal if they were brought to the notice of the authorities. The parties contacted the mediation office which was staffed during office hours, or left a message on an answer phone if contact was made outside office hours. The authorities, especially the police, the prosecutor and the child welfare officers, were encouraged to refer suitable cases to mediation. The guidelines for the suitability were firstly that the cases should be clear-cut, where there is no dispute about the guilt of the person; as it is not an appropriate use of mediation to act as an investigatory service. Secondly the cases should be relatively minor ones, and of a kind where there is room for negotiation and compromise. Particularly suitable were thought to be the cases where the victim of a crime has the onus whether to proceed further with the prosecution, a common assault, when there are no injuries, is one example. Rape and other crimes of this serious nature were ruled out because they were not thought suitable for mediation.

During the two experimental years roughly 140 cases were handled by the service. By the end of 1985, the number of civil cases had declined to almost nothing. The criminal cases were primarily minor violent offences, and minor property offences, including vandalism. In 52 cases a written agreement involving compensation was prepared, and in a further 12 cases an assurance was given that the disputed matter was resolved. Of the 29 agreements in 1984, 25 were fulfilled. The information for 1985 was not adequate enough for the similar figures to be given.

Evaluative Comments

As the total number of cases handled by mediation was relatively low, quantitative analysis becomes very difficult. Breaking down the initially small figures into various categories would make the categories so small that there would not be more than a few cases in each thus making any conclusions drawn from the operation of mediation meaningless. For that reason, only a qualitative, processual analysis seems possible. This form of analysis has examined the various cases as a process, looking for the significant points of interest in each case. Looked at in this way, it is then not important, for example, that an agreement was reached. It is more important to see what is the nature of the case, the characteristics of the participants, and the way in which the agreement either was or was not reached.

From this examination it appears that mediation seems to operate at its best when there is a true conflict discernible between the participants. Therefore it is important to recognise in mediation the different *types* of conflict. A conflict also has to be kept separate from a mere *problem*, which can be either psychological or practical. The techniques of solving problems require different expertise from those of resolving conflicts. Problems in general need expert advice, not mediation skills. Therefore, it is questionable if mediation is an answer for problems, the answer for which seems to lie in individuals, not in the relationship, as is the case with conflicts. As the mediators are trained in communicative skills, they cannot also be expected to act as experts in the multitude of personal problems people have. Even more importantly the mediator should not be expected to act as a lay lawyer; the use of mediation in this way could actually jeopardise the rights of the people using mediation, as mediators cannot be aware of all the legal complexities which people encounter. Similar comments apply to cases where people suffer from personal problems which would require extensive counselling. Again mediation is not a service which is intended for that purpose. At best mediation could act as a referral service when cases identified as problems are brought to them.

An *objective* conflict is the kind when the true conflict is perceived by the parties as such. A *symptomatic* conflict is one where the issue which brought the parties to mediation differs from the true underlying conflict. *Situational* conflict is where the circumstances of the participants bring them into conflict with one another. *Wrong* conflict can occur when the participants are fighting over issues which are not the real issues between them. *False* conflict can occur when there is absolutely no reason for the parties to be in conflict with one another. There could also be *wrong conflict parties* locked into a battle with each other. The task of the mediator is to find out what kind of conflict it is before it can be dealt with appropriately.

It appears that when mediators are dealing with problems rather than interpersonal conflicts, they are stepping into an expert role (psychologist, lawyer), entering into an area in which they are neither trained nor competent to operate. In negotiated settlements in cases which could be classed as problems, the mediators have negotiated compensations when no Finnish court would have done so, and it seems that in some cases the compensation agreement is bigger than a competent court would have settled. In cases where there are personal problems involved, mediators who take the role of a counsellor undertake tasks which can exceed their competence and can also create dependent relationships which the mediators are unable to see through or bring to a satisfactory halt. In cases where the mediators have attempted to deal with the problem as if it were a true conflict situation, the solution cannot be in the best interests of both parties, as it should be in mediation. There are also some indications that a relatively higher failure rate could be related to confusing a problem with a conflict.

When mediators concentrated on interpersonal matters, it usually resulted in the mutual satisfaction of the participants. When the mediators acted as experts by concentrating primarily on fixing compensation, especially monetary compensation, the level of satisfaction was somewhat lower. The recipient of the compensation often felt that it was not enough and the person required to pay it thought it was too much. Serious problems were encountered with the quality of justice, when, for example, unemployed young people agreed to relatively large amounts of compensation, although probably this level of compensation would not have been ordered had the case gone directly to court. Also, the needs of justice probably were not served in cases which were dealt with in court as well after a successful mediation. Although the court may reduce the sentence of conditional imprisonment from, say, six months to three months, the effect felt by the offender is not the same as intended by the court. Before mediation can operate effectively in conjunction with the official criminal justice system in the case of crimes, the prosecution must make more use of the provision of non-prosecution and the court should have more powers and willingness to suspend sentencing in successfully mediated cases.

In the interviews with participants it is overwhelmingly clear that they have welcomed this opportunity to communicate with each other. This seems to be the case particularly with juvenile offenders, who were able to have a voice in their own affairs. Although it is not possible to ascertain from the material available if this method of handling disputes has been utilised by participants in other conflict situations, at least they have been shown that there are other ways of handling their conflicts than those which they thought possible.

While the participants are in general impressed by the informality of mediation, it is apparent that, as the service became more established (in 1985), the formality, routine and bureaucratic way of operating tended to increase. This is evidenced by the kinds of solutions to conflicts that were negotiated. Whilst in the early days of the service a genuine effort seems to have been made to find the kinds of solutions which suited the particular case best, towards the end of the experimental period more and more cases included a purely financial settlement.

While in 1984 approximately 20% of the cases included either full or partial reparation by work, only one agreement in 1985 involved such compensation. This seems to point to the dangers of these types of innovations, as it seems that, without continued attention to the aims and procedures, there is a tendency to resort to those solutions with which people are familiar. The issue of how 'voluntary' mediation is maybe a difficult one, particularly in the case of criminal offenders. When cases came directly from the public, the offender usually agrees to mediation to avoid formal prosecution. In cases which come from the authorities (police, prosecutor, child welfare officer), the issue of voluntariness must be weighed against the expectations of the offenders—*i.e.* whether or not the case should go to court—and usually they anticipate that mediation will provide a better outcome than that offered by prosecution or court appearance. In interviewing the young offenders it was quite apparent that most of them did not even realise that their participation in mediation was operating outside the official system but thought that it was a part of the official system. This was in spite of the fact that it was explained to them when the suggestion to go to mediation was made.

Reasons for agreeing to mediation vary from one case to the next. In the case of juvenile offenders, the victims are motivated by the desire to deal with their case in a more humane way than would happen in the official system. Sometimes the fact that participants knew each other prompted bringing it to mediation. As far as the police were concerned, the motivation for diverting cases to mediation varies from the genuine feeling that a particular case is more suitable for mediation than for processing through the official system, to a desire to divert 'messy' but not particularly serious cases.

Prosecution cases seem to be diverted for similar reasons, although there seem to be some indications that prosecution could be motivated, with the tacit cooperation of the mediation service, by the desire to catch offenders belonging to gangs when some have escaped official notice. From the analysis of successfully mediated cases it is possible to see that, in the cases which come directly from the offenders themselves, the chances of a successful outcome are increased, as the motivational level of both parties is usually high.

The level of participation in the process of mediation by the participants depends a great deal on the role which the mediators take in the negotiations. Some participants felt that the mediator was on the side of one party or another, and this usually did not aid mutual communication. Some mediators experienced problems in communication when the relative power positions of the participants were very different (young versus older persons, articulate versus inarticulate, and so on). Some mediators felt that their role as facilitators of communication was hampered by the self-righteous attitude of some victims of crime, as well as by the sullen attitude of some young offenders.

The decision to use lay mediators seems to have been the right one, in that they are able to adopt the principles of mediation quicker than people trained in the helping professions, who in general find it quite difficult to adjust from their role as a problem solver to that of a communication facilitator. The mediators themselves, when their motivations for joining the service were examined, showed that they had higher than average awareness of community problems and also higher than average interest in dealing with the particular kinds of problems they had encountered in their community. They were not a truly representative sample of community sentiment. Many had personal experience of some of the problems which are involved in the workings of the official criminal justice system. They had, for example, a family member who had been, in their opinion, roughly treated by the official system, or they had observed in their neighbourhood that the way in which the official system operates, especially in the case of younger people, is not to their liking. There were also some law students who wanted to see how community alternatives to justice worked out in practice. Surprisingly few mediators joined the service from the conventional 'do-gooding' need, and those who did quite quickly had to abandon their ideas in the face of the majority opinion of the mediators, who operated from a certain critical and ideological standpoint.

On the whole, it appears that the mediators have proved to be a truly positive community resource. Mediation work has been experienced as a meaningful way of participating in community life. Most mediators think that they are doing a worthwhile job and answering a clear community need. One of the most difficult issues for the mediators to comprehend is that they are primarily only facilitators of communication and not a problem-solving service. Those mediators who in their everyday work deal with people's problems have found it particularly difficult to shift their thinking.

The Place of Mediation in the Modern Community

The area covered by this experimental service was very large, containing some 50,000 inhabitants. Therefore it can be said that its effect on reducing community tensions at the level of the general community would be negligible. So far the effect is felt mainly by direct participants, by mediators themselves and maybe also by certain local authorities who have had a chance to think differently about conflicts in the community they are serving. Mediation is suitable primarily in cases of conflicts where the participants know each other and where there is a chance that they will meet each other in the future. It is best suited to handle interpersonal conflicts and least suited to handle cases where the participants are unwillingly tied to contracts (especially financial ones) over a long period of time. The cost of mediation has not been calculated, as the experimental years would give misleading figures. However, it is felt on the basis of evaluating the various aspects of mediation that its value rests on factors other than financial costs.

The issue of how 'just' mediation is could be looked at in a number of different ways. It is possible to look at it in the 'objective' way by comparing, for example, the amounts of compensation fixed for equivalent cases dealt with by mediation and the official system. Also, it would be possible to look at what could have happened to offenders had they been dealt with in court for similar offences. Both these comparisons are important only to the extent that they give some quantitative measure of mediation. And in this respect, it appears that mediation could be only marginally, if at all, more 'just' than the official justice system. In relation to compensation, it appears that the level agreed in mediation could actually be higher than would have been the case had they been fixed by the courts. With the lack of established possibilities of waiving prosecution in all cases of successful mediation, most offenders who came to mediation through the official system had to face *both* mediation and a court appearance. In so far as the majority of cases were relatively minor ones, where either a fine or a conditional sentence of imprisonment was imposed, a slight reduction in those does not compensate for the dual procedure. It is more important, however, to look at the way in which the participants felt about mediation. Looked at in a qualitative way, the amount of satisfaction felt by the participants after a successful mediation session seems to make the system more 'just' than the official system. People generally felt that they were getting justice, although objectively they actually could have been worse off than without the intermediate step of mediation.[4]

In the Finnish system mediation cannot be said to-reduce the work of the official justice system to any significant degree, as those cases which came from the authorities were usually also dealt with by the official court system. An exception to this was the small category of crimes where the complainant had the power to stop further proceedings after a successful mediation. Such crimes are those involving minor violence, where there were no injuries to the complainant, minor cases of wilful damage, *etc.* In the individual cases which were successfully mediated it can be said that people's conflicts were transferred back to them. An active participation in the disposal on one's case must be a small way towards giving power over their own affairs back to people. The larger issue of community empowerment cannot really be ascertained from this experiment as the mediation service could not be said to have touched very much the general life of the community. However, should mediation spread to many other spheres of community life and become an established way of dealing with various community problems, it could then be said to have transferred power back to the community in a real and concrete way, but that time is still quite a long way off.

Similar comments apply to the effect of mediation on the general society. However, there has been a marked increase in mediation schemes in Finland since the beginning of this experimental project, and at the moment there are schemes either underway or being planned in over 20 cities throughout Finland. So, even if mediation cannot be said to have (yet) had any significant role in a general critique of society, it can be said to have provided a well-wanted service in the community. What can be said is that an uncritical expansion of mediation may not serve the ends of the carefully planned development of mediation. It appears that enthusiasm about mediation has overtaken a considered ideologically grounded establishment of this service in the community. The basis of mediation, even now, is mainly a populist one rather than a political or ideological one.[5]

The idea that people should generally—within limits of their reason and ability—be given a chance to deal with their own conflicts must be supported on the basis of this evaluation. However, as is evident from the examination of the cases in this research, the victims of crimes and offenders, as well as those who are involved in civil conflicts, often start negotiations from quite unbalanced positions of power. This imbalance could be used for gaining an

---

[4] Editors' note: For critical reflections on the problem of introducing mediation without first abolishing the penal apparatus see Cohen. S. (1985)*Visions of Social Control,* Cambridge: Polity Press.

[5] Editors' Note: See discussion by Joe Sim, this volume chapter 8.

advantageous position in negotiations; hence the need for mediators to be trained to balance the power differentials. Should mediation extend widely into many different walks of life the possibility of extortion and naked use of power could actually increase. Therefore, it appears that there should be a check on those cases where this kind of usage is possible, and this seems to speak against the total abolition of the due process model.

Mediation, in the case of criminal matters, seems to be a true alternative to the criminal justice system only in cases where a successfully mediated case does not have to be dealt with by the official system. At the moment both the legal restrictions for waiving prosecution and judicial practice seem to work in such a way that in criminal matters mediation is additional to any other procedure, rather than alternative. When public funds are being used for running mediation, it is much more difficult to institute a totally new way of handling criminal conflicts. The old bureaucratic thinking, which contains elements of judgement and punishment, is so deeply entrenched in the minds of bureaucrats that it seems very difficult to introduce non-judgemental and non-punishing ideas into dealing with criminal matters. When mediation is closely linked to the existing bureaucracy, there are also power games involved. This project has not escaped these, and any bureaucratic power game, when it is connected to mediation, makes mediation less of an alternative than it could ideally be.

The issue of co-option is connected to the previous point, and it is evident from this experiment that the danger of co-option into the official system is quite real. In a climate which views mediation very favourably there are plenty of those who consider mediation only in an instrumental way, either for furthering their own careers, or for the prestige of a particular office, or the prestige of an organisation, hence, there is much competition over the control of mediation. The more the instrumental concerns dominate mediation the less are the chances of considering mediation as an independent system of handling conflicts which benefits the people whose conflicts are being handled by the service.

Bibliography

Cohen. S. (1985) *Visions of Social Control,* Cambridge: Polity Press.

Deutsch M. (1973) *The Resolution of Conflict: Constructive and Destructive Processes,* New Haven: Yale University Press.

McGillis, D. and Mullen H. (1977) *Neighborhood Justice Centers an Analysis of Potential Models*, US Department of Justice.

Sarat, A D (1984) 'The Emergence of Disputes' in *A Study of Barriers to the Use of Alternative Methods of Dispute Resolution*, Vermont Law School Dispute Resolution Project South Royalton, Vermont.

Conclusion

15

'It's a long road to wisdom, but it is a short one to being ignored'[1]: moving forward towards abolition

David Scott and J.M. Moore

> You see, if I look at my own experience ... because I live for more or less a century. I am 84 now... when you have such a large space to see all the things... all the things you have seen change... When you look in such a sort of way on it then... you know that things can change very fast... I am firmly convinced that nobody knows about the future... We should certainly not think that criminal justice could not be abolished.[2]

The papers brought together in this collection were all presented to *European Group for the Study of Deviance and Social Control* annual conferences between 1981 and 1988. Despite the quarter of a century since they were first published being characterised by a period of penal expansion it is important that we, like Louk Hulsman in the quote above, retain a belief in the possibility of penal abolition. Indeed this expansion in the sheer number of people incarcerated (or otherwise supervised by criminal justice agencies) and the growing punitive ideology underpinning many other aspects of social policy, makes abolitionist ideas even more essential in the struggle for social justice. In this conclusion we explore how the contributions included in this collection demonstrate the continuing importance of abolitionist thought in understanding and responding to the contemporary punitive state.

The importance of abolitionist theory

Abolitionism represents a concerted assault upon the logic of the penal rationale and its current deployment in the institutions of the criminal law. It

---

[1] The title is from the lyrics of 'Flowers in your Hair 'by *The Lumineers*
[2] Cited in Roberts, R. (2007) 'What happened to abolitionism? An investigation of a paradigm and a social movement', Unpublished MA Thesis London School of Economics p.36

is therefore essential, as Willem de Haan pointed out in chapter four, for abolitionist analysis to be thoroughly grounded in social theory and moral and political philosophy.   Punishment may well have no moral defence, but abolitionism must have one in order to survive and grow in contemporary societies. By engaging with contemporary social theory abolitionism is not only given a new conceptual language and continued relevance in times of rapidly changing social (and penal) circumstances, but it also helps develop a new rationale and philosophical justification for abolitionism itself. Willem de Haan makes a convincing argument that abolitionists must demonstrate not only that punishment is morally flawed but also that it *is possible* to imagine a world without prisons. Drawing the abolitionist's attention to the value of philosophy, he calls for normative and 'utopian' thinking to show that punishment is not inevitable. Like a number of other abolitionists, perhaps most notably Barbara Hudson,[3] he makes connections between abolitionism and contemporary theories of justice. Both Barbara Hudson and Willem de Haan conclude that punishment is incompatible with justice – in other words justice cannot be created or restored through the criminal law. That we must strive for justice without punishment is an important argument for abolitionists to make.

Central to abolitionist theory is a rejection of taken for granted assumptions about the meaning and nature of 'crime'. Abolitionists recognise that 'crime' is socially constructed and, in the words of Louk Hulsman, has no 'ontological reality' – it has no essence or essential characteristics.[4] As Sebation Scheerer argues in chapter five the formation, deployment and hegemony of the language of 'crime', 'criminals', 'offenders' and so on, has proved to be historically significant in terms of the justifications and expansion of the penal apparatus of the state.   Whilst it is therefore important to reject such language abolitionists neither reject 'reality' nor are they 'utopian' and 'idealistic' as some critics claim. These 'left realist' critiques are effectively responded to by Heinz Steinert in chapter three. Indeed, as many of the chapters in this book clearly demonstrate, detailed accounts of the actual reality of the criminal process provide powerful empirical evidence to support arguments in favour of abolition.

Within abolitionist theory the penal apparatus of the state is firmly located within its socio-economic, historical and political *contexts*. As Joe Sim highlights in chapter eight, prisons are 'warehouses for the poor' and thus to remain both theoretically and politically potent abolitionism must continue to engage with contemporary writings on the political economy of punishment

---

[3] Hudson, B.A. (2003) *Justice in the Risk Society* London: Sage
[4] Hulsman, L. (1986) "Critical Criminology and the concept of Crime" in *Contemporary Crises* Volume 10, pp 63-80

and related disciplines.   It also remains a truism that the increasing authoritarianism in penal regimes and policing practices can only be understood when located within the wider drift towards a more authoritarian 'law and order society'. Raffaele Calderone and Piere Valeriani similarly argue in chapter seven that prisons are 'theatres of class conflict' and therefore it is important, if anti-prison activists are to be successful, that they make connections with left wing political organisations and other social movements promoting freedom, social justice and recognition of common humanity. In chapter three Heinz Steinert calls for abolition to be understood as part of a wider political struggle against repression, domination and inhumanity.   In this sense abolitionism is a broad based liberation movement aiming to emancipate the powerless and dehumanised. As a number of chapters have highlighted, abolitionists search for non-authoritarian ways in which the consequences of 'crime' and troublesome conduct can be minimised.

The consistent failure of criminal justice

Abolitionists recognise that the criminal law cannot provide safety and protection and we cannot achieve liberation and emancipation through punitive means. Criminal processes always fail as they are about domination and as such are incapable of successfully responding to the terrible events and losses that human beings sometimes have to face. The criminal law is clouded in a great deception – that it exists to serve the people – but people are always subservient to the needs of the penal system, which itself serves its masters and the higher interests of the state. As Rene van Swaaningen argues in chapter ten, we should be very wary of those who place the institutions of criminal law on a pedestal and as Jolandeuit Beijerse and Rene Kool argue in chapter twelve, be very sceptical of the apparent seductions of the criminal law.

So what then does the criminal process actually achieve? It is particularly good at damaging human beings and then 'othering' them so that they become social outcasts. It creates false hierarchies, delivers pain and morally degrades the poor and powerless. Significantly, the criminal process is also a means of using people to demonstrate power – *state power*. It has also, as Sebastian Scheerer highlights in chapter five, proved to be very successful in the colonisation of the life world. The penal system, consumed by a 'pathological over-criminalisation', has led to not only the rapid expansion of state bureaucracies and placed new populations of petty offenders under penal control but also has significantly increased the repressive capabilities of state power.[5]

In their opposition to violence abolitionists are particular concerned about the violence of state. For Jacqueline Bernat de Celis prisons are places of brutality, harm and death whilst Joe Sim argues that prison regimes are predicated on violence, drawing specific attention to the institutionalisation of hegemonic masculinity and male violence. He also evidences extreme male violence perpetrated by prison officers. A number of the chapters explored issues around prison staff and highlight how prison officers naturalise the brutality of the prison environment. Under such conditions there appears to be a change in the moral threshold of prison officers. Where a palpable hostility exists between prisoners and prison officers – which Phil Scraton and Kathryn Chadwick in chapter nine argued is generated by the hierarchical nature of prison officer authority – other pains generated by the daily practices of repressive penal regimes are exacerbated even further.[6]

By recognising that prisons are difficult places for people to survive in Scraton and Chadwick challenge the individual pathology underscoring official discourses of why people take their own lives in custody. Self-inflicted deaths in prison are not the result of the failings of 'high risk inadequates' but of the inherent harms of imprisonment. Ida Koch in chapter six also explored these harms detailing the awful long term damage that the mental isolation of solitary confinement inflicted on detainees, destroying previous attachments and making future mutuality virtually impossible. For Raffaele Calderone and Piere Valeriani prisons increase the propensity for dangerousness rather than reduce it. The greater the penal repression, the more austere the penal regime, the more intense the disciplinary techniques deployed, the more likely prisoner resistance, disturbance and outbreaks of physical violence.

Radical alternatives beyond criminal justice

As Joe Sim, in chapter eight, points out any solution to the penal crises must start by closing prisons and other penal institutions and not building new ones. To achieve this requires the creation of alliances with progressive social movements and especially with the people directly impacted by the excesses of the criminal law such as prisoners' families and ex-prisoners. As the chapters by Willemien de Jongste and Marijke Meima make clear, abolitionists must also construct a progressive alliance with feminist, victim and other pro-justice groups based on shared concerns about the harm perpetrated against vulnerable groups. Central to building this coalition is the positive agenda of abolitionism. As Angela Davis has recently argued:

---

[5] See Cohen, S. (1985) *Visions of Social Control* Cambridge: Polity Press
[6] See Scott, D. (2014) *The Caretakers of Punishment* London: Palgrave

> abolition involves much more than the abolition of prisons. It also involves the creation of new institutions that will effectively speak to the social problems that lead people to prison. ... (It requires the) shifting of priorities from the prison-industrial complex to education, housing, (and) health care.[7]

Social inequalities and social injustice are the most significant problems we face. Even when looking at inter-personal and relational conflicts abolitionism points to the need to consider broader structural and political contexts. It is clear that we require solutions based upon equality, equity and social justice rather than penal repression. Abolitionism therefore combines the advocation of change in the penal system with a demand for radical change at a societal level.

New ways of resolving conflicts, troubles and difficulties are needed not only for those problematic behaviours currently processed by the criminal law but which also address the harms of power and interpersonal abuses – such as sexual violence, corporate harms, environmental destruction and state sanctioned killings – problems and conflicts which are largely neglected by the criminal law and penal system. As a number of the previous chapters have noted abolition means adopting a different way of looking at the world – a different way of thinking. Central to this, as Louk Hulsman[8] has highlighted, is the need to learn not to think about 'crime and punishment' – we need to decolonise ourselves of the language of penal repression, domination and authoritarianism. We must learn to take troubles, conflicts and individual and social problems seriously without falling into a punitive trap – to abolish repressive state apparatus and replace them with assistance for conflict resolution and other 'radical alternatives' that in the *real* world actually help people.

A number of key principles underscore these radical alternatives. Abolitionists acknowledge that most problematic and troublesome behaviours are dealt with outside the criminal process – interventions by the penal law are exceptions rather than the norm.[9] Abolitionists also recognise human diversity whilst at the same time that 'offenders' are not exceptional and cannot be othered as 'them'. By recognising the nuances and diversity of struggles for justice abolitionists recognise that there can be no one 'blanket alternative'. Abolitionist alternatives are based on a realistic assessment of

---

[7] Davis, A.Y. (2012) *The Meaning of Freedom,* San Francisco: City Lights Books pp. 52,113
[8] Hulsman, L. (1986) "Critical Criminology and the concept of Crime" in *Contemporary Crises* Volume 10, pp 63-80
[9] Ibid

what is possible, they engage with people's lived experiences and offer realistic ways in which human conflicts and problematic conducts can be managed. In chapter fourteen Marti Gronfors provided a case study of one possible alternative – mediation. He highlights the crucial distinction between resolving conflicts and solving problems – mediation can deal with communication between the parties to a conflict, but problems require more specialist interventions. An abolitionist vision of a future society would see the oppressive and authoritarian penal apparatus – based around repressive policing and pain inflicting prisons – replaced perhaps by a new 'Reconciliation and Conflict Resolution Service' and expert 'Problem Solving Services'. Compensation, support and redress for the person harmed could be the core functions of such services. Drawing upon Willem de Haan's arguments in chapter four we would see the use of 'sanctions' rather than punishments.[10]

Finally, there is the problem of ensuring that abolitionist wisdom informs policy and practice in societies which deploy repressive and authoritarian means in response to 'criminality'. Abolitionists must walk a tightrope between being co-opted by state agencies and being defined out of the dialogue all together. In a crucial contribution to the debate, Thomas Mathiesen talked about the 'competing contradiction' – an argument that could compete with dominant ideologies and discourses on 'crime' and punishment but which at the same time undermined and contradicted their central logic.[11] This idea is essential for abolitionist interventions in the present. As Joe Sim has argued, we must look to 'exploit contradictions' in the existing system whilst engaging in counter-hegemonic struggles and forms of contestation that allow current 'common sense' on 'crime' to be turned into 'good sense'.[12] To achieve this abolitionism needs therefore to take three key steps:

1. *Ensure theoretical and political coherence* by developing an understandable counter-hegemonic set of principles that can challenge common sense and authoritarian ideologies.
2. *Build a social movement* by making alliances and constructing an alternative power base that could have political influence.

---

[10] For discussion here see Boonin, D. (2008) *The Problem of Punishment* Cambridge: Cambridge University Press
[11] Mathiesen, T. (1974) *The Politics of Abolition* oxford: Martin Robertson
[12] Sim, J. (2009) *Punishment and Prisons* London: Sage

3. *Participate in struggles* whilst recognising that effective resistance must come from below and be determined by the people directly involved.

The goal should be to avoid being co-opted but follow the 'hard road' to greater understanding and wisdom without being 'defined out' and thus ignored. This challenge, expressed in the papers delivered at the *European Group* conferences in the 1980s, continues to be central to debates in abolitionism today.

Bibliography

Boonin, D. (2008) *The Problem of Punishment* Cambridge: Cambridge University Press

Cohen, S. (1985) *Visions of Social Control* Cambridge: Polity Press

Davis, A.Y. (2012) *The Meaning of Freedom,* San Francisco: City Lights Books

Hudson, B.A. (2003) *Justice in the Risk Society* London: Sage.

Hulsman, L. (1986) "Critical Criminology and the concept of Crime" in *Contemporary Crises* Volume 10, pp 63-80

Mathiesen, T. (1974) *The Politics of Abolition* Oxford: Martin Robertson

Roberts, R. (2007) 'What happened to abolitionism? An investigation of a paradigm and a social movement', Unpublished MA Thesis, London School of Economics

Scott, D. (2014) *The Caretakers of Punishment* London: Palgrave

Sim, J. (2009) *Punishment and Prisons* London: Sage

Appendix 1

42 Conferences of the European Group for the Study of Deviance and Social Control 1973-2014

1.   1973   **Impruneta, Florence, Italy**
                  *Social Control in Europe: Scope and Prospects for a
                  Radical Criminology*
                  13-16 September 1973

2.   1974   **Colchester, England**
                  *The Development of Social Control and Possible
                  Alternatives*
                  13-16 September 1974

3.   1975   **Amsterdam, Netherlands**
                  Crimes of the Powerful
                  9-12 September 1975

4.   1976   **Vienna, Austria**
                  Economic Change and Legal Control
                  10-13 September 1976

5.   1977   **Barcelona, Spain**
                  The State and Social Control
                  9-12 September 1977

6.   1978   **Bremen, Federal Republic of Germany**
                  Law and Order: Terrorism and state violence
                  7-10 September 1978

7.   1979   **Copenhagen, Denmark**
                Deviance and Discipline
                6-9 September 1979

8.   1980   **Leuven, Belgium**
                *State Control on Information in the Field of Deviance
                and Social Control: Resource, Analysis, Counter
                Strategies*
                4-7 September 1980

9.   1981   **Derry, Northern Ireland**
                *Securing the State: The Politics of Internal Security in
                Europe*
                3-6 September 1981

10.   1982   **Bologna, Italy**
                *Youth and the Economic Crisis: New Forms of Social
                Control and Counter Strategies*
                31 August-3 September 1982

11.   1983   **Hyytiälä, Finland**
                Social Movements, the State and Problems of Action
                9-12 September 1983

12.   1984   **Cardiff, Wales**
                *The State of Information in 1984: Social Conflict,
                Social Control and the New Technology*
                6-9 September 1984

13.   1985   **Hamburg, Germany**
                The Expansion of European Prison Systems
                12-15 September 1985

14.   1986   **Madrid, Spain**
                Civil Rights, Public Opinion and the State
                10-14 September 1986

15.   1987   **Vienna, Austria**
                *Justice and Ideology: Definitions and Strategies for
                the 1990's'*
                10-13 September 1987

16.   1988   **Synnseter fjellstue, Norway**
Gender, Sexuality and Social Control
1-4 September 1988

17.   1989   **Ormskirk, Lancashire, England**
Beyond Domination
31 August-3 September 1989

18.   1990   **Haarlem, Netherlands**
Criminal Justice in a European Legal Order: Migration and Penal Reform
4-7 September 1990

19.   1991   **Potsdam, Germany**
Social Justice and European Transformations: Processes of Marginalisation and Integration. Changes in Social Policies
4-8 September 1991

20.   1992   **Padova, Italy**
Citizenship, Human Rights, And Minorities: Rethinking Social Control in the New Europe
3-6 September 1992

21.   1993   **Prague, Czech Republic**
Control as Enterprise: East and West
29 August 29-1 September 1993

22.   1994   **Komitini, Greece**
The Use and Abuse of Power: Beyond Control
25-28 August 1994

23.   1995   **Crossmaglen, Northern Ireland**
Confronting Control: Theories and Practices of Resistance
31 August- 4 September 1995

24.   1996   **Bangor, Wales**
State Crime and Human Rights
12-16 September 1996

25.   1997   **Kazimierz Dolny, Poland**
                 Europe in transition: Past trends and future
                 Perspectives
                 11-14 September 1997

26.   1998   **Spetses, Greece**
                 Controlling the Movement of People: Critical
                 Perspectives on Practices, Policies and Consequences
                 27-30 August 1998

27.   1999   **Palanga, Lithuania**
                 Criminal Injustices and the Production of Harm
                 2-5 September 1999

28.   2000   **Nyneshamn, Sweden**
                 Punishment enough?
                 31 August-3 September 2000

29.   2001   **Venice, Italy**
                 The Ambivalence of Conflicts and Social Change
                 6-9 September 2001

30.   2002   **Krakow, Poland**
                 Social Control and Violence: Breaking the Cycle
                 29 September- 1 August 2002

31.   2003   **Helsinki, Finland**
                 Critical Perspectives on Crime Prevention
                 30 August- 2 September 2003

32.   2004   **Bristol, England**
                 Critical perspectives on the discipline of criminology
                 and international criminal justice policies
                 16-19 September 2004

33.   2005   **Belfast, Northern Ireland**
                 Crime, Justice and Transition
                 1-4 September 2005

34.   2006   **Corinth, Peloponnes, Greece**
                *The Regulation of Migration, Asylum and Movement
                in the 'N ew Europe'*
                31 August-3 September 2006

35.   2007   **Utrecht, Netherlands**
                Exploring Relations of Power
                30 August-3 September 2007

36.   2008   **Padova, Italy**
                Conflict, Penal Policies and Prison Systems
                4-7 September 2008

37.   2009   **Preston, Lancashire, England**
                *'Crime', Justice, and Control: The Challenge of
                Recession*
                26-29 August 2009

38.   2010   **Lesvos, Greece**
                The Politics of Criminology
                1-5 September 2010

39.   2011   **Chambéry, France**
                No borders? Exclusion, Justice and the Politics of Fear
                3-7 September 2011

40.   2012   **Nicosia, Cyprus**
                *'Beyond the Wire': Regulating Division, Conflict and
                Resistance*
                5-9 September 2012

41.   2013   **Oslo, Norway**
                *Critical Criminology in a Changing World: Tradition
                and Innovation*
                29 August-1 September 2013

42.   2014   **Liverpool, England**
                *Resisting the demonisation of 'the Other': State,
                Nationalism and Social Control in a Time of Crisis*
                3-6 September 2014

Appendix 2

Previously published books of European Group Conference Papers

Bianchi, H, Simondi, M & Taylor, I. (eds) *Deviance and Control in Europe: Papers from the European Group for the Study of Deviance and Social Control,* **(London John Wiley & Sons) 1975**
   1.   Bianchi, H, Simondi, M. & Taylor, I. 'Introduction by the Authors

Part 1: National Reports on the State of Criminology and Deviancy Control
   2.   Cohen, S. & Taylor, L. 'From psychopaths to outsiders: British Criminology and the National Deviancy conference'
   3.   Seppilli. T. & Abbozzo, G.G. 'The state of research into social control and deviance in Italy'
   4.   Bianchi, H. 'Social control and deviance in the Netherlands'
   5.   Schumann, K. 'Approaching crime and deviance: a Note on the contributions by Scientists, Officials of Social Control and Social Activists During the Last Five Years in West Germany'
   6.   Dahl, T.S. 'The state of criminology in Norway: A Short Report'

Part 2: Presentations on the Prison Movement in Europe
   7.   Mathiesen, T. & Roine, W. 'The prison movement in Scandinavia'
   8.   Fitzgerald, M. 'The British Prisoners' Movement: Its Aims and Methods'
   9.   Donzelot, J. 'The Prison Movement in France'
   10. Rauty, R. 'Introductory Note to the Prison Revolts in Italy in 1973'
   11. Modona, G.N. 'Reform of the Italian Prison: A Left Perspective'
   12. Invernizzi, I. 'Class Struggle in the Prisons: Practical and Theoretical Problems'
   13. Dejours, C., Margara, A. & Cohen, S. 'Discussion on Medicine in Prison'
   14. Donzelot, J., Ivernizzi, I., McIntosh, M. & Mathieson, T. 'Discussion on Women in Prison

Part 3: Selected Conference Papers
   15. McIntosh, M. 'New Directions in the Study of Criminal Organization'
   16. Makela, K. 'The Societal Tasks of the System of Criminal Law'
   17. Ciacci, M. 'Psychiatric Control: A Report on the Italian Situation'
   18. Hepworth, M. 'The Criminalisation of Blackmail'

The European Group for the Study of Deviance and Social Control (eds.)
Terrorism and the Violence of the State: Working Papers in European Criminology No. 1. (Hamburg: EGSDSC) 1980

1. de Sousa Santos, B. 'Some notes on 'Terrorism' and State Violence'
2. Scheerer, S. "Law Making in a State of Siege: Some regularities in the legislative response to political violence'
3. Schwinghammer, T. 'Theory and Practice: 'The Comments of the Commandos''
4. Muckenberger, U. 'The 'Mescalero Affair' has become a Legal Scandal'
5. de Wit, J. & Ponsaers, P. 'The Mescalero Case'
6. Bruckner, P. 'Principils obsta. or: Incitement to Discord'
7. EGSDSC, 'Declaration of the European Group'
8. EGSDSC, 'Advertisement placed in the Weser Kurier published 14.9.1978'

Brusten, M & Ponsaers, P. (eds.) *State Control on Information in the Field of Deviance and Social Control: Working Papers in European Criminology No. 2.* (Leuven: EGSDSC) 1981

Brusten, M. & Ponsaers, P. 'Introductory Note'
General Overview of the subject
1. Brusten, M. & Van Outrive, L. 'The relationship between state institutions and the social sciences in the field of deviance and social control'
2. Baratta, A. & Smaus, G. 'Comments on the paper of M. Brusten and L. Van Outrive'
National Reports
3. Brusten, M. 'Social control of criminology and criminologists'.
4. Schumann, K. 'On proper and deviant criminology - Varieties in the production of legitimation for penal law'.
5. Behr, C-P., Gipsen, D., Klien-Sconnefeld S., Naffin, K. & Zillmer, H. 'The use of scientific discoveries for the maintenance and extension of state control - On the effect of legitimation and the utilization of science'.
6. Jepsen, J. 'Control of criminologists - state and science and the state of science in the state of Denmark'.
7. Faugeron, C. 'Les conditions de la recherche en sociologie de la déviance et du contrôle sociale en France'. (With English Summary)
8. Stangl, W. 'Considerations about the process of everyday control over science'.
9. Lapis, T. 'The political economy of the development of Italian Criminology'.
10. Squires, P. 'The policing of knowledge: Criminal statistics and criminal categories'.

Contributions on specific themes
11. Van Kerckvoorde, J. & Kerstemont , F. 'La position des citoyens devant l'automatisation croissante de l'information'. (With English Summary)
12. Young, J. 'The manufacture of news: a critique of the present convergence in mass media theory.'

Hillyard, P. & Squires, P. (eds.) *Securing the State: Politics of Internal Security in Europe: Working Papers in European Criminology No. 3.* (Bristol: EGSDSC) 1982

Hillyard, P. & Squires, P. 'Introductory Note'

I. Production of Insecurity
1. Dalstra, K. 'The Immanent Structure of Crime Control'.
2. Wright, S. 'The International Trade in the Technology of Repression'.

II Administering Insecurity
3. Brusten, M. 'Police and Politics: Analytical Aspects and Empirical Data Against the Ideology of a 'politically neutral police force'.
4. Jorgensen, B. 'Defending the terrorists: Queen's Counsel before the Diplock Courts'.
5. Hualde, G. & Lezana, J. 'Police action in the Basque Country: the development of repressive measures'.

III Social Insecurity
6. Squires, P. 'Internal security and Social Insecurity'.
7. Miralles, T. & Munagorri, I. 'State Control and the Internal Security in Spain'.
8. Mosconi, G. & Pisapia, G. 'The stereotype of the repentant terrorist: his nature and functions'.
9. Smith, P. 'Emergency legislation: the Prevention of Terrorism Acts'

IV Carceral Insecurity
10. Heatley, P. & Tomlinson, M. 'The Politics of Imprisonment in Ireland: some historic notes'.
11. Caldarone, R. & Valeriani, P. 'Prison Politics and Prisoners Struggles in Italy'.

Squires, P. & Hillyard, P. (eds.) *Disputing Deviance: Experience of Youth in the 80s: Working Papers in European Criminology No. 4.* **(Bristol: EGSDSC) 1983**

Mosconi, G. & Pavarini, M. 'Introductory Note'

I. Theoretical Controversies

1.   Pitch T. 'Adequacy or Obsolescence of the Notion of Deviance'.
2.   Stangl, W. 'The Effect of Penal Control on Society'.
3.   De Leo, G. 'Decline or Eclipse of Juvenile Delinquency'.

II Youth and Social Control

4.   Ella, N. 'Transition from Youth Protection to Youth Control'.
5.   Ambroset, S., Carrer, F., Capolucci, A. & Gazzola, A. 'Juvenile Delinquency in Italy'.
6.   Herriger, N. 'The Prevention of Juvenille Delinquency and the Widening net of Social Control'.
7.   Loney, M. 'The Youth Opportunities Programme: Requiem and Rebirth'
8.   Malinowski, P. 'Youth is it a Social Problem'.
9.   Ericsson, K. & Stangeland, P. 'Is the Social Control of Youth Really Tightening'.

III Social movements and Social Control

10.   Lodi, G. 'The Collective Mobilisation of Youth in the 1970s and 80s'.
11.   Uusitalo, P. 'Policing Environmental Conflicts in Finland and Norway'.
12.   Gisper, D., Klein-Schonnefeld, S., Naffin, K. & Zillmer, H. 'Analyses on Terrorism'.

Hillyard, P., Rolston, B. & Tomlinson, M. (eds.) *Social movements and Social conflicts: Working Papers in European Criminology No. 5.* **(EGSDSC) 1984**

Hillyard, P., Rolston, B. & Tomlinson, M. 'Introductory Note'

1.   Alapuro, R. 'On Collective Action and the State in Finland, 1900-1930'.
2.   Bjornshauge, L. 'Youth riots - Marginal Deviance or Fundamental and Concrete Criticism of Society?'
3.   Lezana, J. & Miralles, T. 'Youth in the Basque Country: A Social Movement or a Marginal minority?'
4.   Stalstrom, O. 'Profiles in Courage: Problems of Action of the Finnish Gay movement in crisis'.
5.   Haukaa, R. 'The Women's Liberation Movement in Norway'.
6.   Moerings, M. 'Protest in the Netherlands: Developments in a Pillarised Society'.
7.   McCartney, J. 'The Falls Road Taxi Association: A Case Study in the Management of Political Stigma'.
8.   Rolston, B. 'The Republican Movement and Elections: An Historical Account'
9.   Hillyard, P. 'Popular Justice in Northern Ireland'.

Rolston, B. (ed.) *The State of Information in 1984: Conflict, Social Control and New Technology: Working Papers in European Criminology No. 6.* (Jordanstown: EGSDSC) 1985

Rolston, B. 'Introduction'

I. Wales – Society, Economy and Politics
1. Welsh Campaign for Civil and Political Liberties, 'Women and the Strike: It's a whole way of life'.
2. Evans, J. 'The Peace Movement in Wales'.
3. Rees, T. 'Youth Unemployment, Migration and the Employment of Men and Women in Wales'.
4. Mainwaring, L. 'The South Wales Economy in the Post-War Period'.

II New Technology and its Contradictions
5. Pounder, C. 'The British Police and Computers: Recent Trends and Developments'.
6. Beaulieu, M. 'The Use of Computers by the Correctional Service of Canada to Registers and Disclose information on Federal Inmates: Comments on the Practices and Principles"
7. Bevere, A. 'Coercive Apparatus and the Use of Computers in Italian Legislation'.
8. Brieske, R. 'New Technology and the deskilling of female Employees'.
9. Scanagatta, S. 'Young People's Use of Microelectronics in Italy'.
10. Stodolsky, D. 'Personal Computers in Educational and Democratic Processes: the American Experience and the Danish Context'.
11. Mathiasen, K. 'The People's Data Project: An Alternative Use for Computers'.

III Ideology and the Control of Information
12. Mathiesen, T. 'Criminal Policy at the Crossroads: Report at 'Anhorung zur Situation des Strafvolluges in hessen', Hessichen Lantag, 6 September 1984'.
13. Grőnfors, M. & Stålstrőm, O. 'Ethical Aspects of the Production of Information on AIDS'.
14. Powell, C. 'Control of Criminology and Legal Policy: the case of Finnish 'Neo-Classicism''.
15. Lloyd, C. & Scola, J. 'Policing Two Nations: Community Crime Prevention and Public Order Policing'.
16. Ward, T. 'Coroners, Police and Deaths in Custody in England: a Historical Perspective'.

Rolston, B. & Tomlinson, M. (eds.) *The Expansion of European Prison Systems: Working Papers in European Criminology No. 7.* (Belfast: EGSDSC) 1986

de Haan, W. & Tomlinson, M. 'Introduction'

A. Expansion of Prison Systems
1. de Haan, W. 'Explaining Expansion: The Dutch case'.
2. Scheerer, S. 'Dissolution and Expansion'.
3. Mosconi, B. 'References for a Real Alternative to Prison'
4. Sim, J. 'Working for the Clampdown: Prisons and Politics in England and Wales'.
5. Miralles, T. 'The Spanish Prison Situation in 1985'.
6. Moerings, M. 'Prison Overcrowding in the United States'.
7. Fox, J. 'Conservative Social policy, Social control and Racism: the Politics of new York state Prison expansion, 1975-1985.'

B. Prison Regime
8. Boock, J.B. 'Conditions for Remand prisoners'.
9. Koch, I. 'Mental and Social Sequelae of Isolation'.
10. Siegmeier, U. 'Women in Prison'
11. Pecic, D. 'Imprisonment of Mothers, Punishment for Children: the situation in the Federal Republic of Germany'.
12. Schick, H. 'Everyday Life of Male Prisoners'.
13. Scraton, P. & Chadwick, K. 'The Experiment that went Wrong: the crisis of deaths in Custody at the Glenochil Youth Complex'.

C. Special Categories
14. Rolston, B. & Tomlinson, M. 'Long-Term Imprisonment in northern ireland: Psychological or Political Survival'.
15. Schubert, M. 'Political Prisoners in West Germany: their situation and some consquences concerning their rights in respect of the treatment of political prisoners in international law'.
16. Janssen, H. 'Political Prisoners: some thoughts on the status of politically motivated offenders in Europe'.
17. Tengeler, S. 'Political justice in Stammheim: the case of Peter Jűrgen Boock'.
18. Klaus, M. with Prison Justice Group, 'Life Imprisonment in the Federal Republic of Germany'.

D. Ideological 'Alternatives' and Net-Widening
19. Stålstrőm, O. & Grőnfors, M. 'Internment or Information? On Different Strategies for Containing the AIDS Crisis'.
20. Schwenkle-Omar, I. 'An Outline Of Division in Hamburg'.
21. Powell, C. 'Televising Penal Policy for Young Men: a view from Wales'.

Rolston, B. & Tomlinson, M. (eds.) *Civil Rights Public Opinion and the State: Working Papers in European Criminology No. 8.* (Belfast: EGSDSC) 1987

Rolston, B. & Tomlinson, M. 'Introduction'

Part One
1. de Haan, W. 'Fuzzy Morals and Flakey Politics: the Coming Out of Critical Criminology'.
2. McMahon, M. 'The State of Policing Reform in Toronto'.
3. Durieux, H. 'The Rotterdam Junkie Union and Affiliates'.
4. Smith, S. 'Neglect as Control: Prisoners' Families'.
5. Levi, M. 'Public Opinion, the State and the Control of Business Crime'.
6. Jepsen, J. 'Moral Panics and the Spread of Control Models in Europe'.
7. Wright, S. 'Public Order Technology: 'Less-Lethal Weapons''.
8. van Swaaningen, R. 'The Image of Power: Abolitionism, Emancipation, Authoritarian Idolatry and the Ability of Unbelief'.
9. van Kerckvoorde, J. 'Statistics, Official Statements and Public Rumour'.
10. Campbell, D. & Lee, B. 'Policing Contemporary Britain: Re-Addressing the Balance'.

Part Two
11. Folguera, P. 'Women: Protagonists of Social Change in Spain, 1975-1986'.
12. Bennun, M. 'The Judiciary in Franco's Spain and in South Africa'.
13. Pastor, S. 'Liberty Versus security: Should Drugs be Illegal?'
14. Carrion, J.S. 'Drugs and the Mass Media: The Social Construction of a Reality'.

Rolston, B. & Tomlinson, M. (eds.) *Justice & Ideology: Strategies for the 1990s. Working Papers in European Criminology No. 9.* (Belfast: EGSDSC) 1989

1. de Celis, J. B. 'Whither Abolitionism?'
2. Chambliss, W.J. 'State Organized Crime'.
3. de Haan, W. 'The Necessity of Punishment in a Just Social Order: A critical Appraisal'.
4. Fijnaut, C. 'The Contemporary Evolution of Criminology in the Netherlands'.
5. Hirvonen, A. 'Forget Criminology: The Radical Strategies of Abolition and Deconstruction'.
6. Knauder, S. 'Justice and Imprisonment in the Light of their Effects on the Ex-Convicts in Two Cultural Settings'.
7. Lacombe, D. 'The Demand for the Criminalisation of Pornography: A State-Made Ideological Construction or a Demand Articulated in Civil Society?'

8. Minkkinen, P. 'The Criminal Myth and Ideology: An Outline for an Exercise in the Semiotics of Criminology'.
9. Mosconi, B. 'The Gozzini Law: Conflict in Reform'.
10. Nielsen, B.G. 'Criminal Justice and Social Service: Conflict or Cooperation in Incest Cases?'
11. Pilgram, A. 'The Politics of Crime Control in Austria: History and Theory'.
12. Platek, M. 'Ideology and Justice: Some Practical Polish Connotations'.
13. Ruggiero, V. 'An Encounter with Realist Criminology'.
14. Ryan, M. & Ward, T. 'Left Realism Against the Rest Revisited: Or Some Particularities of the British'.
15. Stangl, W. 'Who Has the Right to Prosecute? The Reform of Criminal Procedure in the Nineteenth century and the Abolitionist Trend in Contemporary Criminology'.
16. Steinert, H. 'Marxian Theory and Abolitionism: Introduction to a Discussion'.
17. Powell, C. 'Contemporary Criminology: Whatever Happened to the Anarchic Impulse'.
18. Gronfors, M. 'Mediation: An Experiment in Finland'.
19. van Ransbeek, H. 'Reflections on Abolitionist Practice: Some Results of Abolitionist Research on "Petty Crime" in Two Social contexts'.
20. van Swaaningen, R. 'Strategies of Reform: Some Historical Examples'.
21. Wantula, H. 'Deviance and Social Control in Western Europe and Poland'.
22. Weber, H-M. & Wilson, C. 'What is to be Done about Marginalisation and Criminalisation? Some Thoughts on a Comparison between England and Wales and the Federal Republic of Germany'.
23. Van Kerckvoorde, J. 'Criminal Statistics. Crime and the Administration of Criminal Justice'.
24. Hes, J. 'Suppressed Minorities and the Need for Protection and Moral Disapproval'.

Rolston, B. & Tomlinson, M. (eds.) *Gender Sexuality & Social Control: Working Papers in European Criminology No. 10.* (Belfast: EGSDSC) 1990

1. Widerberg, K. 'Female Sexualisation - Learning Subordination through the Body: A New Method and a New Knowledge?'
2. Durieux, H. 'Metaphors on Order and Deviance from the Work of Julia Kristeva'.
3. Kellough, G. 'The 'Ideological Ceiling' of Male Culture'.
4. Eggert, A. & Rolston, B. 'Exporting the Problem: Abortion and the Law in Ireland'.
5. O'Malley, S. & Hall, G. 'I Have No Past'.

6. Wiemann, B. 'The Rise and Decline of the Care System for Unmarried Mothers and Changing Forms of Social Control'.
7. Ryan, J., Ryan, M. & Ward, T. 'Feminism, Philanthropy and Social Control: The Origin's of Women's Policing in England'.
8. Skidmore, P. 'Genderising Deviance: News Media Constructions of Women and Crime'.
9. Prieur, A. 'The Male Role and Sexual Assault'.
10. Berge, A. 'Sexual Violence: The Gender Question as a Challenge to Progressive Criminology and Social Theory'.
11. Smyth, M. 'Kincora: Towards an Analysis'.
12. Finstad, L. 'Sexual Offenders out of Prison: Principles for a Realistic Utopia'.
13. van Swaaningen, R. 'Feminism, Criminology and Criminal Law: Troublesome Relationship'.
14. Meima, M. 'Sexual Violence, Criminal Law and Abolitionism'.
15. Berjerse, J. & Kool, R. 'The Traitorous Temptation of Criminal Justice: Deceptive Appearances? The Dutch Women's Movement, Violence against Women and the Criminal Justice System'
16. de Jongste, W. 'The Protection of Women by the Criminal Justice System? Reflections on Feminism, Abolitionism and Power'.

Ruggiero, V. (ed) *Citizenship, Human Rights and Minorities: Rethinking Social Control in the New Europe [XX Conference of The European Group for the Study of Deviance and Social Control, Padova 3-6 September 1992]* (Athens: Ant. N. Sakkoulas Publishers). 1996

1. Ruggerio, V. 'Introduction'.
2. Melossi, D. 'Weak Leviathan and strong democracy: two styles of social control as they apply to the construction of a European Community'.
3. Van Outrive, L. 'Legislation and decision making in Europe. International police cooperation and human rights'.
4. Van Outrive, L. 'European Parliament Committee on civil liberties and internal affairs working document on police cooperation'.
5. Pastore, M. "Boundary' conflicts around and inside the European Community'.
6. Krarup, O. 'The democratic 'no' and its legal meaning'.
7. Klovedal Reich, E. 'A utopia for a living people'.
8. Dahlerup, D. 'More women than men said 'no' to Maastricht'.
9. Wilson. C. "Going to Europe': Prisoners' right and the effectiveness of European standards'.

10. Yeates, N. 'Appeals to citizenship in the unification of Europe: the political and social context of the EC's third programme to combat poverty'.
11. Calamti, S. 'The violation of human rights in Northern Ireland'.
12. Ruggiero, V. 'The Italian political refugees in Paris'.
13. Edwards, J. 'Group rights v. individual rights – The case of race conscious policies'
14. Scholter, M. & Trenx, H-Z. 'The social construction of the 'asylum abuses' in the Federal Republic of Germany'.

Georgoulas, S. (ed) *The Politics of Criminology: Critical studies on deviance and social control* **[38th Annual Conference of European Group] (Zurich: LIT). 2012**

Georgoulas, S. 'Introduction'.
Part 1 Critical criminology: From the past to the future
1. Georgoulas, S. 'Radix of radical criminology – Hesiod'.
2. Malloch, M. & Munro, B. 'Crime, Critique and Utopia'.
3. Bell, E. 'Neoliberal crime policy: Who profits?'.
4. Ruggiero, V. 'Criminal enterprise, identity and repertoires of action'.

Part 2 Contemporary Critical Criminology Case Studies
5. Orr, D. 'Lehman brothers, Obama and the case for corporate regulation'.
6. Norris, P. 'Public order policing in the UK: From paramilitary policing to neighbourhood policing?'.
7. Hayes, M. 'The imposition of internment without trial in Northern Ireland, August 1971: Causes, consequences and lessons'.
8. Delimitsos, K. 'Restructuring government's expertise on violence and delinquency in France'.
9. Karamalidou, A. 'The educative and emancipatory potential of human rights in prisons: Lessons from English and Dutch prisons'.
10. Sorvatzioti, D. 'Poor criminals in prison: violation of their fundamental human rights'.
11. Nikolopoulos, G. 'The criminalisation of the migration policy and the new European territorialities of social control'.
12. Ericson, C. 'Programmes for abusive men – results from a Swedish evaluation study'.
13. Peroni, C. 'Gender, violence and law in the post-feminist and queer debate in Italy'.
14. Harris, J. ''Little innocents no more': criminalising childhood and sexuality in the UK'.

Part 3 Introducing Critical Criminological Research – University of the Aegean

15. Sotiris, P. 'Revolt or deviance? Greek intellectuals and the December 2008 revolt of the Greek youth'.
16. Voulvouli, A. 'LGBT movements, biopolitics and new criminology: a preliminary research in Eastern Mediterranean Region'.
17. Demeli, T. 'Going through the gates: Prison and motherhood, adjustment and solidarity'.
18. Kitsiou, A. 'Focus group, a research method to analyse free software movement and social construction of crime'.
19. Sarantdis, D. 'A participant observation of police culture in Greece'.
20. Rinis, N. 'Cinema codes and crime: qualitative analysis of the movie 'Hoodwinked''.
21. Kouroutzas, C. 'Forensic science and criminology: the role of medical coroners: a pilot qualitative research'.

Bell, E. (ed) *No Borders: Immigration and the Politic of Fear* (Chambery: Universite' de Savoie). 2012

Scott, D. 'Foreword: The European Group for the Study of Deviance and Social Control'.
1. Bell, E. 'Introduction'.
2. Blanchard, E., Clochard, O. & Rodier, C. 'The new frontiers of immigration policy'.
3. Kaczmarek-Firth, A. 'An examination of the effects of contradictions in Globalisation on Europe's Migration laws'.
4. Fischer, N. 'Policing and the rule of law: a critique of the French deportation of unauthorised immigrants'.
5. Santorso, S. 'Migration and detention: changes in Italian legislation'.
6. Crocitti, S. 'Do immigration policies work? The case of Italy'.
7. Bracci, F. 'The 'Chinese deviant': Building the perfect enemy in a local area'.
8. Fabini, G. 'Buongiorno, documenti'. Police identity checks in Italy: Stories from migrants and local police officers'.
9. Parra, C. 'Latinos by nationality and illegal by ethnicity: otherness and the condition of fear in the US'.'
10. Michalowski, R. 'Re-bordering social space in Arizona's war on the immigrant 'other''.
11. Hoenig, R. 'Monsters on the borderscape of detention: Some Australian print media depictions of residents of Woomera Village and asylum seekers in immigration detention'.

Gilmore, J., Moore, J. M. and Scott, D. Critique and Dissent: An Anthology to mark 40 years of the European Group for the Study of Deviance and Social Control, (Ottawa: Red Quill Books) 2013

1. Joanna Gilmore, J.M. Moore and David Scott 'Critique and Dissent: An Introduction'.

Section A: Theoretical priorities of the European Group

2. Gilmore, J., Moore, J.M. and Scott, D. 'Towards a 'Critical, Emancipatory and Innovative Criminology'.
3. McMahon, M. and Kellough, G. 'An Interview with Stanley Cohen'.
4. European Group for the Study of Deviance and Social Control 'Manifesto 1974'
5. Ciacci, M. and Simondi, M. 'A New Trend in Criminological Knowledge: The Experience of the European Group for the Study of Deviance and Social Control'.
6. Swaaningen, R. van 'Inspirations and Aspirations of a Critical Criminology?
7. Scraton. P. 'Marginal to What?'
8. Beckmann, A. 'Louk Hulsman - In Memoriam'.
9. Cohen, S. 'Panic or Denial: On whether to Take Crime Seriously'.
10. Scott, D. 'A disobedient Visionary with an Enquiring Mind:An Essay on the Contribution of Stan Cohen'.
11. Working Group on Prison, Detention and Punishment Manifesto 2013

Section B: Critique

12. Gilmore, J., Moore, J.M. and Scott, D. 'The Resources of Critique'.
13. Scheerer, S. 'Law Making in a State of Siege: Some Regularities in the Legislative Response to Political Violence'.
14. Bell, E. 'Neo-liberal Crime Policy: Who Profits'.
15. Lacombe, D. The Demand for the Criminalisation of Pornography:A State-Made Ideological Construction or a Demand Articulated in Civil Society?'
16. Berge, A. 'Sexual Violence: The Gender Question as a Challenge to Progressive Criminology and Social Theory'.
17. Behr, C. Gipsen, D., Klien-Sconnefeld, S., Naffin, K. and Zillmer, H. 'State Control: The Use of Scientific Discoveries'.
18. Hillyard, P. 'Zemiology Revisited: Fifteen Years On'.

Section C: Dissent

19. Gilmore, J., Moore, J.M. and Scott, D. 'The Politics of Dissent'.
20. Schumann, K. 'On Proper and Deviant Criminology - Varieties in the Production of Legitimation for Penal Law'.
21. Stalstrom, O. 'Profiles in Courage: Problems of Action of the Finnish Gay Movement in Crisis'.

22. Welsh Campaign for Civil and Political Liberties, 'Women and the Strike: It's a Whole Way of Life'.
23. Rolston, B. and Tomlinson, M. 'Long-Term Imprisonment in Northern Ireland: Psychological or Political Survival?'
24. Smith, S. 'Neglect as Control: Prisoners' Families'.
25. Leander, K. 'The Decade of Rape'.

Appendix 1 41 Conferences of the European Group

Appendix 2 Table of Contents from Books of Conferences Proceedings

Appendix 3 Coordinators of the European Group 1973-2013

Appendix 3

A selection of Louk Hulsman's writings published in English

Hulsman. L., (1972), "Strategies of Changing Legal Systems", in *Symposium of the Research Committee on Sociology of Law,* ISA Proceedings

Hulsman, L., (1973), "The Decriminalization, in Transactions of Colloquium of Bellagio", *General Report of the International Association of Penal Law*, pp. 59-68.

Hulsman, L. (1974), "The Penal System as a Social Problem", in *Issues and Answers* Minnesota: The Rural Crime and Justice Institute

Hulsman, L., (1977), "Penal and Penitentiary Aspects of Road Traffic", *General Report for the Fourth International Colloquium of the International Penal and Penitentiary Foundation*. Proceedings of the Fourth International Colloquium of the IPPF, Rotterdam, June 1977.

Hulsman, L., (1977), *Violence as a Challenge to Modern Society*, Institute Universitaire International, Luxembourg.

Hulsman, L., (1978), "The Dutch Criminal Justice System from a Comparative Legal Perspective," in D. Fokkema et al. (eds.) *Introduction to Dutch Law for Foreign Lawyers*, Deventer, pp. 289-381.

Hulsman, L., (1979), "The Causes and Manifestations of Recent Trends in Juvenile Delinquency - Their Impact on Policies of Prevention, Treatment and Rehabilitation of Offenders", in *New Approaches in the Treatment of Young Offenders*. European Social Development Program, New York, UN. European Social Development Program, New York, UN.

Hulsman, L., (1979), *An abolitionist Perspective on Criminal Justice system and a scheme to Organize Approaches to 'problematic situations'*, Colloque international pour le 50ème anniversaire de l'Ecole de criminologie de Louvain, 22-26 May 1979.

Hulsman, L. (1980) *Report on Decriminalisation*, Strasbourg: Council of Europe

Hulsman, L. (1981), "Penal Reform in the Netherlands. Part 1 - Bringing the Criminal Justice System under Control". *Howard Journal of Penology and Crime Prevention*, Volume 20, Number 3, pp. 150-159.

Hulsman L. (1982), "Penal Reform in the Netherlands. Part 2 - Criteria for Deciding on Alternatives to Imprisonment". *Howard Journal of Penology and Crime Prevention,* Volume 21, Number 1, pp. 35-47.

Hulsman LHC, (1983), On the Relation between Social Control inside and outside Criminal Justice, Report at the International Congress on Criminology, Wien,

Hulsman, L., (1983), *On the relation between social control inside and outside the Criminal Justice,* Report at the International Congress on Criminology, Vienna,1983

Hulsman LHC, (1984), together with others, Toward a Victim Policy in Europe HEUNI Publ., series 2, Helsinki

Hulsman LHC, together with others, (1984), *Report on the Discussions and Proposed Resolutions,* Actes du Colloque international de l'AIDP (Tokyo 1984), Revue internationale de droit pénal, 54, 3, "Déjudiciarisation et médiation".

Hulsman LHC, (1985), "Conflicts as Property: Fear of Crime, Criminal Justice and the Caring Community, in Jayoder (ed.), Support Networks in a Caring Community, Dordrecht, Martinus

Hulsman LHC, (1985), Critical Criminology and the Concept of Crime, in International Conference on Prison Abolition, Amsterdam, 24-27 June 1985, V, 37,

Hulsman L, (1986), "Critical Criminology and the Concept of Crime". *Contemporary Crisis,* Volume 10, pp. 63-80.

Hulsman LHC, (1986), "Critical Criminology and the Concepts of Crime", in H. Bianchi and R. van Swaaningen (eds.), *Towards a Non-Repressive Approach to Crime,* Amsterdam.

Hulsman, L., (1989), "The Right of the Victim not to be subordinated to the Dynamics of Criminal Justice", in Separovic, ZP (ed), *Victimology, International Action and Study of the Victims,* Zagreb. pp. 25-35.

Hulsman, L. (1991), "The Abolitionist Case: Alternative Crime Policies". *Israel Law Review,* Volume 25, Number 3-4, Summer-Autumn, pp 681-709.

Hulsman, L., (1998), "Struggles about Terminology: 'problematic situation' vs. Crime," in Cartuyvels Yves, Francoise Digneffe, Robert Phillippe (eds), *Politique, police et justice au bord du futur. Mélanges pour et avec Lode van Outrive,* pp. 45-56 , Paris et Montreal, l'Harmattan.

CPSIA information can be obtained at www.ICGtesting.com
Printed in the USA
LVOW01s1911120315

430303LV00007B/455/P